The Coit Tower Murals

The Coit Tower Murals

New Deal Art and Political Controversy in San Francisco

ROBERT W. CHERNY

UNIVERSITY OF ILLINOIS PRESS
Urbana, Chicago, and Springfield

Manufactured in the United States of America
1 2 3 4 5 C P 5 4 3 2 1
♾ This book is printed on acid-free paper.

Library of Congress Cataloging-in-Publication Data
Names: Cherny, Robert W., author.
Title: The Coit Tower murals : New Deal art and political controversy in San Francisco / Robert W. Cherny.
Description: Urbana : University of Illinois Press, [2024] | Includes bibliographical references and index.
Identifiers: LCCN 2024018773 (print) | LCCN 2024018774 (ebook) | ISBN 9780252046285 (cloth) | ISBN 9780252088353 (paperback) | ISBN 9780252047565 (ebook)
Subjects: LCSH: Mural painting and decoration, American—California—San Francisco—20th century. | California—In art. | Coit Memorial Tower (San Francisco, Calif.) | Public Works of Art Project (U.S.) | Art—Political aspects—California—San Francisco—History—20th century. | Art and society—California—San Francisco—History—20th century.
Classification: LCC ND2638.S36 C49 2024 (print) | LCC ND2638.S36 (ebook) | DDC 751.7/30979461—dc23/eng/20240523
LC record available at https://lccn.loc.gov/2024018773
LC ebook record available at https://lccn.loc.gov/2024018774

To Richard Rothman and Jon Golinger,
steadfast defenders of San Francisco's New Deal art

Prejudices grow; they might even grow to the actual point of having the murals destroyed. Then next would come the books.

—Ralph Stackpole, 1941

In the 2022–23 school year, from July 1, 2022, to June 31, 2023, PEN America recorded 3,362 instances of book bans in U.S. public school classrooms and libraries. These bans removed student access to 1,557 unique book titles, the works of over 1,480 authors, illustrators, and translators. . . . PEN America recorded 1,406 book ban cases in Florida, followed by 625 bans in Texas, 333 bans in Missouri, 281 bans in Utah, and 186 bans in Pennsylvania.

—PEN America, *Banned in the USA*

Contents

Preface and Acknowledgments

Between mid-December of 1933 and the early months of World War II, the New Deal art projects produced a rich collection of art, among which public murals are best known today. San Francisco has a particularly rich collection of New Deal artworks, especially murals. But they remain vulnerable. From mid-1934 until the early 1950s, there were occasional efforts to destroy some murals because they were alleged to be Communist propaganda. Recently there have been efforts to destroy some murals because they are deemed to be offensive on other grounds or simply because administrators found it inconvenient to continue their stewardship of the art. That long history began with the murals created at Coit Tower between December 1933 and June 1934.

I don't recall the first time I saw the Coit Tower murals, but I *really* saw them when Masha Zakheim, daughter of one of the artists, gave me a personal tour and a copy of her book about them. That was sometime in the 1990s, when I began offering senior proseminars and graduate seminars on California in the Great Depression. I later led optional field trips to Coit Tower for my seminar members.

From Masha Zakheim's book, I learned a bit about Victor Arnautoff, one of the muralists. In 2011, as a fund-raiser for the Presidio Historical Society, I agreed to give a lecture on a later mural by Arnautoff, at the Presidio of San Francisco. That lecture led to a book, *Victor Arnautoff and the Politics of Art* (2017). In researching that book, I learned a good deal more about the Coit Tower muralists and their murals, which led to a journal article in 2017 and to an invitation to join Katherine Petrin and Jon Golinger in preparing an amendment to the listing of Coit Tower in the National Register of Historic Places, which was approved in 2018.

The history of the Coit Tower murals includes political controversy, the destruction or alteration of some original artwork, later efforts to remove parts of the murals, vandalism, and long-term neglect, but also recognition of the historic and artistic significance of the murals and repeated restorations. Coit Tower and its murals are now listed on the National Register of Historic Places, and plans are under way to nominate them as a National Historic Landmark.

My biography of Arnautoff involved me in what became a nationally prominent controversy over his New Deal murals at San Francisco's George Washington High School. At an early school board meeting when the subject came up, I tried to explain to the school board my understanding of Arnautoff's intent, based on my research. In response, a board member loudly claimed that I had insulted and offended him by my comments. Months later, at another board meeting, when I tried to explain that the board's pending vote to destroy or cover the murals violated state law, I was ignored. (Later, my letter was among evidence cited by the judge who ordered the school board to reverse their decision.) That experience led to another article about the long-term history of San Francisco's rich collection of New Deal artworks. Some have been subject to political attacks, some have been allowed to deteriorate, and some have been carefully restored to their original splendor. And that led to my involvement in yet another controversy, over plans by the University of California, San Francisco (UCSF), to demolish a set of New Deal murals by Bernard Zakheim because they wanted to replace the building in which they were located. That controversy was resolved by the careful removal and storage of the murals, but UCSF has yet to produce a plan to reinstall them. And all of that led to this book.

We live in a world where public art is sometimes threatened. The history of the Coit Tower murals, and San Francisco's New Deal art more generally, may provide a valuable lesson when some new controversy over public art surfaces, as it is certain to do.

This book would not have been possible without the pioneering work of Masha Zakheim, whose book was published by the company of her sister, Ruth Zakheim Gottstein. It has been a privilege to have met both Zakheim sisters and also Ruth's son, Adam Gottstein. I am grateful to the San Francisco Arts Commission for providing the high-resolution color photographs of the murals that appear in chapter 3 and especially to Allison Cummings for her assistance in dealing with the city attorney's office regarding the licensing requirements. Sarah Mackay, assistant curator of the Achenbach Foundation for Graphic Arts, Fine Arts Museums of San Francisco, was very helpful with locating the original sketches and drawings done by the Coit Tower artists. Emilia Mickevicius, curatorial associate in photography at the San Francisco Museum of Modern Art, was similarly helpful in locating photographs of the artists at work. Christina

Morreta, photography curator at the San Francisco History Room, San Francisco Public Library, was, as usual, efficient and helpful with that institution's large stock of historic photos. Jane Glover provided access to the Walter Heil files held by the Fine Arts Museums of San Francisco. I arrived at the Archives of American Art in Washington early in the morning of a January day and discovered that all federal offices had been closed due to an ice storm. A staff member found me sitting on the floor in the hallway and generously allowed me to come inside and begin my work although they were officially closed.

I owe thanks to the following for permission to draw upon my previous publications: the University of Illinois Press for *Victor Arnautoff and the Politics of Art* (University of Illinois Press, 2017); the San Francisco Historical Society for "The Controversy at Coit Tower, 1934," in *The Argonaut* 28 (Summer 2017); and the University of California Press for "San Francisco's New-Deal Murals in Long-Term Perspective: Controversy, Neglect, and Restoration," *California History* 97 (February 2020).

Several people read and commented on early drafts, and I appreciate the comments of Richard Rothman, Harvey Smith, and the anonymous reviewers chosen by the University of Illinois Press. Mark Dean Johnson was especially helpful in directing my attention to legacies, which led to a separate chapter on the subject. Jon Golinger was both perceptive in his comments and generous in sharing his rich collection of primary source material. Special thanks must also go to Bill Issel, a colleague and friend for more than fifty years, whose advice was helpful throughout but especially as I was focusing on the final chapter.

Thanks are also due to the editorial staff at the University of Illinois Press, especially Alison Syring, Tad Ringo, and to Jill Hughes, who did her usual outstanding copyediting.

And, of course, I owe special thanks to my family: Rebecca, my wife and partner of fifty-seven years; Sarah, our daughter, who, among her many gifts to us, does her best to keep us healthy; and Cerys and Sabina, our granddaughters, who took part in their COVID-caused Zoom classes in our dining room and my study while I worked on my projects in the living room. Only grandparents will understand what a pleasure it was to have them in the house for those many months.

The Coit Tower Murals

1

The Origin of the Coit Tower Murals

The Great Depression, Coit Tower, San Francisco Artists, the Mexican Muralists, and the New Deal Art Projects

The spectacular murals at Coit Tower resulted from the convergence of four elements: the San Francisco arts community; the influence of Mexican muralists, especially Diego Rivera; the availability of bare walls in the new Coit Tower; and the first federal program to provide work relief for artists. And all of these existed within the larger context of the Great Depression.

In October 1929 the New York stock market crashed. It continued to fall over the following weeks, months, and years. From a high point of 381.17 on September 3, 1929, the Dow Jones Industrial Average fell to 41.22 on July 8, 1932, a decline of nearly 90 percent. The crash set off the Great Depression. As the economy spiraled downward, banks were unable to meet their obligations, declared bankruptcy, and closed their doors. Credit dried up. Amid this, the Federal Reserve raised interest rates, further contributing to the credit crunch. The economy lurched toward paralysis. Unemployment rose from 3 percent in 1929 to 25 percent in 1933, with much higher rates in manufacturing areas. By 1933, the average annual family income had dropped by 35 percent.[1]

In San Francisco, manufacturing companies reduced production. Fewer ships came to the port, the center of much of the city's economy. Unemployment grew. Those without work became eligible for work relief: a week's labor on some city projects brought a family a three-week supply of groceries. In 1929 some seventeen hundred families received such relief each month; by 1933 some eighteen thousand families were receiving relief—almost 10 percent of all families. The demand for work relief soon outstripped city funds, but voters approved bond issues in 1931 and 1932 to continue relief programs. The city also drew on bond issues to construct public infrastructure, thus providing some jobs and economic stimulation. Those projects included several school buildings and two great bridges, one across the Golden Gate and the other across San Francisco Bay, linking San Francisco with Oakland.[2]

The Coit Memorial Tower was another new construction project, but it was not financed by a bond issue. When Lillie Hitchcock Coit died in 1929, her will contained two bequests to the city, one to memorialize the city's firefighters and the other to beautify the city. The former was accomplished through statuary in Washington Square, the latter by construction of Coit Memorial Tower, a commemorative monument and observation tower in Pioneer Park, at the top of Telegraph Hill, the highest point along the city's waterfront. Designed by Arthur Brown Jr. and rendered by Henry Howard, the tower is 182 feet high and constructed with unpainted, reinforced concrete. It is a three-part cylindrical composition (fluted shaft, belvedere, and lantern) that rises from a squared, cubic base. The belvedere and lantern levels at the top form observation platforms, accessible by both an elevator and stairs. High-relief sculptures over the entrance comprise the only exterior decoration. There, Robert Boardman Howard, brother of Henry Howard, sculpted a phoenix, the mythical bird that is reborn from its ashes, a symbol of San Francisco since the 1850s, and, flanking the phoenix, two fasces, traditional symbols of republican government since Roman times. The tower was completed and dedicated in October 1933.[3]

Public construction and local work-relief programs failed to restore the city's economy. Unemployment reached 32 percent. For some, economic crisis fueled interest in radical solutions. The Communist Party (CP) organized unemployment councils, and their demonstrations drew far more people than the CP's dues-paying membership. In early 1931 the CP organized a "hunger march" in San Francisco that attracted some three thousand demonstrators. In the 1931 and 1933 city elections, Communist candidates drew more than ten thousand votes. In 1933 the Communist-led Cannery and Agricultural Workers International Union carried out a series of strikes by farmworkers, culminating in October with a strike by some twelve thousand workers in the cotton fields of the southern San Joaquin Valley. The party's newspaper, the *Western Worker*, was available in most parts of the city. By February 1934 the CP counted 2,532 dues-paying members in California, about half of them in the Bay Area.[4]

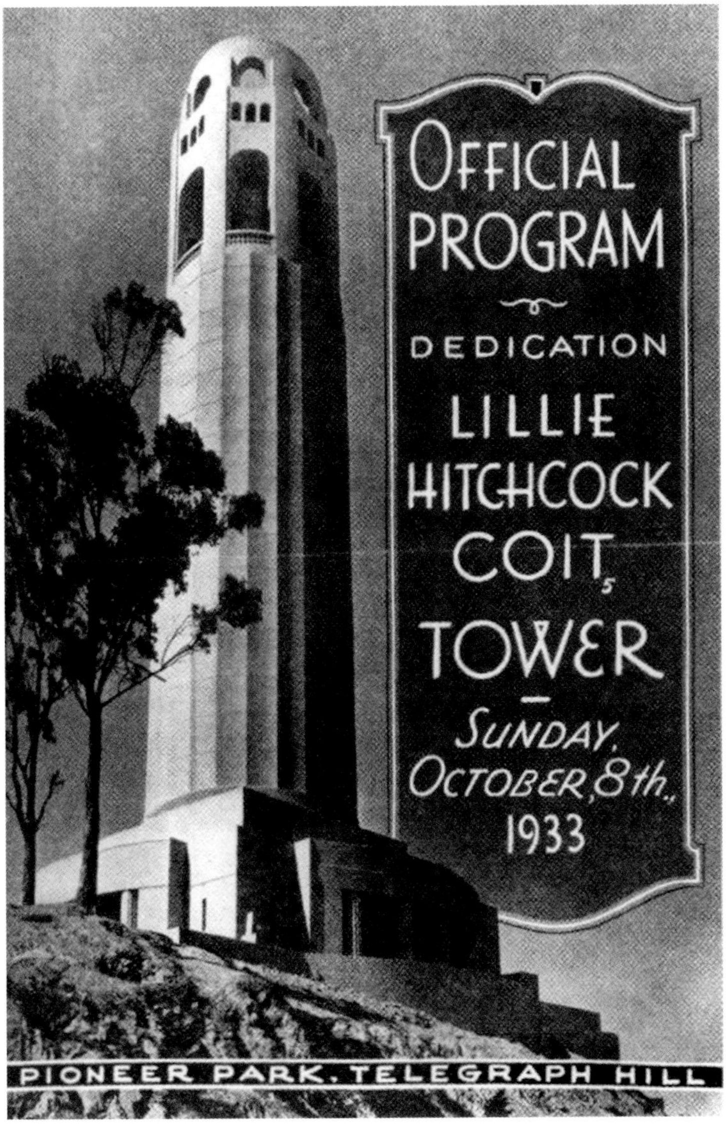

Figure 1.1. The Lillie Hitchcock Coit Memorial Tower was completed in October 1933. (Source: Masha Zakheim, *Coit Tower, San Francisco: Its History and Art* (2009), courtesy of the heirs of Masha Zakheim.)

Though San Francisco's artists were hard hit by the Great Depression, the large majority left no record of attraction to the CP. The city's major art enclave had long been the neighborhood surrounding the intersection of Montgomery and Washington streets. There, old buildings with low rents attracted artists and fostered a bohemian subculture. Many artists had studios in the Montgomery Block, a four-story building that dated to the 1850s, often called the "Monkey Block," and other artists maintained studios in several buildings to its north. A group of artists organized a cooperative gallery, the Art Center, at 728 Montgomery in the block between Washington and Jackson streets, a building filled with artists'

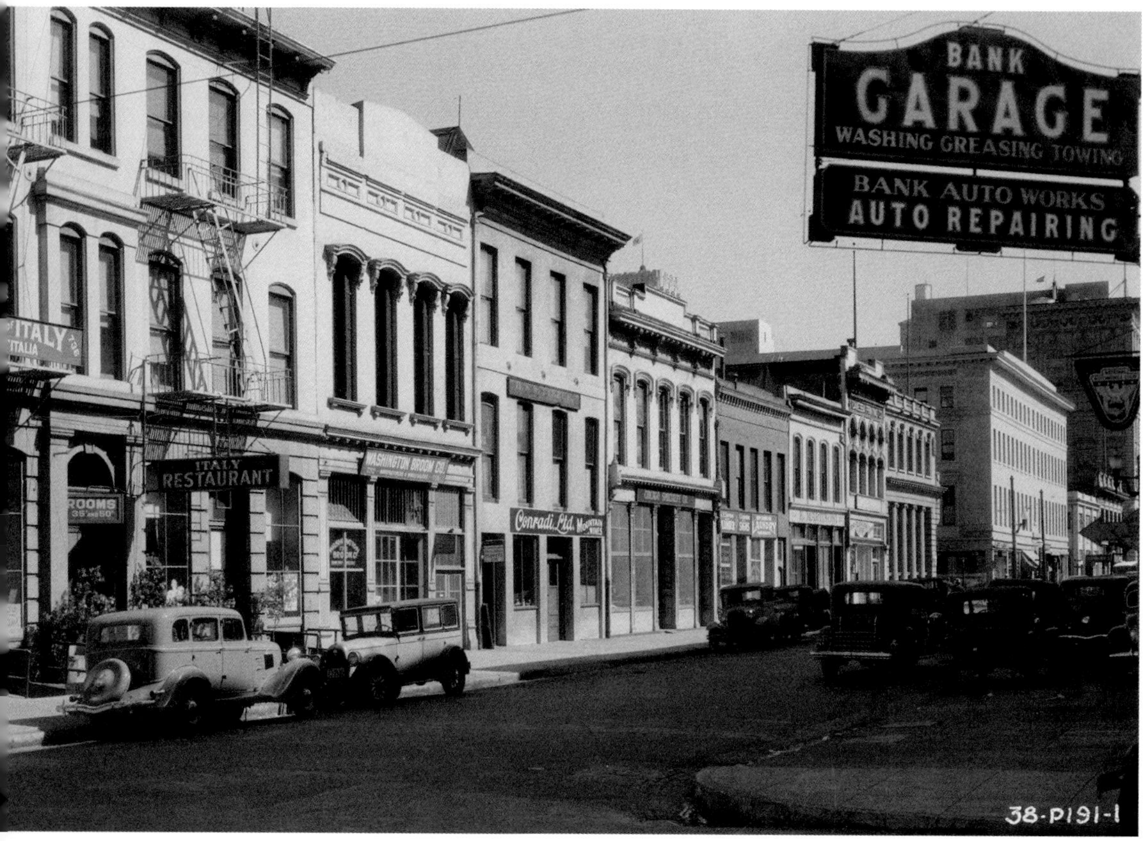

Figure 1.2. Montgomery Street between Washington and Jackson, c. 1930. The Montgomery Block is the light-colored, four-story building on the right. The Art Center was at 728 Montgomery. The building to the right of it, 722 Montgomery, also had artists' studios. (Source: Historic American Building Survey CA-1474, accessed through LOC.GETarchive.net.)

studios. In 1931 the *San Francisco Chronicle* described the Art Center group as "radical"—but based entirely on their modernist approach to art, not their politics. The artists who clustered in this enclave included many who would have been at home in the bohemian districts of New York or Paris. The city's largest Italian neighborhood began just steps to the north, where even poor artists could usually afford a plate of spaghetti and some red wine, which was generally available throughout Prohibition.[5]

The California School of Fine Arts (CSFA) was the other pole of the city's arts community. Perhaps the leading art school on the Pacific Coast, the CSFA had recently opened a new campus at Chestnut and Jones streets, a twenty-minute walk from Montgomery and Washington. Several faculty members had studios near Montgomery and Washington; other artists with studios there had been students at the school. The San Francisco Art Association (SFAA) oversaw the CSFA and mounted

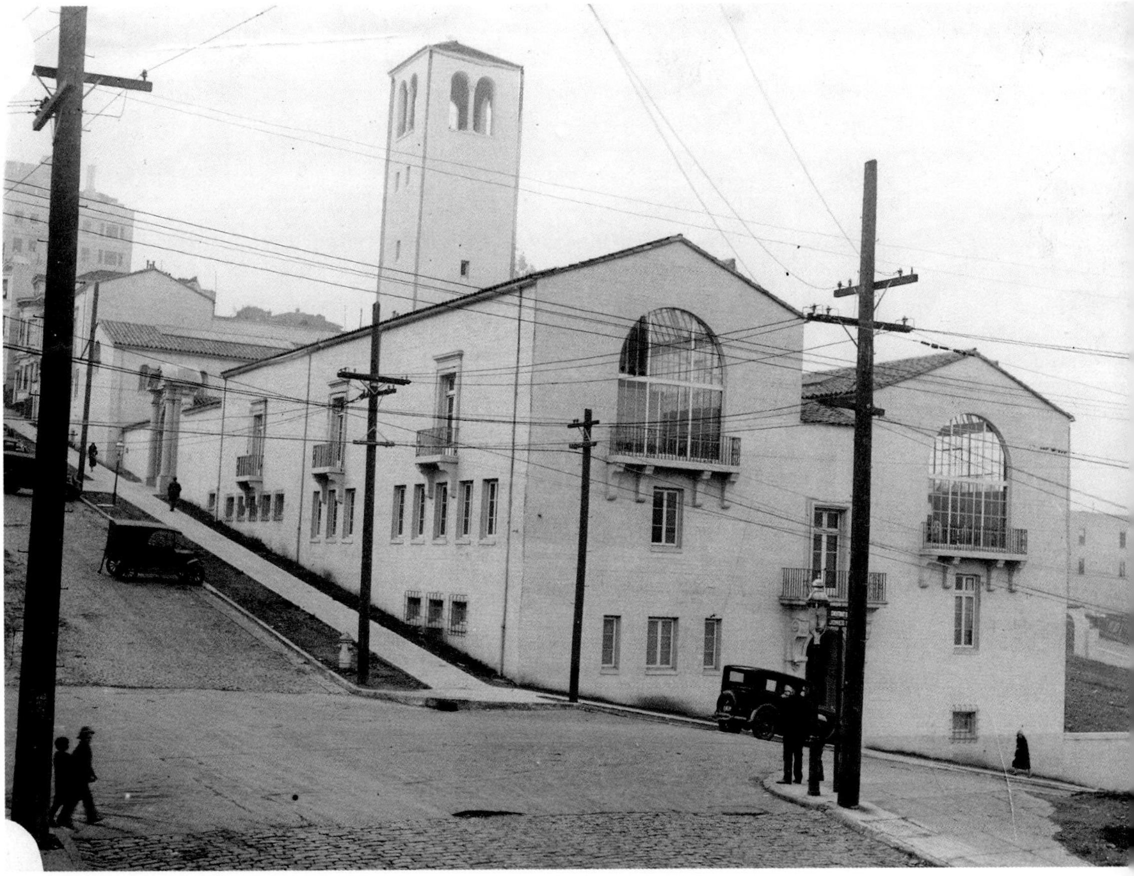

Figure 1.3. The new campus of the California School of Fine Arts (later the San Francisco Art Institute) was designed by Arthur Brown Jr.; this photo is from 1927. (Source: Photo AAD-7797, courtesy of San Francisco History Center, San Francisco Public Library.)

annual exhibitions. Organized in 1871, the SFAA membership included both artists and art patrons, but its leaders came from a quite different social milieu than most artists: the board of directors reads like a list of the city's social elite. Would-be artist members of the SFAA had to be vetted and approved before their membership could be accepted. During the 1930 census, more than a thousand San Franciscans recorded themselves as "artists, sculptors, teachers of art," but the SFAA counted only ninety-one artist members in 1931, and many of the SFAA's artist members had some connection to the CSFA.[6] Both the Monkey Block and the CSFA campus were easily visible from the windows of Coit Tower, which was a fifteen- or twenty-minute walk from both.

In the late 1920s and early 1930s, some CSFA faculty members were involved in creating large murals in buildings open to the public. In 1928 Raymond Boynton completed an elaborate mural project, partly in fresco, around the sides and above the center stage of the new music hall at Mills

College, in Oakland. The central panel, not fresco, was of a California landscape but with bold colors and patterns suggestive of the influence of the Mexican muralists; the side panels were allegorical depictions of joy, on one side, and sorrow, on the other, featuring nudes in idealized landscapes. From 1931 to 1932 Gottardo Piazzoni created *The Land*, five large murals depicting the area's landscape, and *The Sea*, five murals depicting the area's seascapes, for the second-floor loggia surrounding the staircase of San Francisco's Main Library.[7]

Ralph Stackpole, a leading CSFA faculty member best known as a sculptor, was among the most prominent California artists in the 1920s. He had begun his art studies at a predecessor of the CSFA and continued in Paris at the École des Beaux-Arts, one of the leading art schools in the world. While in Paris, he befriended Diego Rivera, and their friendship persisted after each returned home. Before returning to San Francisco, Stackpole studied briefly in New York with Robert Henri, a leader in the "Ash Can" school, which emphasized painting from everyday life, especially the urban working class. Stackpole's studio, at 716 Montgomery Street, in the block north of Washington, was a popular gathering place for local artists.[8]

San Francisco had two major art museums in the early 1930s. The California Palace of the Legion of Honor had opened in 1925, housed in a copy of the *palais* by the same name in Paris. Its first exhibition featured contemporary French art. The new museum was quite unlike the city's older De Young Museum, which had long reflected the eclectic tastes of its founder and longtime chief patron, Michael De Young, whose death, also in 1925, marked the beginning of the transformation of the De Young Museum into a more professional art museum.[9]

In late 1932, amid the economic disaster of the Great Depression, Americans held a presidential election. Franklin D. Roosevelt, the Democrat, swept to victory, winning almost two-thirds of the vote in San Francisco. Upon taking office in March 1933, he summoned Congress into special session. Within a hundred days, Roosevelt and Congress wrote into law measures intended to reverse the economic paralysis, initiate economic reforms, provide relief for the unemployed, and end Prohibition. Roosevelt's programs were quickly labeled the New Deal. Among the early New Deal programs was the Federal Emergency Relief Act of 1933, designed initially to allocate funds to states to provide work relief for the unemployed. Roosevelt appointed Harry Hopkins, a former social worker, to head the Federal Emergency Relief Administration. Unhappy with the slow pace of relief in many states, and concerned about the approach of winter, Roosevelt and Hopkins created the Civil Works Administration (CWA) as a temporary measure to provide direct federal relief through the winter of 1933–1934 by hiring jobless people to work on federal, state, and local projects. The CWA was intended to provide work for as many unemployed people as possible and also to create permanent public infrastructure. For the first time, the federal government directly provided relief to the unemployed.[10]

The creation of the CWA coincided with efforts by George Biddle, a wealthy artist and art patron, to encourage President Roosevelt, his former classmate, to create a federal art program. Biddle had traveled to Mexico in the late 1920s and returned enthusiastic about the work of Mexican artists in transforming public buildings with murals in a style soon labeled Mexican Modernism. The murals were bold, colorful, and usually carried a message. Those murals began in the early 1920s under President Álvaro Obregón, whose administration focused on land reform and guaranteeing basic human rights. Education Minister José Vasconcelos commissioned artists to paint murals in public buildings as a way to celebrate the Mexican Revolution (1910–1920) and the values of the Obregón administration; to honor ordinary Mexicans, including the indigenous population; and to provide instruction on the nation's history and accomplishments. The most prominent among these Mexican muralists were Diego Rivera, José Clemente Orozco, and David Alfaro Siqueiros, the trio becoming known as *Los Tres Grandes*.[11]

Biddle was not alone in his regard for the Mexican muralists. By 1933 many American artists and art patrons had become familiar with the work of the Mexican muralists and had traveled to Mexico to see the murals and watch the muralists at work. Rivera had completed two large murals in San Francisco and a smaller one nearby in 1930–1931 as well as an extensive project in Detroit in 1932–1933. In March 1933 he began a major mural in New York City. Orozco had studied at CSFA and lived in the Montgomery Block in 1917–1919 before he created murals in Los Angeles and New York City; he returned to San Francisco for a brief visit in 1930, shortly before Rivera began his first mural in San Francisco. In 1933 Orozco was completing a set of murals at Dartmouth College in New Hampshire. And Siqueiros had created two murals in Los Angeles.[12]

Biddle explained the significance of the Mexican mural movement and its relation to the Roosevelt administration in a letter to Roosevelt in early May 1933, two months after Roosevelt took office:

> The Mexican artists have produced the greatest national school of mural painting since the Italian Renaissance. Diego Rivera tells me that it was possible only because Obregón allowed Mexican artists to work at plumbers' wages in order to express on the walls of the government buildings the social ideals of the Mexican revolution.
>
> The younger artists of America are conscious as they have never been of the social revolution that our country and civilization are going through; and they would be eager to express these ideals in a permanent

> art form if they were given the government's co-operation. They would be contributing to and expressing in living monuments the social ideals that you are struggling to achieve. And I am convinced that our mural art with a little impetus can soon result, for the first time in our history, in a vital national expression.[13]

Roosevelt agreed with Biddle that his administration should promote contemporary art in public buildings, and he connected Biddle with Edward Bruce, an official in the Treasury Department. Bruce, a former lawyer and banker, was also an artist and art collector. He had lived in San Francisco for a time but left in 1932 to go to Washington, D.C. Biddle and Bruce worked with other federal officials to create a program using CWA funds to provide work relief for unemployed artists so they could create art for public buildings. Bruce took charge of the new program, the Public Works of Art Project (PWAP), launched in early December 1933 through a meeting with a dozen museum directors from around the country. Eleanor Roosevelt, wife of the president, also took part. (A photograph of Bruce, Eleanor Roosevelt, and other federal officials examining a map of the sixteen PWAP regions became the basis for part of Lucien Labaudt's mural at Coit Tower.) Bruce appointed Forbes Watson as technical director, the person most directly involved with the artists.[14]

The PWAP was the first New Deal program to employ artists and fund public arts projects. Its goals were twofold: to support professional artists and thereby create quality public art, and to educate the public to appreciate professional artists, but to do so without threatening patriotism or violating conventional art traditions. Bruce wrote to each PWAP artist in mid-January to emphasize the latter purpose of the program:

> I am sure that you are approaching the work with a feeling that we all have down here, that you are going to give to it the finest that is in you and help to make of this work not only a record of which our country may be proud but to sell to the American people the idea that art is and should be an integral part of our civilization. . . . We should all recognize that art is an expression of national culture and that it takes artists of all schools and types to make this expression a rounded one. It is time that all of us forget ourselves and our individual interests and personal preferences for the sake of a great cause.[15]

The CWA, and PWAP as a part of it, were always defined as temporary, to provide work relief over the winter of 1933–1934. PWAP was scheduled to last for just nineteen weeks. During that time, the agency engaged more than three thousand artists to adorn public buildings with murals, easel paintings, sculptures, and other artworks. The artists were removed from the PWAP payroll as soon as they completed their individual commissions but by April 28 at the latest, whether they had finished or not.

Soon after, in a letter on May 2, 1934, Bruce made clear that some federal art program would survive: "The President . . . and Mrs. Roosevelt have indicated a keen interest not only in the success of the Public Works of Art Project, but in the propriety of a continued effort on the part of the Federal Government to foster the art movement in this country. This attitude is shared by a large group of important officials in the Government."[16]

What emerged were two different approaches to federal funding for the arts. Bruce was committed both to democratizing art by bringing it to large numbers of Americans and to maintaining a high level of quality. He headed the Treasury Department's Section of Painting and Sculpture (1934–1942), renamed the Section of Fine Arts in 1938. Usually called "the Section," Bruce's agency oversaw the creation of art, often murals, in federal buildings, especially the many new post offices and other federal buildings that were part of the New Deal's program to stimulate the economy by construction of permanent infrastructure. Bruce's insistence on quality came up against the desire of other New Deal officials to provide work for as many unemployed artists as possible. The result was the Federal Art Project (FAP) within the Works Progress Administration (WPA; 1935–1943), the New Deal's major work-relief program. The WPA/FAP provided work relief for artists to create art for local and state public buildings. A similar work-relief program existed briefly in the Treasury Department called the Treasury Relief Art Project (TRAP; 1935–1938).[17]

The PWAP set important patterns for the subsequent New Deal art programs. PWAP artists were instructed to paint "the American Scene," a theme that was central to all subsequent federal programs. Previous art in federal buildings and in many, if not most, state and local governmental buildings had been as classical as the buildings' architecture. References to classical antiquity, historical allegories, and the early history of the United States abounded in much of the previous public art. The New Deal programs' emphasis on the American scene reflects in part the influence of the Mexican muralists, who drew upon Mexican themes in most of their bold public murals; it also reflects the influence of early twentieth-century American artists who had chosen to paint what they saw around them, notably the Ash Can school of the early twentieth century and the American Scene artists, centered in the Middle West, of the 1920s and early 1930s. As Belisario R. Contreras indicates in his *Tradition and Innovation in New Deal Art* (1983), "The American scene . . . pointed to the rejection of the European influences that had dominated American art during the 1920s." The emphasis on the American scene also largely excluded abstract art.[18]

Lenore Clark, in her biography of Forbes Watson, Bruce's chief assistant in administering the PWAP, provides this account of the significance of the American scene for PWAP artists: "The assumption was that art depicting images from daily life was most likely to touch average citizens. . . . To requests for clarification of 'American scene,' they [Bruce and Watson] responded in general terms, encouraging artists to draw from local life and lore. Watson, who could barely tolerate the 'scholastic frumpery' of academic muralists, suggested that artists use contemporary rather than historical topics."[19] There is no evidence that the Coit Tower muralists had any direct contact with Watson, but they did exactly what Watson suggested.

The four New Deal arts programs—PWAP, Treasury Section, WPA/FAP, and TRAP—created an unprecedented outpouring of public art in all parts of the country. As Marlene Park and Gerald E. Markowitz explain in their book *Democratic Vistas* (1984), "New Dealers developed the most innovative and comprehensive program for government art patronage in American history," employing more than ten thousand artists to produce one hundred thousand easel paintings, eighteen thousand sculptures, thirteen thousand prints, and more than four thousand murals. Park and Markowitz further explain, "The New Deal sought to change the relationship between the artist and society by democratizing art and culture. . . . The projects were a uniquely American blend, combining an elitist belief in the value of high culture with the democratic ideal that everyone in the society could and should be the beneficiary of such efforts." Further, they point out, "New Dealers expected that the art projects would help create a national culture."[20]

Although public murals were the smallest in number among the results of the New Deal art programs, they have since provided the most visible examples of New Deal art. The easel paintings may have ended up in museums, offices, and courtrooms (and, for some, the scrap pile), but many—probably a significant majority—of the New Deal murals remain on the walls of post offices, schools, libraries, and other public buildings all across the country. As a result, murals have come to be considered typical of New Deal art. They continue to be of interest to scholars and members of the public, as witness the large number of books in recent decades that have surveyed surviving New Deal murals within a single state or region.[21]

The Coit Tower murals represent one of the largest collections of New Deal murals outside Washington, D.C. They were the first New Deal art project to involve a large number of artists at one site. Later projects involving multiple artists at sites in Washington, D.C., were completed over several years,[22] but most of the twenty-eight murals at Coit Tower were done by seventeen artists in about four months, and the remainder were done by eight artists in less than seven months.[23] And the Coit Tower murals were the first New Deal art project to generate a national controversy, one that significantly affected later New Deal art projects.

2

Creating the Coit Tower Murals

In 1964 Bernard Zakheim looked back at the depth of the Depression. "The artists were in a terrible financial condition," he said, and recounted how one was cleaning toilets for a living while offering a one-man show at the Legion of Honor, and another was threatening to commit suicide because he had nothing to eat.[1]

Zakheim, born in Poland, had come to the United States in 1920. Trained as a furniture maker, he engaged in that trade while taking art classes at the predecessor of the CSFA. In the early 1930s, he went to Mexico to meet Rivera and then studied painting in Paris and learned fresco painting in Hungary. Returning to San Francisco in 1932, he received a commission for a fresco mural at the new Jewish Community Center. By 1933 he had joined the Communist Party but often kept his membership secret. That year, he recalled, he teamed up with Kenneth Rexroth, an organizer for the John Reed Club—the CP's organization for intellectuals—who was then at the beginning of his career as a poet. Zakheim recalled that they "went around from studio to studio talking to each artist separately" and promoting the notion of getting "commissions from the government." In early December, Ralph Stackpole assisted them in gathering a group of artists at Maynard Dixon's studio, one of the many at 728 Montgomery. Zakheim recalled that Stackpole had "a friend, a financial expert and artist from San Francisco" who might be of help—Edward Bruce—which suggests that Stackpole knew something of the events then percolating in Washington. Pooling their pennies, the artists collected enough for Stackpole to send Bruce a night letter about the destitution of artists and their need for jobs.[2]

National developments were rapidly converging to create exactly what the San Francisco artists wanted. On December 8, Bruce's planning group met in Washington, with Eleanor Roosevelt present. They agreed to Bruce's approach and divided the country into sixteen regions. Northern California, Nevada, and Utah became PWAP Region 15. On December 10 Bruce appointed Walter Heil, recently named as director of San Francisco's De Young Museum, to head Region 15 and encouraged him to act quickly to commission works of art and locate appropriate public buildings where art might be installed. Zakheim, apparently unaware of the events in Washington, attributed this to the artists' letter to Bruce: "In an amazing short time, came a telegram to the De Young Museum to Heil, to get the artists together and send them on a project."[3]

Heil immediately created an advisory committee to discuss locations and themes for public art. Coit Tower quickly came to the fore as a site. Originally intended to house an exhibition of artifacts and works of art from pioneer days, the tower remained vacant except for the caretaker's apartment. When the tower was proposed as a site for murals, Arthur Brown Jr., the tower's architect, reluctantly agreed; he was not enthusiastic about the idea of modernist murals but may have agreed to putting them in Coit Tower as a way to keep them out of his recently completed opera house. In keeping with the directive that PWAP projects depict the American Scene, Heil's committee directed that the Coit Tower murals should depict contemporary California, a theme that was unusual for a public building up to that time but fully in keeping with the goals of Bruce and Watson. Now all the first- and second-floor interior walls and the spiral staircase between the first and second floors were to be adorned with murals depicting a contemporary and local version of "the American Scene," centered on everyday life in San Francisco and the Bay Area.[4]

On December 15 the *San Francisco Chronicle* reported that local artists "by the score" were "descending upon Dr. Walter Heil," and "Many of the artists are being assigned immediately to draw up sketches for the decoration of municipal, State or Federal buildings." In fact, only municipal buildings were involved. And oral histories make it clear that some who were "descending" on Heil were responding to an invitation to do so. With advice from Stackpole, Heil assigned 50 master artists and assistants to the Coit Tower project and sent 130 others to projects in or for other city buildings.[5] Stackpole was well positioned to advise; he was something of a father figure to many of the younger painters, several of whom had been his students at the CSFA. For Coit Tower, Heil's final report lists 25 master artists, 14 assistant artists who were assigned to one or more of the master artists, 5 "general" assistant artists, a "mural coordinator" assistant artist, 2 plasterers, and 2 volunteer assistants. The assistant artists were all artists in their own right. In keeping with Bruce's commitment to quality, those chosen included some of the region's best-known artists, a large majority of whom had some connection to the CSFA. Stackpole,

Ray Boynton, Otis Oldfield, and Lucien Labaudt taught there, and several others had been their students.[6]

By then, Diego Rivera had established a reputation as the most prominent muralist in the Americas and the role model for other muralists.[7] He had recently created three murals in the Bay Area: at the new Pacific Coast Stock Exchange tower in San Francisco's Financial District, at the family home of Sigmund and Rosalie Stern in Atherton, a suburb south of San Francisco, and at the CSFA.[8] Unlike the recent murals in Oakland by Ray Boynton or those in San Francisco by Gottardo Piazzoni, Rivera's murals in San Francisco were filled with images of people, some of them identifiable San Franciscans, and some of them were simply going about their everyday work. Among the master artists at Coit Tower, many had some experience with Rivera. Victor Arnautoff had spent two years as Rivera's assistant in Mexico, working on the murals at Cuernavaca and on the initial phases of the mural over the stairway at the National Palace. When Rivera came to San Francisco, he left Arnautoff in charge of finishing up at Cuernavaca and beginning at the National Palace. Clifford Wight, another master artist at Coit Tower, had assisted Rivera in Detroit. Five other master artists—Stackpole, Boynton, Zakheim, Maxine Albro, and Parker Hall—had visited Rivera in Mexico and observed his technique. All were familiar with Rivera's recent works in San Francisco. Albro and Wight had assisted him, and many of the rest had watched Rivera at work while in the city. Arnautoff was designated as technical coordinator for the Coit Tower project. He had spent the most time working with Rivera, was well experienced working with large-scale fresco murals, and had recently completed fresco murals in Palo Alto, in his studio on Washington Street, and in another artist's studio. According to Heil, "The artists established for themselves one scale and also one palette consisting of elementary earth colors," much the same palette used by Rivera.[9]

There is no indication in the available evidence that Heil and Stackpole were consciously selecting a diverse group of artists for Coit Tower, but the final twenty-five master artists were nonetheless representative of general patterns within the city's arts community and the city itself. Seven (35 percent) were born outside the United States, as compared with 24 percent of the city's population; twenty-three (92 percent) were white, as compared with 94 percent of the city's population. The major disproportion is in gender. The four women made up 16 percent of the total, but according to the 1930 census, women made up 38 percent of all "artists, sculptors, and teachers of art" in San Francisco, and as of 1934, women accounted for three of the sixteen members (19 percent) of the Artists Council of the San Francisco Art Association.[10]

All but four of the master artists agreed to work in *buon fresco*, the technique used by Rivera and the other Mexican muralists. Otis Oldfield,

José Moya del Pino, and Rinaldo Cuneo agreed to the palette but preferred to use oil paint on canvas. They were assigned a separate space, the elevator lobby. They did not work on site but in Cuneo's studio on Montgomery Street. Jane Berlandina preferred to use egg tempera, which involves painting on dry plaster, and also preferred a more abstract style and a different palette. She was also given a separate room, at the end of the second-floor corridor.[11]

The Coit Tower project was overseen by the San Francisco Art Commission. Its Committee on Architecture reviewed both scaled drawings of the proposed murals and, for the fresco painters, the detailed, full-scale drawings prepared by the individual artists on the walls. The artists produced their preliminary sketches in mid- and late December, transferred them to the walls as soon as sandblasting was complete in mid-January, and then began to work in earnest. While the murals were being executed, the tower was a busy and crowded place, especially in the first month or more, when all the artists were working from scaffolds, usually with powerful portable lighting. In addition to the master artists, assistant artists, and plasterers, there were seven laborers, a few volunteers, and several park department employees—more than sixty people in all, plus reporters and curious members of the public. The three working with oil on canvas seem to have visited the tower regularly.[12]

A comment by Maxine Albro in her 1964 oral history suggests that Arnautoff was involved in the organization of the murals within the ground floor. Albro had received the commission to do the largest mural on agriculture, and Arnautoff was to do the largest one on city life. According to Albro, Arnautoff traded sites with her because, "his subject matter . . . would work better on that wall."[13] In fact, Arnautoff (and likely others in the planning process) was placing the largest murals quite consciously: his treatment of city life faces the south window, looking out over the city; Albro's study of agriculture faces the east window, the direction of California's interior with its agricultural cropland; and Stackpole's mural of industry faces west, overlooking industrial sites along the north waterfront.[14] The smaller murals on the ground floor are arranged topically around the largest ones.

By focusing on contemporary life and employing the techniques of the Mexican muralists, especially Rivera, the Coit Tower fresco artists were among those breaking new ground for public art. Nearly all the Coit Tower murals exhibit a social consciousness—an awareness of their own society. Nearly all feature ordinary people engaged in a wide range of everyday activities, including working. Like much of Rivera's art, some of the Coit Tower murals exhibit social realism—that is, they not only depict their own society but also pose a critique of it. In their social consciousness and social realism, the Coit Tower artists helped to expand the boundaries

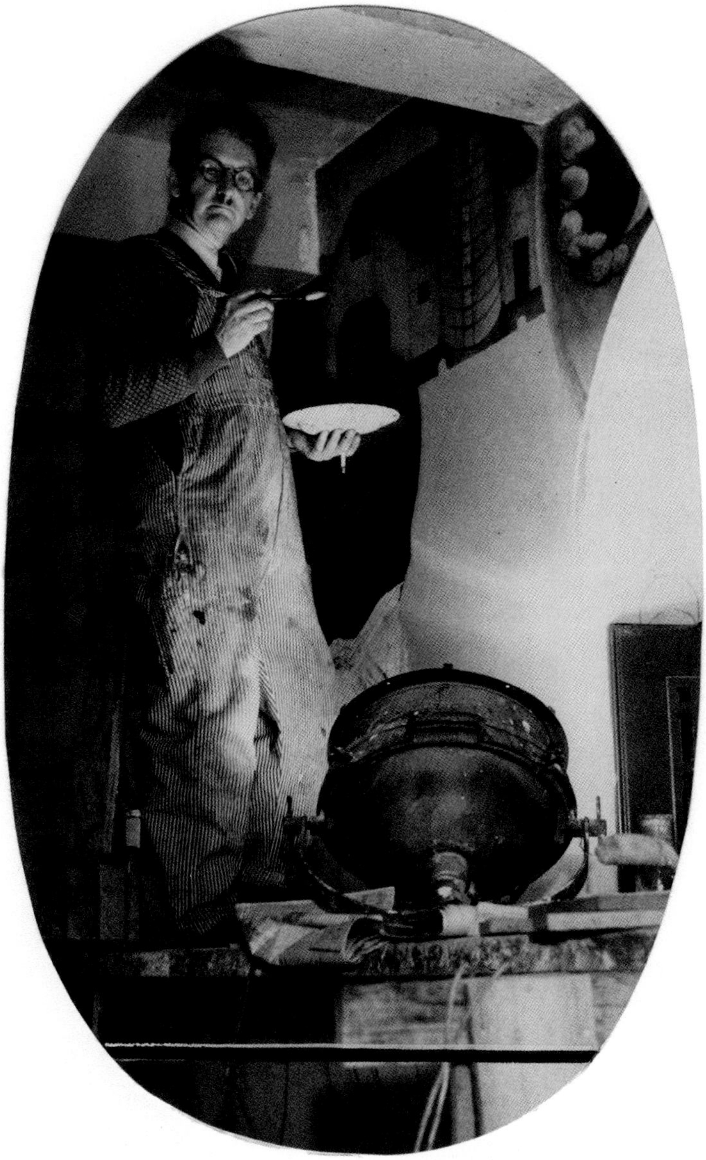

Figure 2.1. Fresco artists necessarily worked from the top down. Ray Boynton was high on a scaffold, working with a portable light, on February 5. (Source: Photo MOR-0668, courtesy of San Francisco History Center, San Francisco Public Library.)

of what had been acceptable in public art. Both of these themes became prominent in later New Deal art projects.

Much of the enthusiasm and esprit de corps among the artists at Coit Tower came from the opportunity to work in fresco. Some of the artists had not worked with that medium before the project. Boynton, however, had begun working in buon fresco in 1917 and was teaching classes in that medium at the CSFA by the mid-1920s. At least eight of the Coit Tower muralists had been Boynton's students at the CSFA. At Coit Tower he provided instruction and dispensed advice.[15]

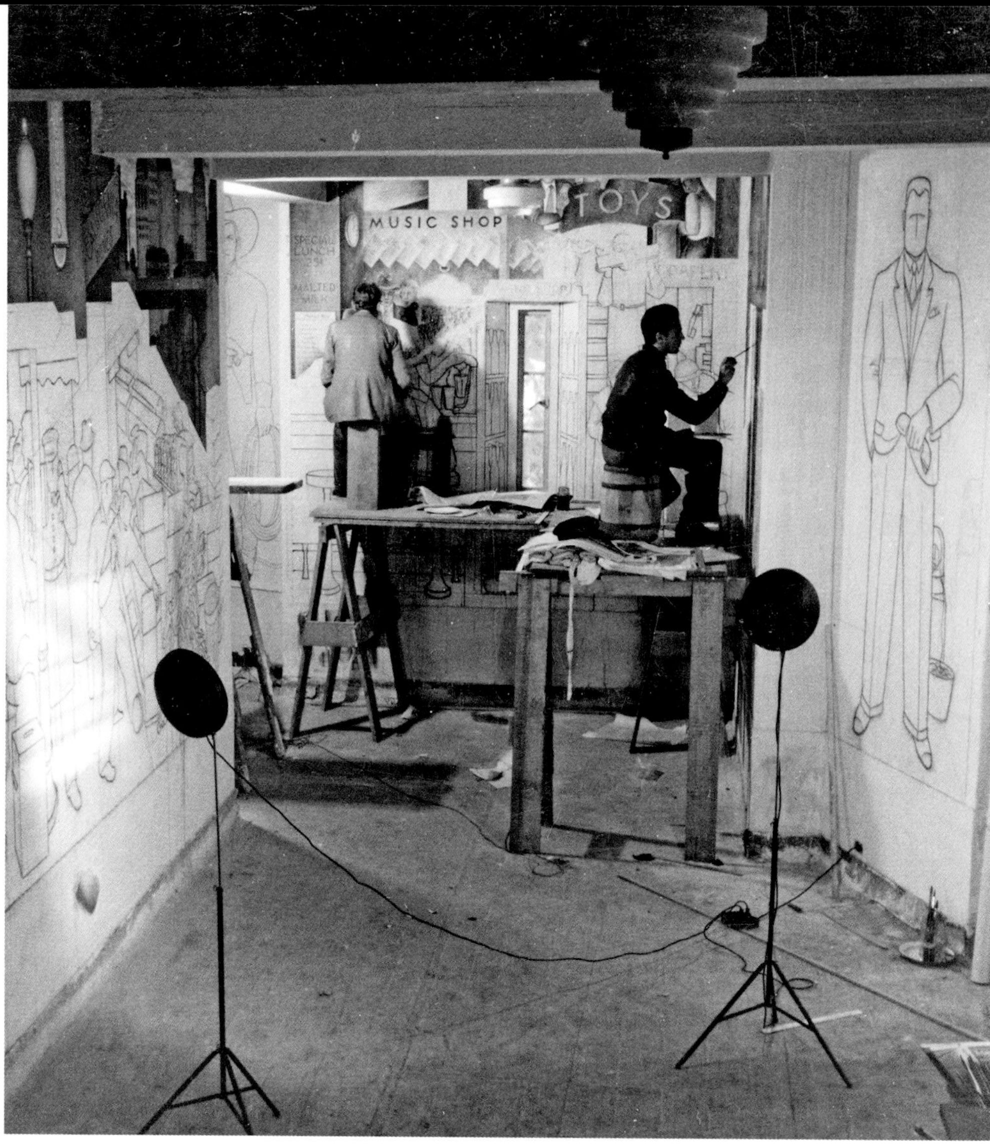

Figure 2.2. Frede Vidar (left) and George Harris, were both working on scaffolds, apparently in early February. Arnautoff's work is visible in the foreground on the left; Dean's is on the left. (Source: Photographer unknown, artists at work, Coit Tower, 1934; United States General Services Administration, formerly Federal Works Agency, Works Progress Administration [WPA], allocation to the San Francisco Museum of Modern Art; courtesy of the San Francisco Museum of Modern Art.)

The Coit Tower artists working in buon fresco followed the Mexican artists' version of the ancient Italian tradition. In this process, fine marble dust is mixed with slaked lime to create the painting surface. A plasterer prepares the surface with this plaster, and the artist then applies ground pigment mixed with water as long as the surface remains moist. As the plaster dries, the pigment becomes part of the wall. Edward Johnson and Farwell Taylor, assistant artists directed by Arnautoff, were responsible for grinding all the pigments, assuring overall color uniformity among the fresco muralists. Other assistant artists filled in details while the master artists attended to the major features. Shirley Staschen, an assistant to Zakheim, remembered that work hours were quite casual and that the master artists typically painted for five or six hours—about the time it took to complete one square yard of wet plaster—and then began to prepare for the next day's work. However, the artists did not typically work with a square of fresh plaster; instead, the fresh plaster was placed within the outline of some feature so that the border of one day's work fit into a line in the final mural, thus concealing the lines between different days' work as much as possible. The work schedule also reflected the close quarters: Suzanne Scheuer, one of the master artists, recalled that the artists painting on adjoining walls sometimes worked in shifts and that her shift began at 5:00 a.m.[16]

Harold Mack, a leading member of Heil's committee and a longtime friend of Bruce, wrote to Bruce on January 9 that the artists "have changed from a sullen, suspicious group, suffering greatly from inferiority complexes, into a cooperative, intelligent body, far easier to deal with than the various commissions with which we have been forced to come in contact."[17]

Mack did not mention the Art Commission specifically, but the commission was moving at a snail's pace. It tentatively approved the list of topics and probably also the scaled drawings on January 8. Although the Art Commission waited until February 27 to grant its final approval, the artists had already begun to work based on the earlier approval of topics and scale drawings. On January 23, Heil described Coit Tower as "a swarming beehive of master artists, assistants and plasterers, as well as newspaper reporters." Those painting on canvas made quick progress. Oldfield had substantially completed his landscape by early March, and Moya del Pina finished his landscape at about the same time. The fresco artists took longer. Sandblasting to prepare the walls took until mid-January. Next the artists placed detailed drawings of their murals on the walls. The Art Commission's Committee on Architecture reviewed and tentatively approved those drawings on January 27.[18]

The murals are on two levels. The ground-floor corridor forms a square, with the entrance on the north and large windows in the center of the east, south, and west walls. The ground floor was designated for California agriculture, industry, and city life resulting from both, with the four largest murals on the interior walls, facing the windows and entrance. Eight smaller murals are on the exterior walls. Tall figures (reminiscent of Rivera's giant construction worker at CSFA) are on either side of the three windows; the artists who did those figures also decorated the area above the windows. More murals were done along the stairway to the second floor and along the hallway and in a room on that floor. Most of the large sites were assigned to experienced fresco muralists, and some of the smaller murals were also by artists experienced in fresco.

When entering, agricultural scenes are to the left, including the use of draft animals in farming (Boynton); lumbering, dairy farming, and cattle raising (Gordon Langdon); and meatpacking and sausage making (Ray Bertrand). Maxine Albro's large mural featuring viticulture, fruit and vegetable raising, flower raising, and haying faces the east windows. Clifford Wight's tall figures of a farmer and a cowboy are on either side of those windows, and he also painted agricultural symbols in the area above the windows.[19] Frede Vidar's department-store lunch counter and wine shop, at the south end of the east wall, link to Bertrand's sausage making and Albro's winery and provide a more general transition from food production to food consumption and city life more generally.

The murals along the south corridor present city life, including George Harris's mural depicting the grain exchange (another transition from agriculture), banking, the stock market, and a law library. Arnautoff's kaleidoscopic depiction of city life, facing the south window, includes many city landmarks and bustling city streets. On the right as one faces the mural, Arnautoff depicted the city's produce market, linking to the agricultural murals around the corner. On the left, he showed industrial scenes, connecting to the murals around the corner on that side. Opposite Arnautoff's mural, on either side of the south windows, are Harold Mallette Dean's tall figures of a stockbroker and a scientist-inventor; Dean was also responsible for the area over the windows.[20] On the west end of the south exterior wall, Zakheim painted a public library, with books and people reading books on the left and people reading newspapers on the right.

The west corridor and the western section of the north wall present industry. On the west wall, around the corner from Zakheim's depiction of people reading newspapers, is Suzanne Scheuer's mural of newspaper publishing (news gathering, editing, and printing), providing the transition between city life and industry. Ralph Stackpole's large mural facing the west windows presents several Bay Area industries, including food processing, metalworking, and oil refining. Clifford Wight placed a steelworker and a surveyor, representative of the construction industry, on either side of the west windows and decorated the area above them.[21] On the north end of the west wall is William Hesthal's mural of railroad and maritime transportation. Around the corner, on the west end of the north wall, is John Langley Howard's mural showing an oil field, a hydroelectric dam, and mining, along with a group of protesting workers and homeless victims of the Depression. The half of Boynton's mural, subtitled *Wealth*, and facing Howard's, is of industrial machinery, hydroelectric power, and large-scale construction. The small area over the entry door, originally part of Howard's space, was given to Fred

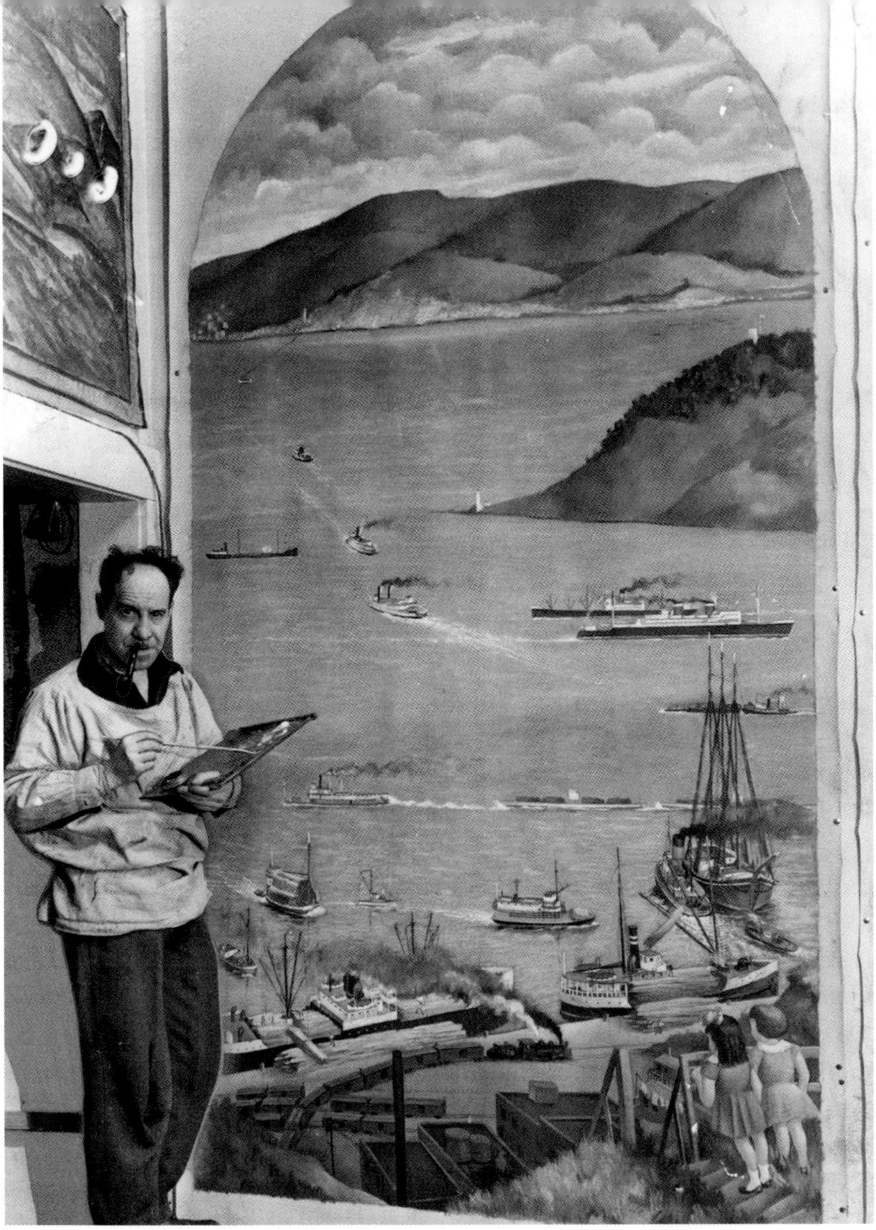

Figure 2.3. Otis Oldfield (seen here), José Moya del Pino, and Rinaldo Cuneo, all of whom used oil on canvas, worked in Cuneo's studio on Montgomery Street. This photo is from March 17. (Source: Photo AAZ-0019, courtesy of San Francisco History Center, San Francisco Public Library.)

Olmsted late in the process. Originally hired as an assistant, Olmsted depicted a left fist arising from flames.[22]

The elevator lobby, opposite the entrance and with its entrance in the middle of Boynton's mural, presents oil-on-canvas paintings of Bay Area landscapes by Otis Oldfield, José Moya del Pino, and Rinaldo Cuneo. Oldfield also painted two lunettes of aquatic birds over the doors to the concessions area and the stairs to the second floor and a lunette of a Bay Area map over the entrance to the elevator. Labaudt painted the largest single mural along both sides of the curving stairway from the elevator lobby to the second floor, depicting life along San Francisco's Powell Street as it rises steeply toward Nob Hill. Murals on the second floor depict sports (Hall, Takeo Edward Terada), children at play (Ralph Chessé), hunting (Edith Hamlin), outdoor recreation (Ben Cunningham), and home life (Berlandina).[23]

Because the large majority of the artists had some connection with the CSFA or the city's art colony that centered on Montgomery and Washington Streets, nearly all had some acquaintance with one another before the project began. Hamlin later recalled "a great camaraderie among the artists." Chessé remembered that they all had "picnic lunches together at noontime." Hebe Daum, an assistant, added, "We'd buy big slabs of cheese and salami and bread [easily available nearby in the Italian neighborhood in North Beach], breaking off bread and sitting around talking." Oldfield reminisced that when one of the artists finished, they all celebrated with sherry or wine—recently legalized with the end of Prohibition. Albro and Hall had traveled together to Mexico and were married a few years later.[24]

In a further indication of the collegiality among the Coit Tower artists, many of the muralists used as models the other artists and assistant artists, other members of the city's arts community, and their own and other artists' family members. Labaudt included many of the artists in his murals. Stackpole's likeness appears in several murals. Some artists included self-portraits. Zakheim painted himself reading a book in Hebrew. Arnautoff's self-portrait looks at the viewer over his shoulder, much like the self-portrait of Rafael in his *School of Athens*. Arnautoff, Zakheim, and Oldfield depicted their own children, and the Oldfield girls also appear in Labaudt's mural. Of the hundreds of faces in the murals, only a very few are of nationally prominent individuals. Dean's stockbroker was modeled on Bank of America founder A. P. Giannini and his scientist-inventor was based on Nobel Prize winner Albert Michelson. Labaudt reproduced members of the group in the photograph of the December 8 planning meeting for the PWAP, including Edward Bruce, Eleanor Roosevelt, Forbes Watson, and L. W. Roberts, a Treasury official, but Labaudt placed them at the foot of Power Street in San Francisco.[25]

The vast majority of the art demonstrates what Masha Zakheim, the daughter of Bernard Zakheim and author of the only book devoted entirely to the murals, termed "everyday life without incident."[26] Nearly all the ground-floor and staircase murals include people at work, in a variety of settings, rural and urban. Various murals also show people at lunch, browsing a newspaper, reading a book, and strolling along city streets. The second-floor murals show other aspects of everyday life: sports, camping, picnicking, hunting, and a family at home. The muralists captured San Francisco and the Bay Area at a specific moment. San Francisco's hotels, cable cars, restaurants, newspaper headlines, billboards, and clothing fashions all convey a keen sense of life in late 1933 and early 1934. The muralists, many of whom lived or had their studios nearby, drew inspiration and ideas from several places within walking distance of Coit Tower, notably the salami factories and food processing plants of North Beach and the views from Telegraph Hill. The murals themselves demonstrate that some of the muralists roamed the city or the area with sketchpad in hand. In his mural, Moya del Pino portrayed himself watching Oldfield sketching. Labaudt and Arnautoff reproduced identifiable city buildings, both prominent and ordinary. Scheuer visited the *San Francisco Chronicle*'s offices and printing plant to prepare for her mural.[27]

Several artists painted newspapers in their murals as a way of referring to current events, locally, nationally, and internationally. Zakheim created the most. His headlines include references to the street battles between the political left and right in Austria in mid-February, fraud in the Hoover administration also in mid-February, a moratorium on mortgage-related evictions in North Dakota in mid-March, and violations of New Deal regulations by oil companies in late March. He had completed his mural by late March/early April. Others of Zakheim's headlines celebrated San Francisco sculptor Beniamino Bufano and wryly announced, "Art Commission Awakens from Its Deep Sleep." Arnautoff's newsstand had only one visible headline, "Police Robbed, Accuse Dillinger" (a nationally prominent gangster), a reference to events in Indiana in mid-April. The newspaper in Vidar's mural includes references to conflict in Paris and Adolf Hitler. One of Howard's two newspapers referred to Roosevelt and the other to a strike by pea pickers.[28]

Several artists incorporated references to the New Deal into their murals. Boynton included a direct statement: "The decoration of the interior in fresco was authorized as a PUBLIC WORKS OF ART PROJECT and undertaken by the artists of San Francisco and completed in 1934." Zakheim listed Heil, Mack, and two other members of the advisory board under the headline "Tower Decoration Com." One of Howard's newspaper headlines states, "'I'm a Tough Guy,' F.R. Warns Congress." Vidar and Zakheim referred to the CWA in their newspaper headlines. Labaudt drew upon the photograph of the December 8 meeting that launched the PWAP. The blue-eagle logo of the National Recovery Administration (NRA), the New Deal's major effort to bring about economic recovery, had quickly became a symbol of the New Deal more generally. Albro, Scheuer, and Stackpole all featured the blue eagle in their murals, and one of Zakheim's headlines refers to NRA code violations.

Today's visitors to Coit Tower may note that the murals mostly depict white people. The original plan for the ground floor included the notation "Various Races of Population," and the murals do include people

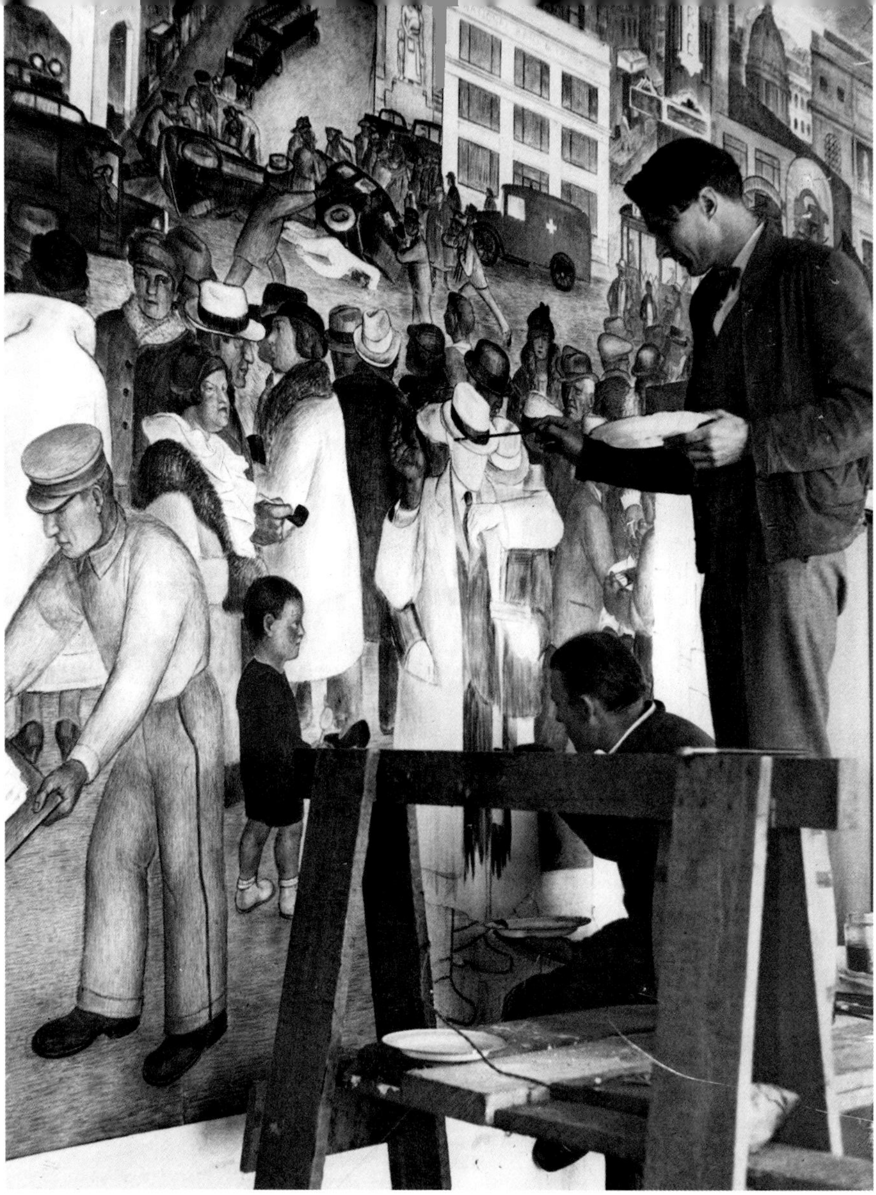

Figure 2.4. Victor Arnautoff and an unnamed assistant were working on the lower third of his mural on April 19. (Source: Photo AAA-5412, Courtesy San Francisco History Center, San Francisco Public Library.)

of color—Blacks, Latinos, and Asians—in the murals by Harris, Hesthal, Howard, Labaudt, Stackpole, Terada, Zakheim, and perhaps Arnautoff—but they are integrated into the overall design of those murals. In presenting mostly white people, the Coit Tower artists were depicting what they saw around them. Data from the 1930 census indicate that San Francisco was 94 percent white, and the rural farm population of the six surrounding counties was 92 percent white. Given that reality, even though Asian, Black, and Latino faces are relatively few in number in the murals, their very presence likely reflects the social consciousness of the artists. Similarly, the absence of such faces does not necessarily reflect a conscious choice by other artists who were painting the faces they saw in the streets.[29]

In mid-February 1934, with the Coit Tower project under way, a national uproar arose over the destruction of Diego Rivera's mural *Man at the Crossroads*, in New York City's Rockefeller Center. Work on the mural had been halted prior to its completion because Rivera included a portrait of Lenin and perhaps also because of his unflattering portrayal of John D. Rockefeller Sr. Nelson Rockefeller, in charge of the project, paid Rivera his commission and had the fresco covered for some time. Then, during the night of February 9, Rockefeller's workers destroyed the fresco. That event and the resulting condemnation by artists and artists' groups nationwide appeared in the San Francisco daily press on February 13.[30]

The next day, the San Francisco Artists and Writers Union, a recently organized group, held a protest meeting in front of Coit Tower. A photograph shows twenty-five people in attendance, mostly Coit Tower artists and assistant artists. According to the *San Francisco News*, the meeting was convened at "the instigation of artists working on the Coit Memorial Tower frescoes and other artists employed on federal public works of art projects." Albro, a member of the union's executive committee, presented a resolution condemning the destruction of the Rivera work as "outrageous vandalism and political bigotry." Vidar and Zakheim incorporated references to the destruction of the Rivera mural in the newspapers in their murals. Albro included a large stand of calla lilies in her mural, likely an homage to Rivera, given his repeated use of the calla lily in his paintings.[31]

Scheurer put "April" into a newspaper headline announcing completion of the murals. Saturday, April 28, was the target date for all the murals to be completed, and Heil's final report indicates that seventeen of the twenty-five master artists had completed their work and been paid by then. On May 10, Heil forwarded glossy photographs of many of the Coit Tower murals to Washington, for use in newspaper articles and perhaps in exhibitions. As of April 28, however, the eight largest murals were not yet finished. Heil secured funds from the State Emergency Relief Administration (SERA), itself funded by the Federal Emergency Relief Administration, so that all the artists could complete their murals. Boynton worked until May 19. Howard, the only artist to put a specific date into his signature, specified May 17; he, Albro, and Arnautoff were all paid through May 26. Cunningham, Labaudt, Langdon (who started later than the others), and Stackpole received their last pay on June 2. Six of the assistant artists also continued until May 26 or June 2, and the two plasterers were paid through June 9, perhaps to help with cleanup. Some of them seem to have continued past their final paycheck, as a newspaper reporter noted a few of them there in mid-June, putting in some final touches or cleaning up.[32]

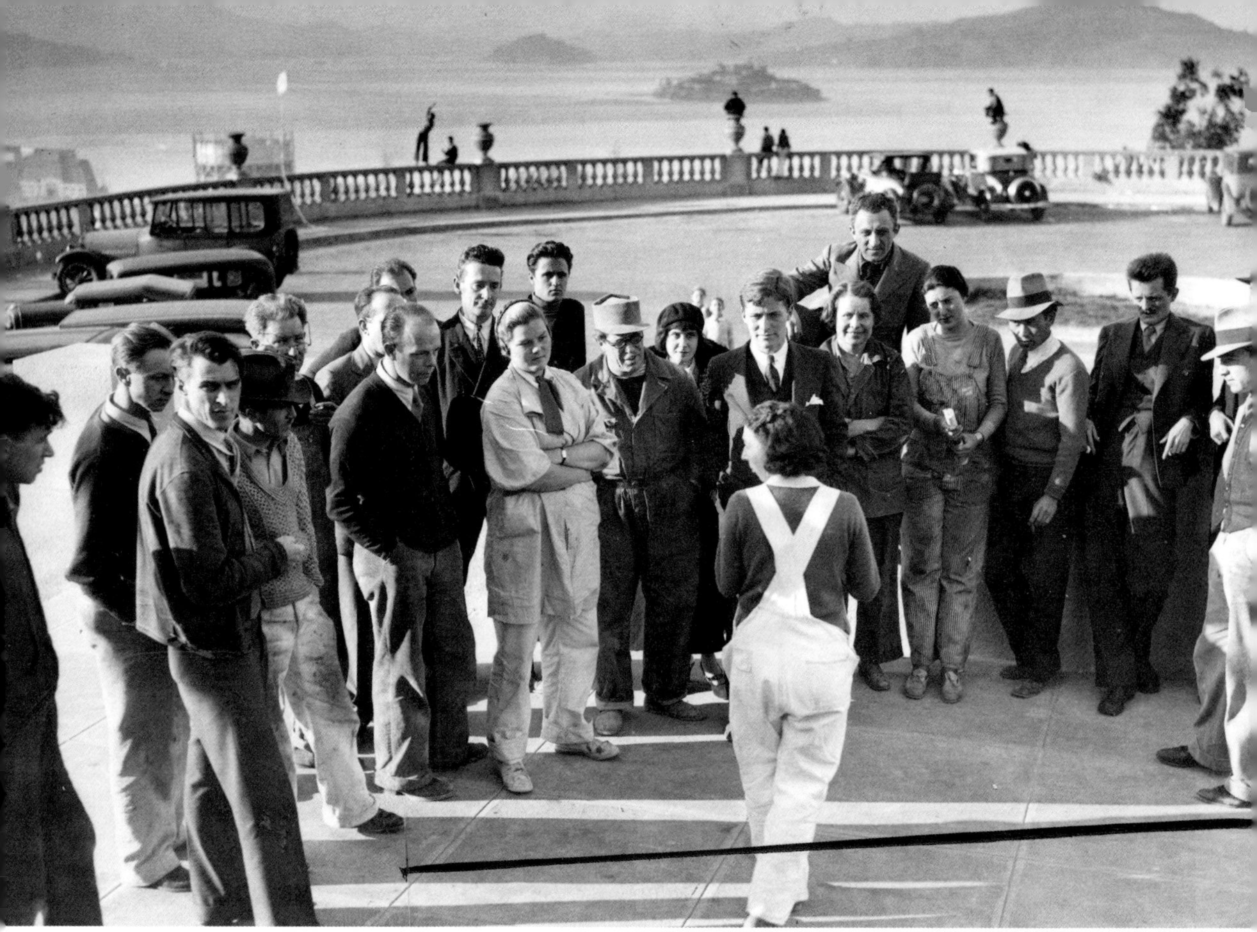

Figure 2.5. Maxine Albro led the protest meeting on February 14. She is in the center, with her back to the camera. Victor Arnautoff is third from left, facing the camera. Ray Boynton, with glasses, is fifth from left. Clifford Wight is standing in back, ninth from left. Helen Clement, an assistant, is in front of Wight. George Harris is in back, tenth from left. Bernard Zakheim is in the back row sitting on a ledge, seventh from right. Suzanne Scheuer is in front of Zakheim. Takeo Edward Terada, wearing hat and holding a cigarette, is fourth from the right. (Source: Photo MOR-0350, courtesy of San Francisco History Center, San Francisco Public Library.)

On April 22, a week before the deadline for completion, H. L. Dungan, writing in the *Oakland Tribune*, provided a glowing account of the murals. Coit Tower, he said, "will stand for a long time," and visitors will go there "to see the tower's frescoes and murals, which tell the tale and show pictures of our generation." He continued: "Uncle Sam—you and I and some generations yet unborn—will pay the bill, but we shall not complain, I hope, for the cost will be small to compare with the lasting enjoyment. . . . The whole is so exciting—that seems about the word to use—that there should be no fussy criticism about any part of it." He remarked on the "amazing uniformity of standard" among such a large group of artists and walked his readers through the tower, hall by hall, floor by floor, adding, "I walked around the inner wall so often I got dizzy."

Harold Mack, an influential member of the regional committee, was also highly enthusiastic about the project. In a May 3 letter to President Roosevelt, Mack called it "unique in the art history of the United States" and quoted Jo Davidson, a prominent sculptor, as confirming that "the results achieved in this building surpass anything heretofore accomplished in this country."[33]

Dungan, the *Oakland Tribune* reporter, had specified, "there should be an opening day celebration of sufficient size, dignity, warmth and enthusiasm to compare with the works the San Francisco artists are doing. But, no doubt, some one has thought of that." And, in fact, the Art Commission and the Park Commission had scheduled Coit Tower for a grand opening on July 1.

3

The Murals

The following pages present the Coit Tower murals. The entrance to the ground floor is from the north. The photos begin there, then move to the left, with the murals dealing with agriculture, then those showing city life, and finally those presenting industry. All color photos are courtesy of the San Francisco Arts Commission.

Figure 3.1 is the original plan for the ground floor. William Gaw later withdrew, and Cuneo did that mural as well as his own in the elevator lobby.

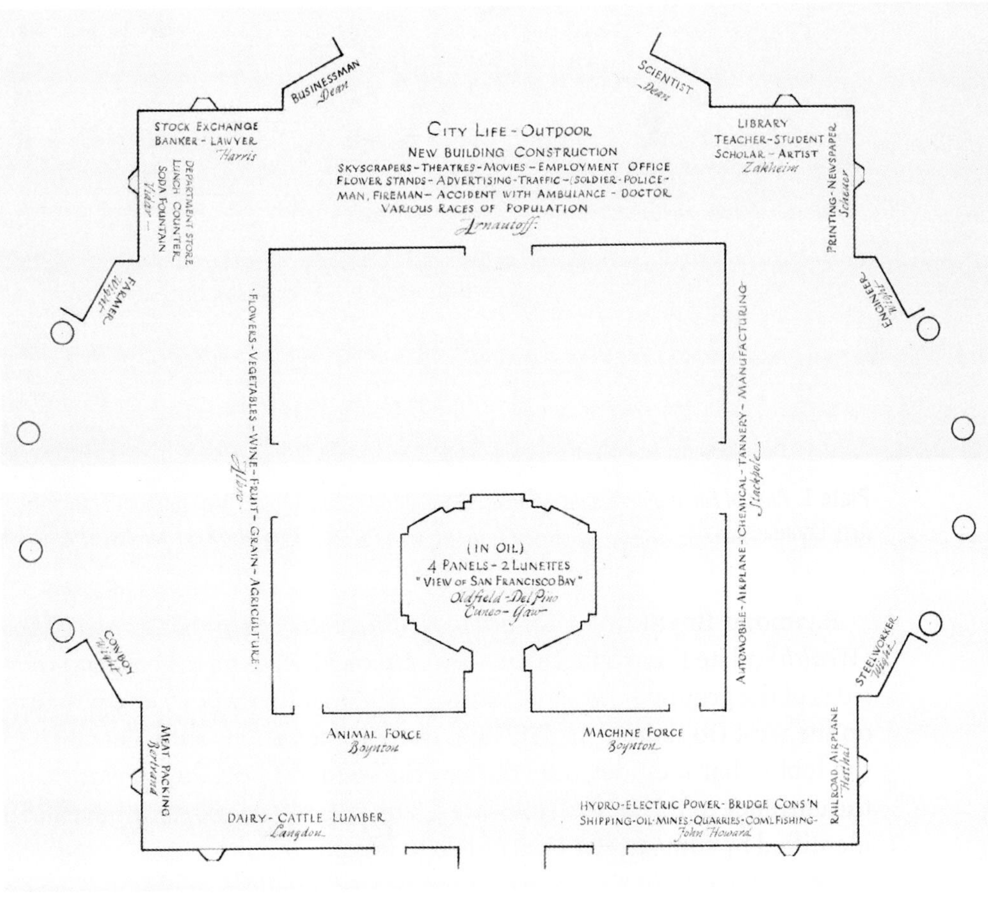

Figure 3.1. Original plan for the ground floor. (Source: Unknown designer, *Coit Tower, Floor Plan for the Murals [Ground Floor]*, black ink on paper, 17½ x 23 in. [445 x 584 mm], December 1933, Federal Art Project, FA9513.2, photograph by Randy Dodson, courtesy of the Fine Arts Museums of San Francisco.)

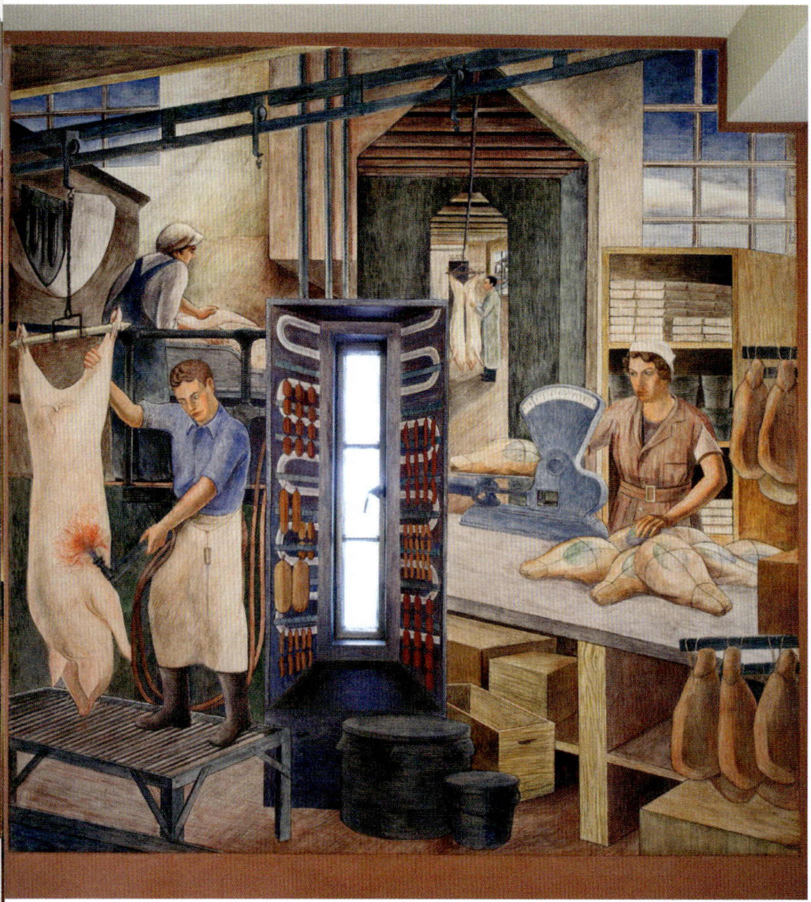

Plate 5. *Meat Industry*, Raymond Bertrand. Courtesy of the San Francisco Arts Commission.

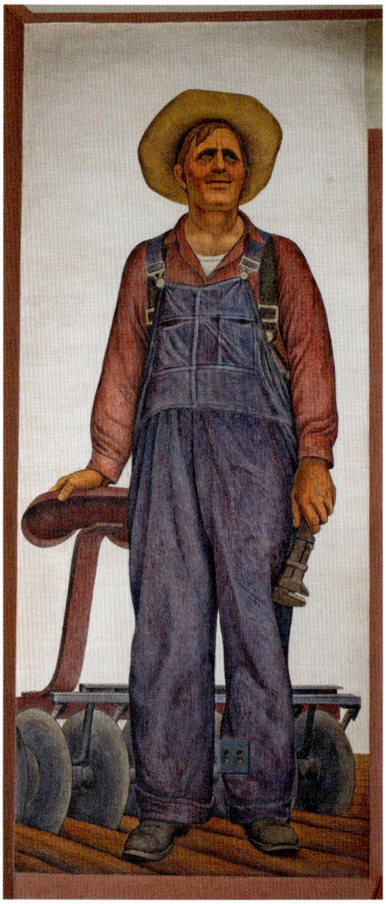

Plate 6. *Farmer*, Clifford Wight. Courtesy of the San Francisco Arts Commission.

These murals line the east outside wall. Ray Bertrand's *Meat Industry* (plate 5) continues the depiction of California agriculture. His portrayal of a slaughterhouse, sausage factory, and butcher shop is next to the beef-raising section of Langdon's mural.

Clifford Wight's *Farmer* and *Cowboy* (plates 6 and 7) were on either side of the three large windows in the center of that wall. They are reminiscent of the giant worker in the center of Diego Rivera's mural at the California School of Fine Arts.

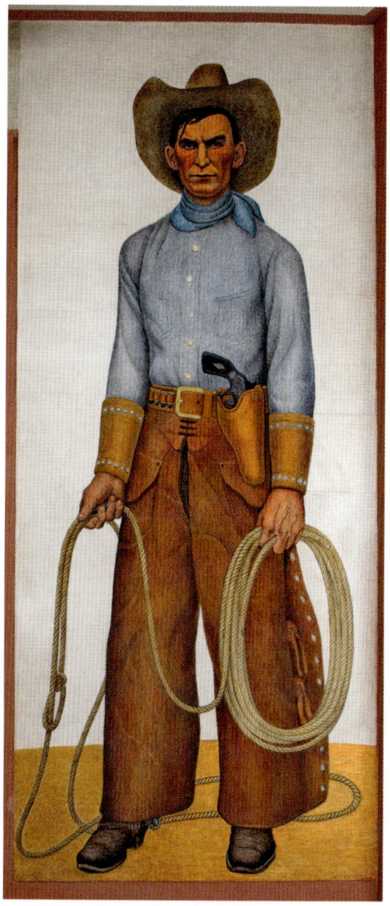

Plate 7. *Cowboy*, Clifford Wight. Courtesy of the San Francisco Arts Commission.

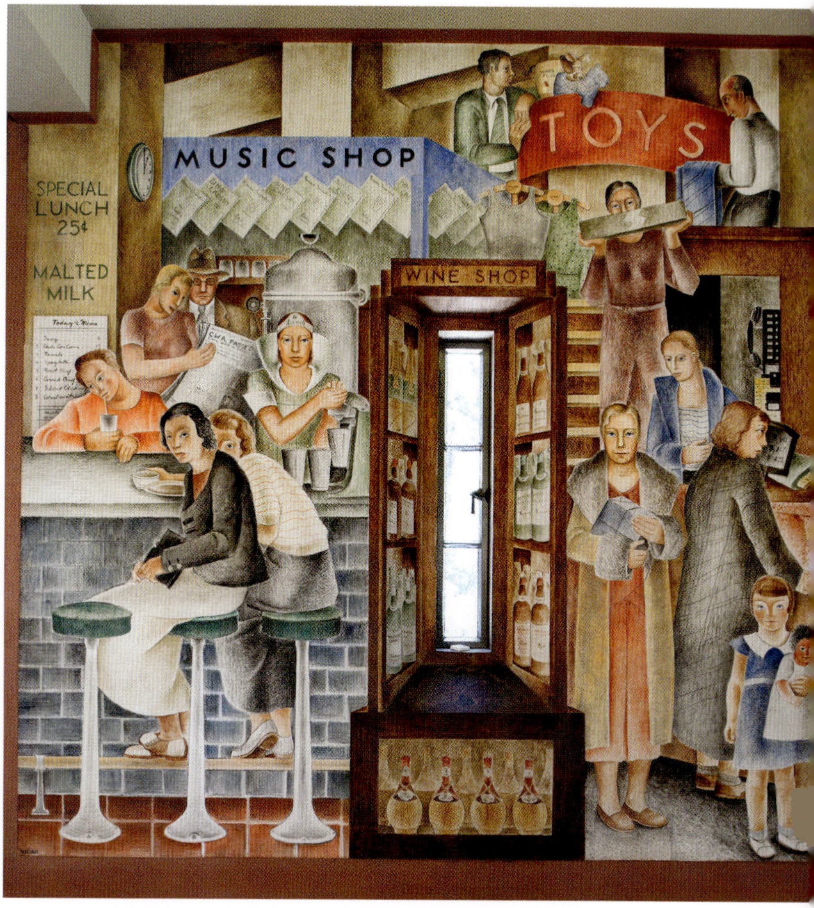

Plate 8. *Department Store*, Frede Vidar. Courtesy of the San Francisco Arts Commission.

Frede Vidar's *Department Store* (plate 8) includes a lunch counter that continues the agricultural theme by depicting the consumption of agricultural products. The wine shop subtly refers to the repeal of Prohibition in December 1933 and connects more directly to the winery in Albro's mural (see plate 9). Vidar's department store also provides a transition to the murals of city life on the south walls. One of the newspaper headlines in Vidar's mural refers to the destruction of Rivera's mural at Rockefeller Center and another mentions Hitler.

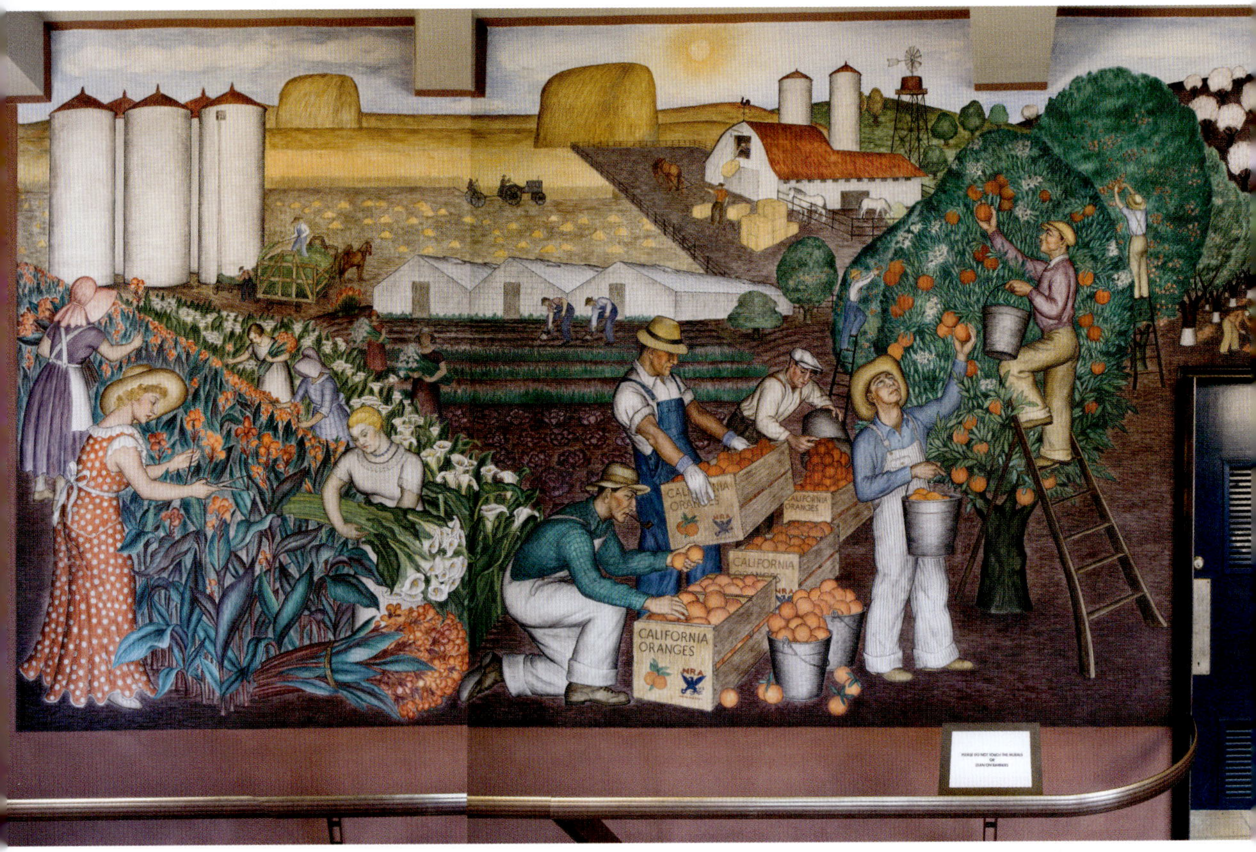

Plate 9. *California Agriculture,* Maxine Albro. Courtesy of the San Francisco Arts Commission.

Maxine Albro's *California Agriculture* (plate 9) faces the murals by Bertrand, Wight, and Vidar. In it, she depicts viticulture and wine making on the right, fruit orchards in the center, flower raising, haying, vegetable raising, and greenhouse cultivation on the left. Albro modeled several of the people on her fellow artists, including Stackpole and Parker Hall (her future husband). Her depiction of calla lilies may have been intended as a subtle homage to Diego Rivera, who was already known for his depictions of that flower by the time Albro created this mural. The woman holding them is modeled on Helen Clement, Albro's assistant, who took part in the protest against the destruction of Rivera's mural (see fig. 2.5).

Albro's mural is one of several to include an acknowledgment of the New Deal, which she did by depicting the blue eagle of the National Recovery Administration, the Roosevelt administration's initial effort to plan the recovery of the economy (see plate 10). Each industry was to draft a code of fair competition and in return was permitted to display the blue eagle.

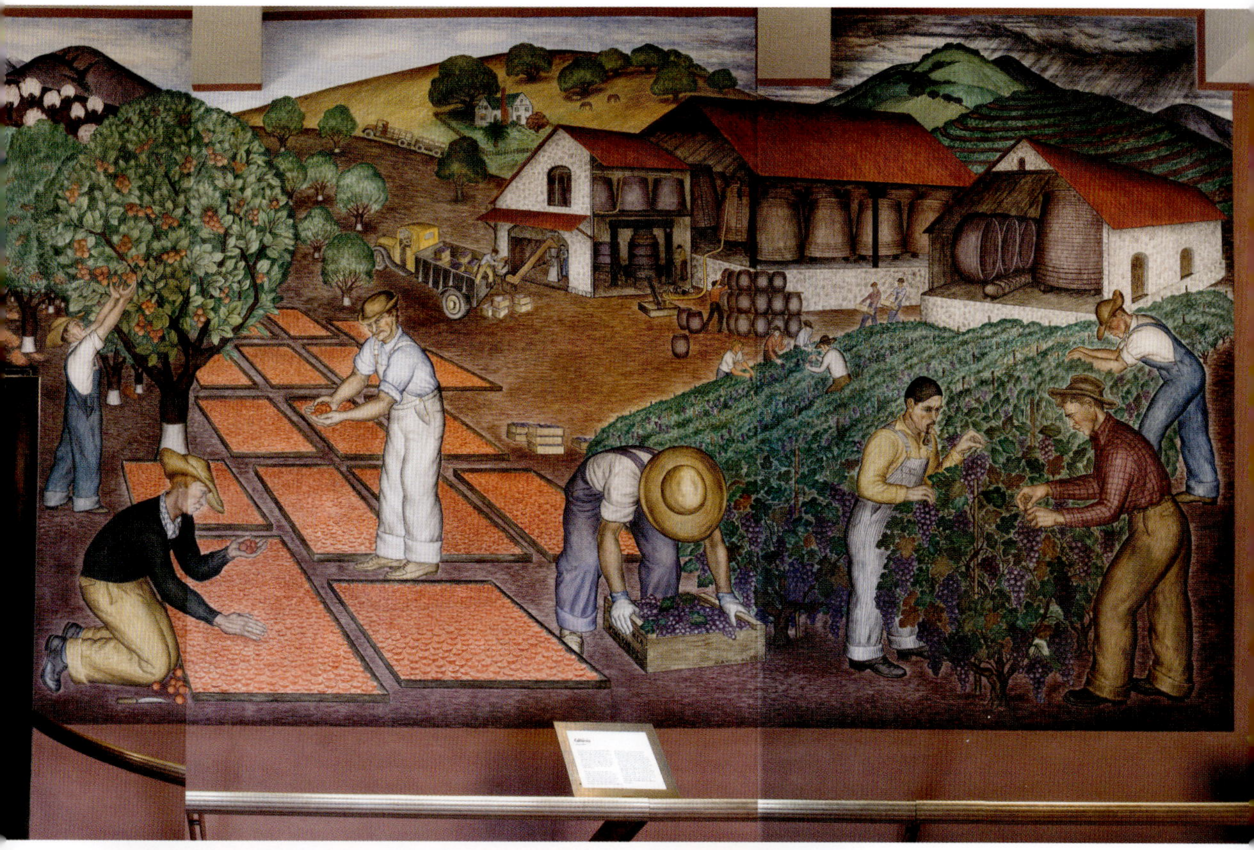

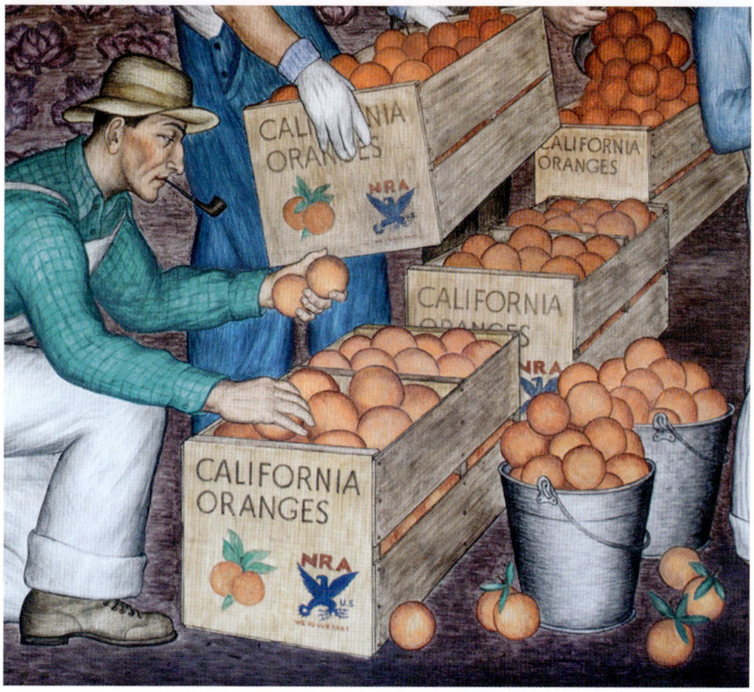

Plate 10. Detail from Albro's *California Agriculture.*

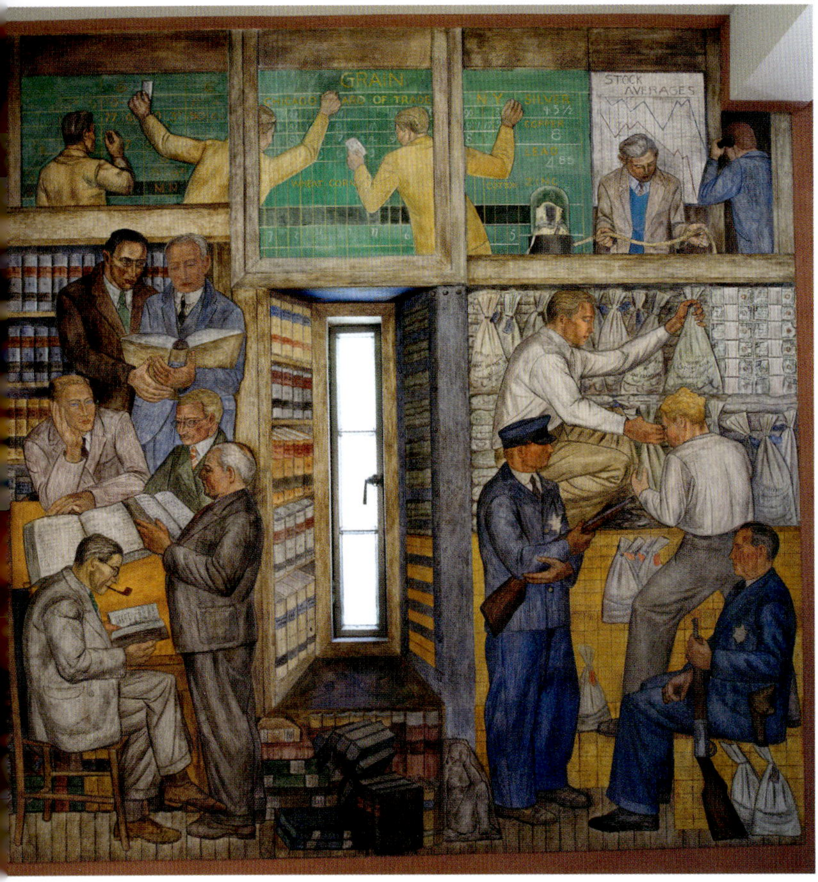

Plate 11. *Banking and Law,* George Harris. Courtesy of the San Francisco Arts Commission.

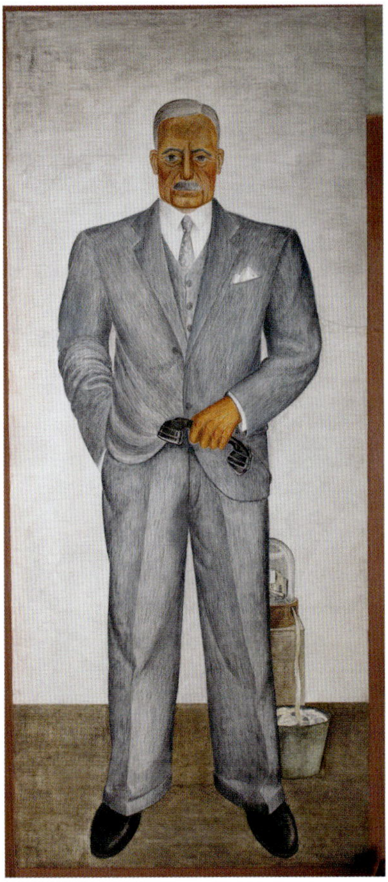

Plate 12. *Stockbroker,* Harold Mallette Dean. Courtesy of the San Francisco Arts Commission.

The murals on the south exterior wall depict aspects of urban life. George Harris's *Banking and Law* (plate 11) includes a law library in the lower left, the commodities exchange in the upper left (an urban connection to the agricultural murals around the corner to the left), the Twelfth District Federal Reserve Bank in the lower right, and a stock market ticker and chart of falling stock prices in the upper right. Harris's law library includes a variety of titles, some typical of actual law books but many providing humorous references to other artists.

Harold Mallette Dean's *Stockbroker* (plate 12) was modeled on A. P. Giannini, founder of the Bank of America. His *Scientist-Inventor* (plate

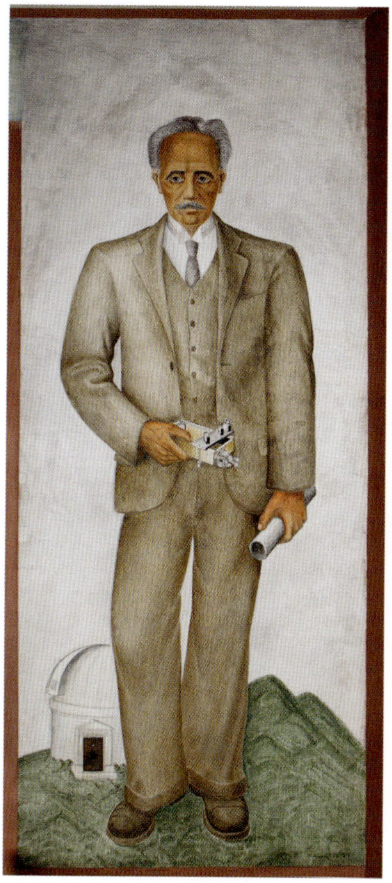

Plate 13. *Scientist-Inventor*, Harold Mallette Dean. Courtesy of the San Francisco Arts Commission.

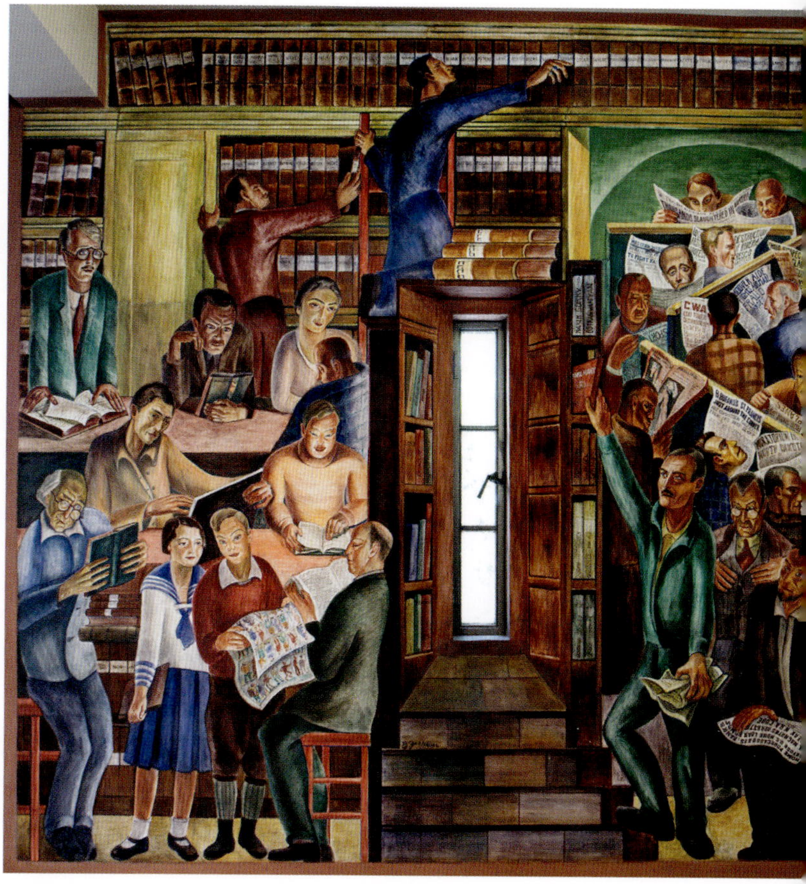

Plate 14. *Library*, Bernard Zakheim. Courtesy of the San Francisco Arts Commission.

13) was modeled on Nobel Prize winner Albert Michelson. They were on either side of the three south windows.

Bernard Zakheim's *Library* (plate 14) provides a parallel to Harris's law library. The girl in the blue sailor suit was modeled on Zakheim's daughter, Ruth, and Zakheim included a self-portrait of him reading the Torah. The man in the green jacket, modeled on John Langley Howard, is reaching for a copy of Marx's *Das Kapital*. Book titles include several by leftist authors. The newspaper headlines on the right include major events from February through March 1934.

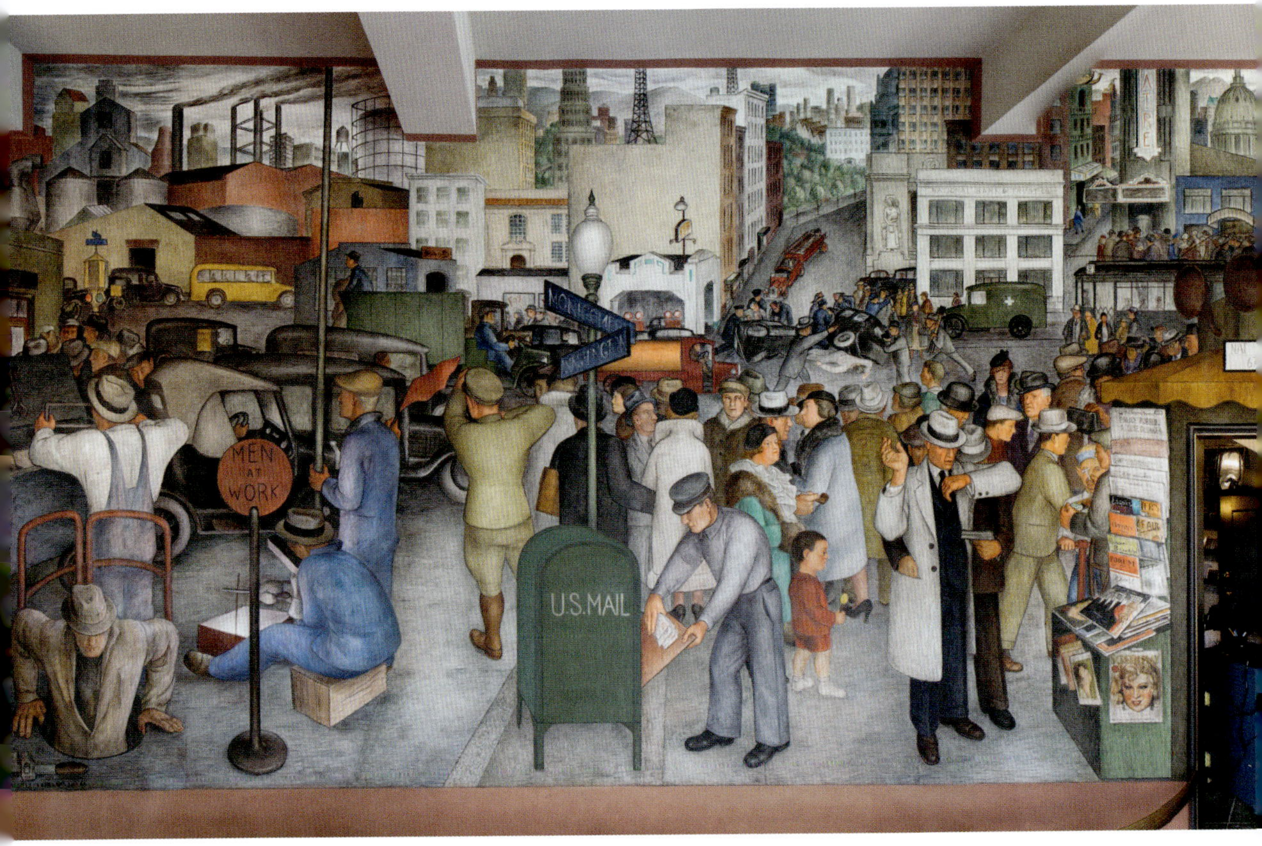

Plate 15. *City Life*, Victor Mikhail Arnautoff. Courtesy of the San Francisco Arts Commission.

Victor Arnautoff's *City Life* (plate 15) faces the south windows. The produce market, on the right, links to the agricultural theme around the corner, and the industrial scenes, on the left, providing a transition to the theme of industry around the corner to the left. Arnautoff disguised the door in the center of the mural as the back entrance to a newsstand. The street sign next to the mailbox on the left is for the intersection of Washington and Montgomery, the center of the arts community and also the northern limit of the Financial District. The newsboy to the right of the door is modeled on Arnautoff's son Michael, and Arnautoff's self-portrait in a gray hat faces the newsboy and the viewer.

Arnautoff's painting of an automobile crash in front of the Pacific Coast Stock Exchange (plate 16) may be his way of depicting the stock market crash.

His depiction of a well-dressed man being robbed in broad daylight by two other well-dressed men (plate 17) may be Arnautoff's wry comment on life in the Financial District.

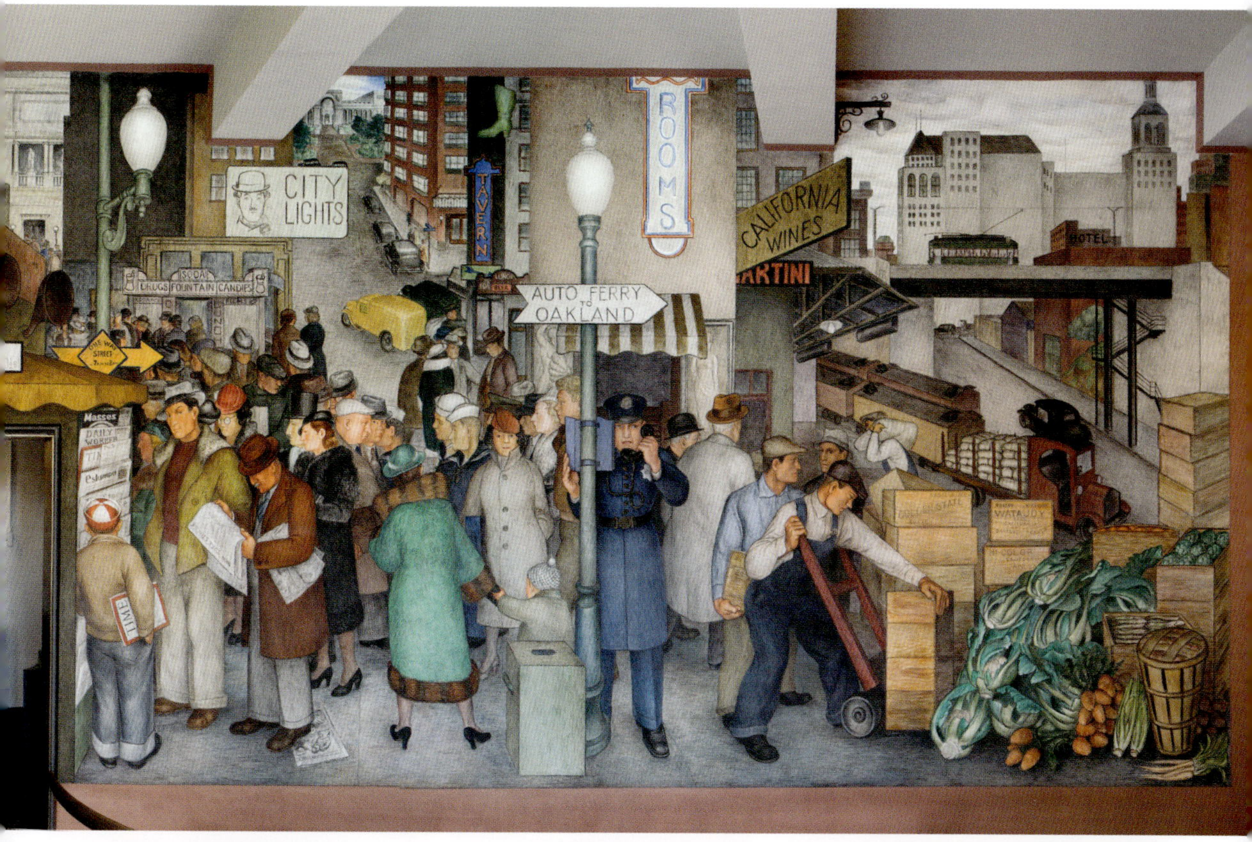

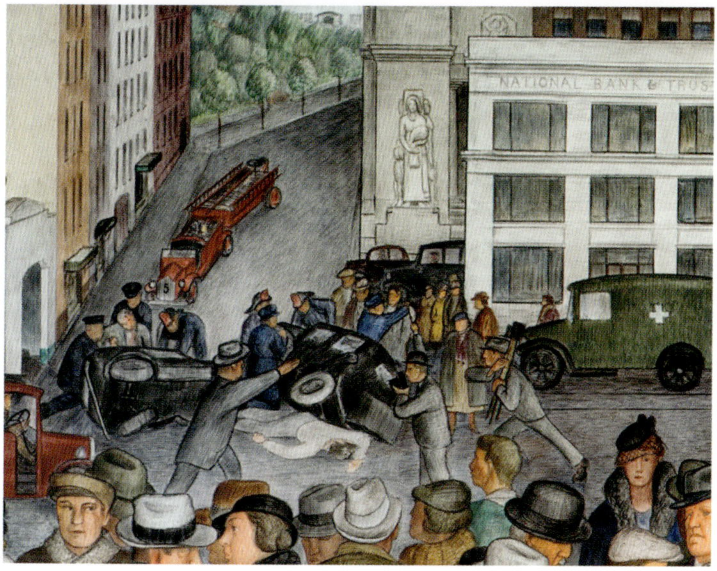

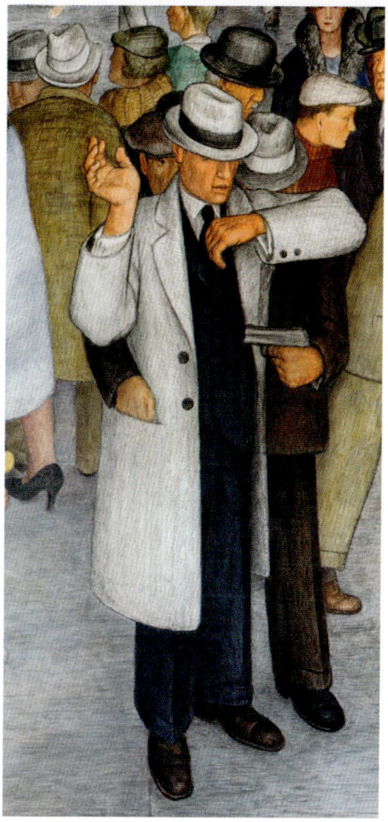

Plate 16. (above) Detail from Arnautoff's *City Life*.

Plate 17. (right) Detail from Arnautoff's *City Life*.

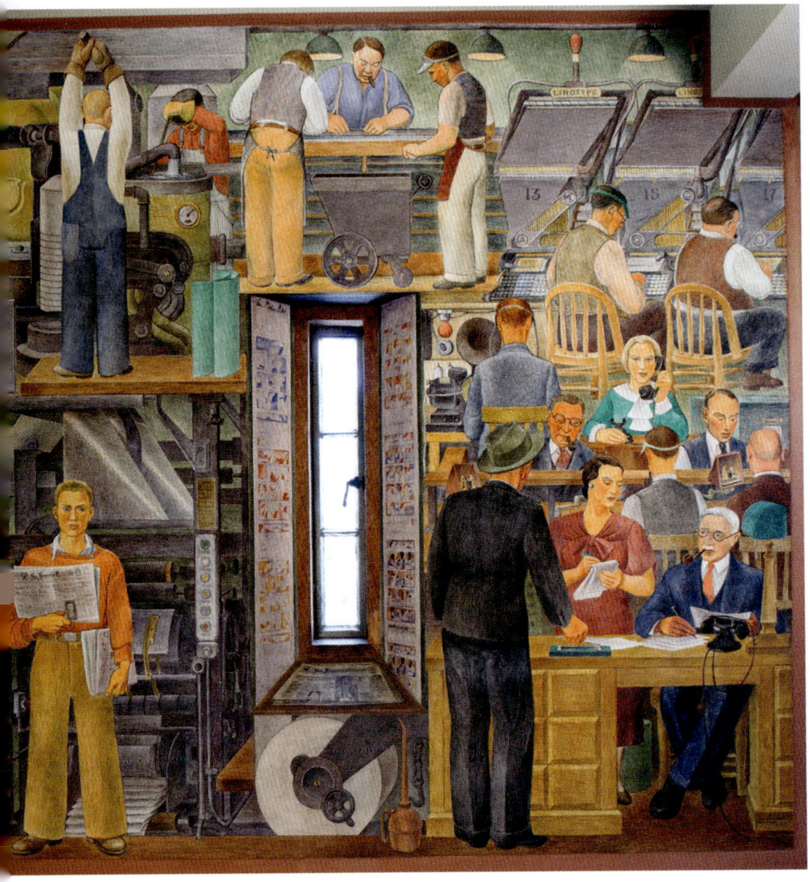

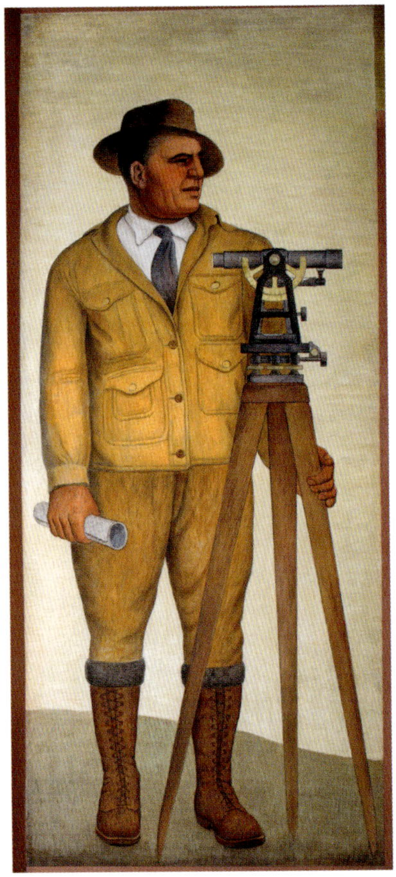

Plate 18. *Newsgathering*, Suzanne Scheuer. Courtesy of the San Francisco Arts Commission.

Plate 19. *Surveyor*, Clifford Wight. Courtesy of the San Francisco Arts Commission.

The murals on the west exterior wall (plate 18) present various aspects of industry—publishing, construction, and transportation. Suzanne Scheuer's *Newsgathering* begins on the lower right with reporters and editors at work, then depicts typesetting and printing at the top, and ends with a newsboy selling the latest edition at the lower left. Nearly all the artists had to deal with windows or doors in their murals; Scheuer used the sides of the window to present newspaper comics. She also included a blue eagle on the newspaper.

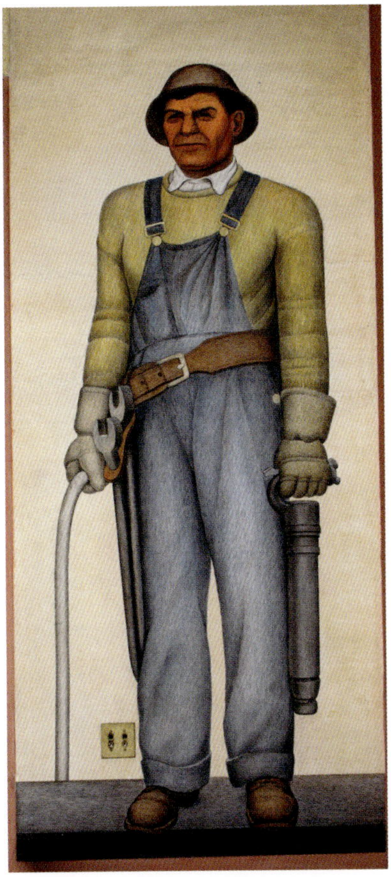

Plate 20. *Ironworker*, Clifford Wight. Courtesy of the San Francisco Arts Commission.

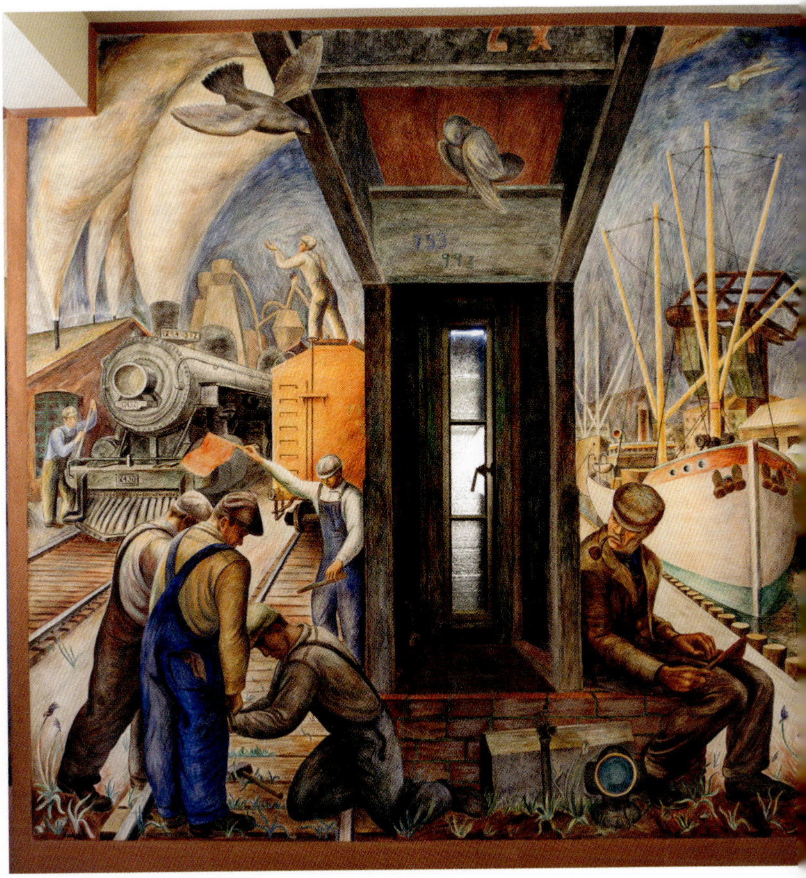

Plate 21. *Railroad and Shipping*, William Hesthal. Courtesy of the San Francisco Arts Commission.

Clifford Wight's *Surveyor* (plate 19) and *Ironworker* (plate 20), representative of the construction industry and reminiscent of Rivera's giant workman at the CSFA, are on either side of the three west windows.

William Hesthal's *Railroad and Shipping* (plate 21) treats major Bay Area transportation industries. On the left, a flagman warns workers who are clearing the track for an approaching car. Some have suggested that Hesthal was symbolically depicting the economy beginning to move again after it had stalled during the Depression.

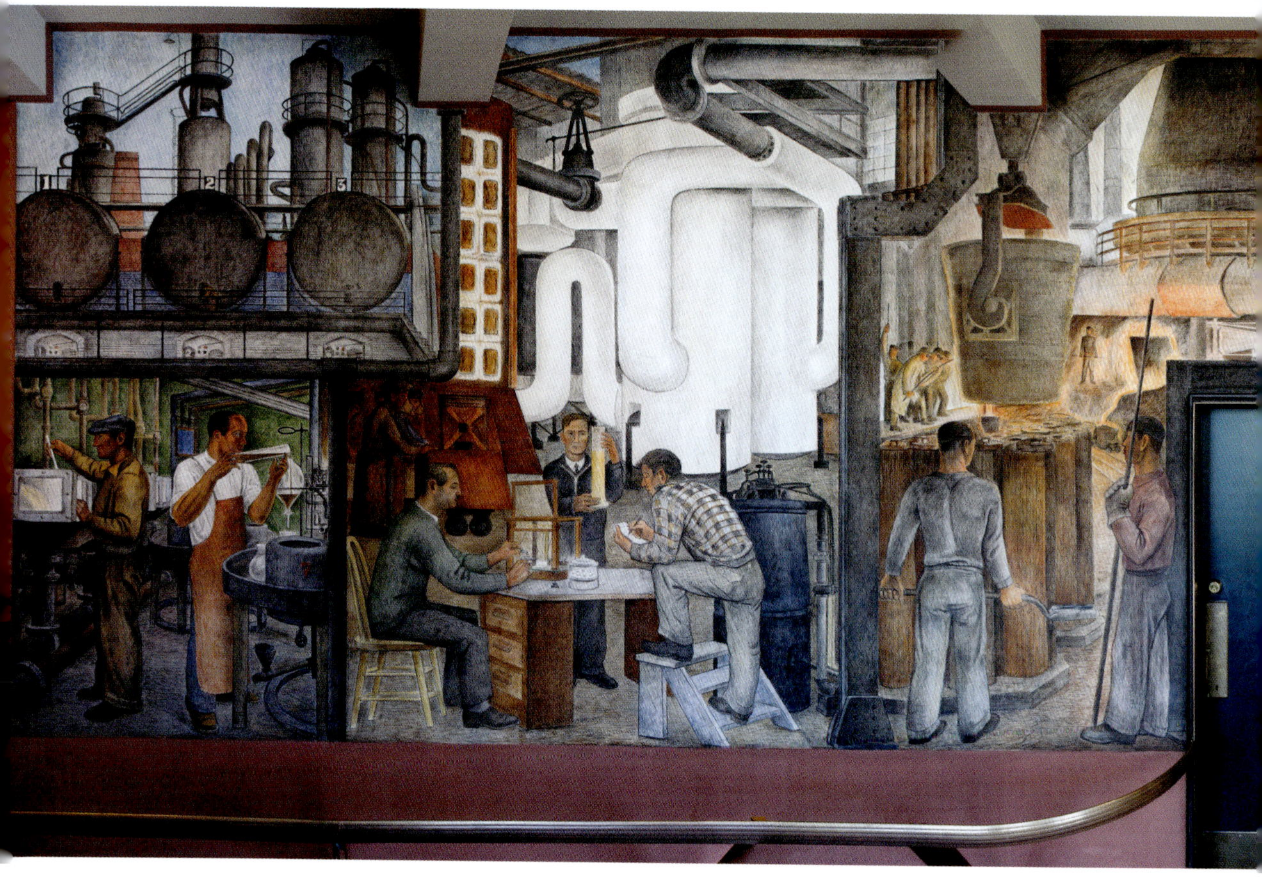

Plate 22. *Industries of California*, Ralph Stackpole. Courtesy of the San Francisco Arts Commission.

Ralph Stackpole's *Industries of California* (plate 22), facing the west windows, includes major industries then prominent in the San Francisco Bay Area, including petroleum refining and chemicals on the left, metalworking in the center, and food processing on the right.

The cannery workers include a number of Asian faces (see plate 23).

The bags of refined sugar provide another example of the appearance of the blue eagle of the NRA (see plate 24).

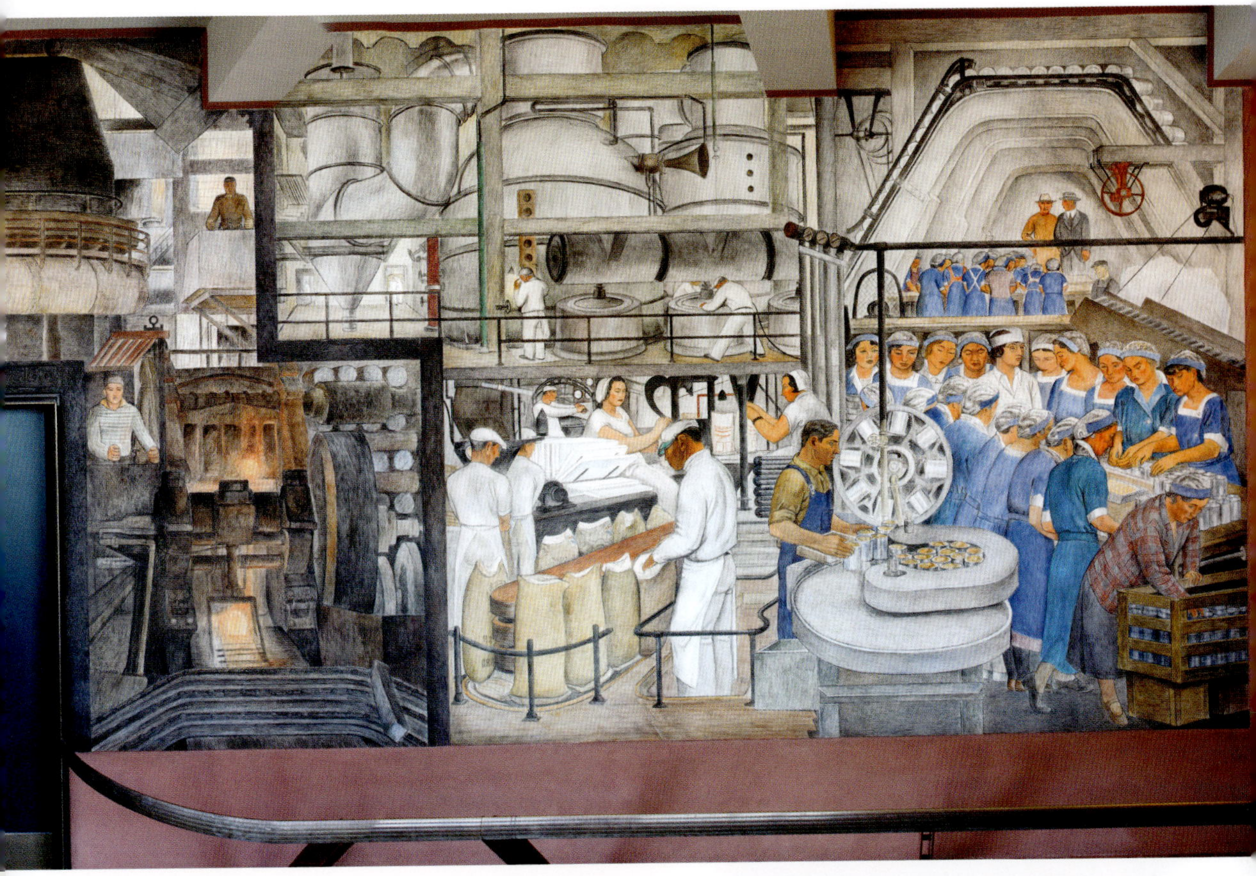

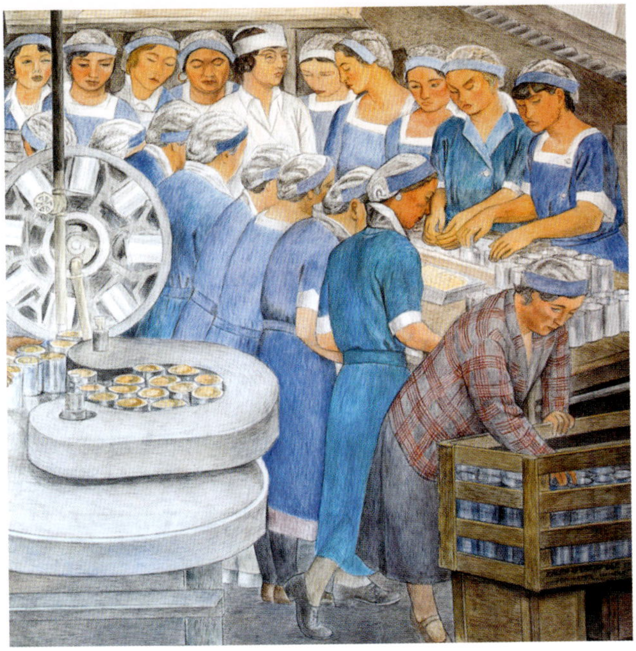

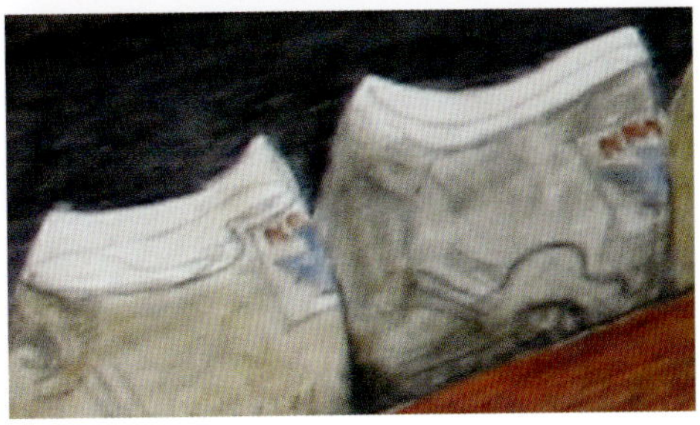

Plate 23. (left) Detail from Stackpole's *Industries of California*.

Plate 24. (above) Detail from Stackpole's *Industries of California*.

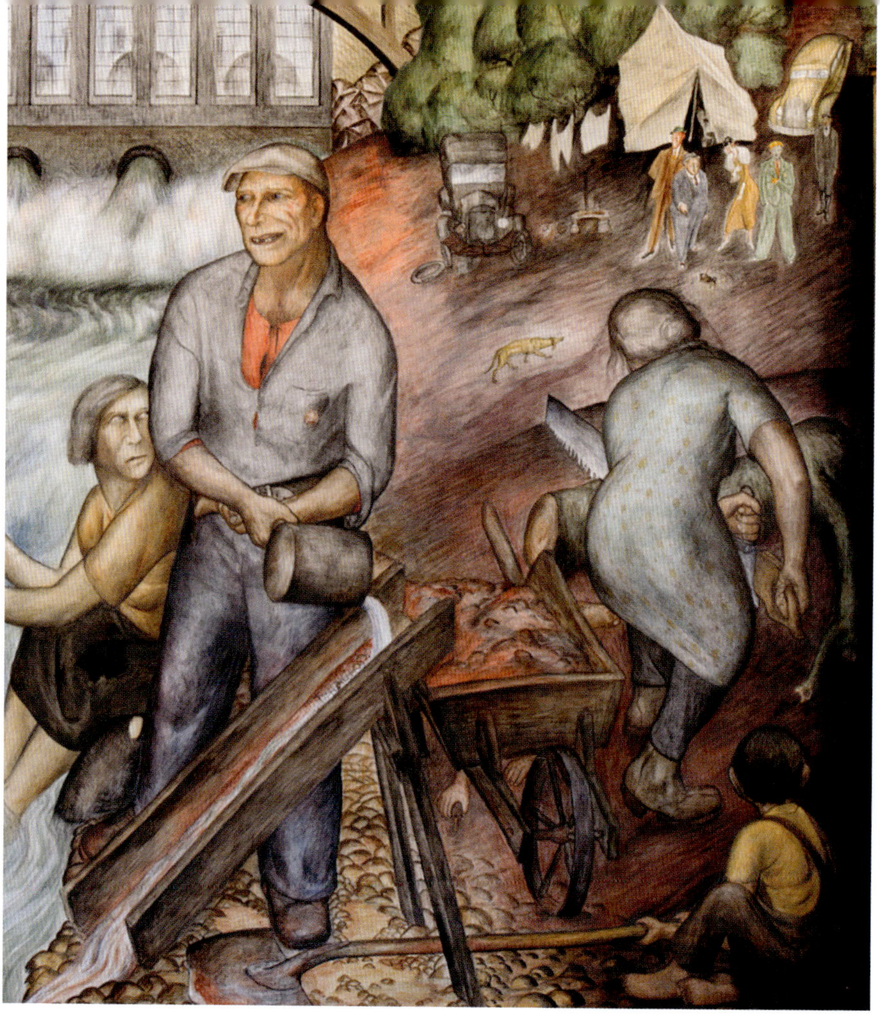

Plate 26. Detail from Howard's *California Industrial Scenes.*

Howard also presented these men demonstrating on May Day against unemployment and in support of striking farmworkers (plate 27). One of the marchers holds a copy of the *Western Worker*, the newspaper of the Communist Party. Howard must have been aware of the irony of posing these images of the Depression opposite Boynton's mural with its subtitle of *Wealth*.

Frederick Olmsted's *Power* (plate 28) is over the main entrance, facing the entrance to the elevator lobby. Originally this was to be part of Howard's mural, but late in the process he gave the area to Olmsted, his assistant. Olmsted left no explanation for depicting a left fist emerging from flames.

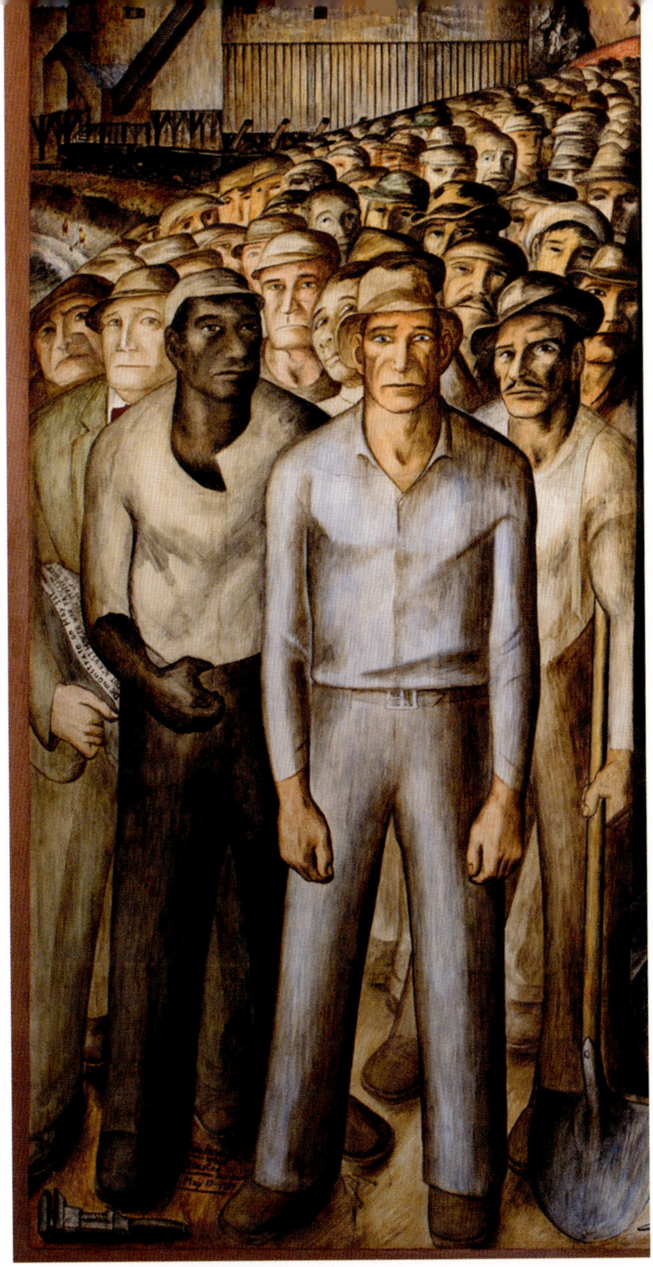

Plate 27. (left) Detail from Howard's *California Industrial Scenes*.

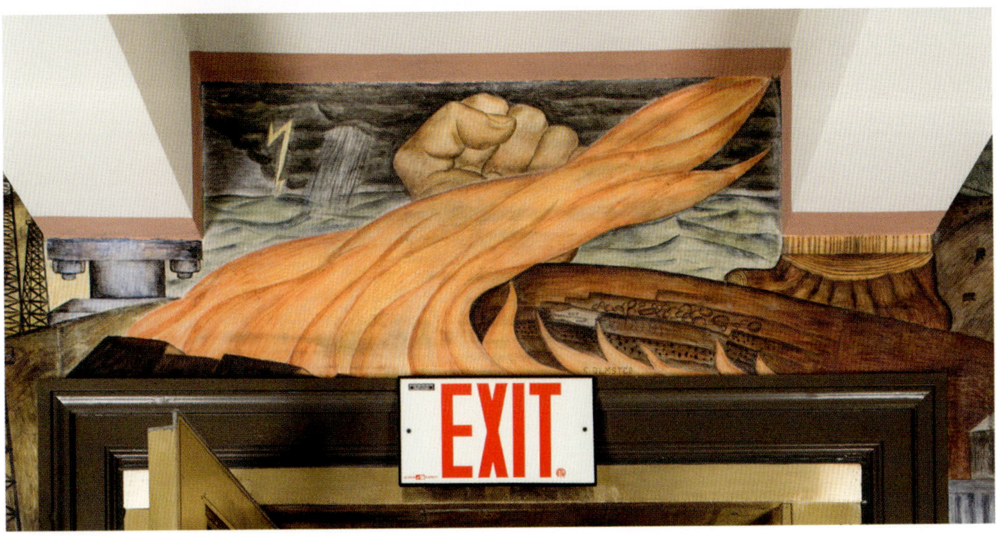

Plate 28. (below) *Power*, Frederick Olmsted. Courtesy of the San Francisco Arts Commission.

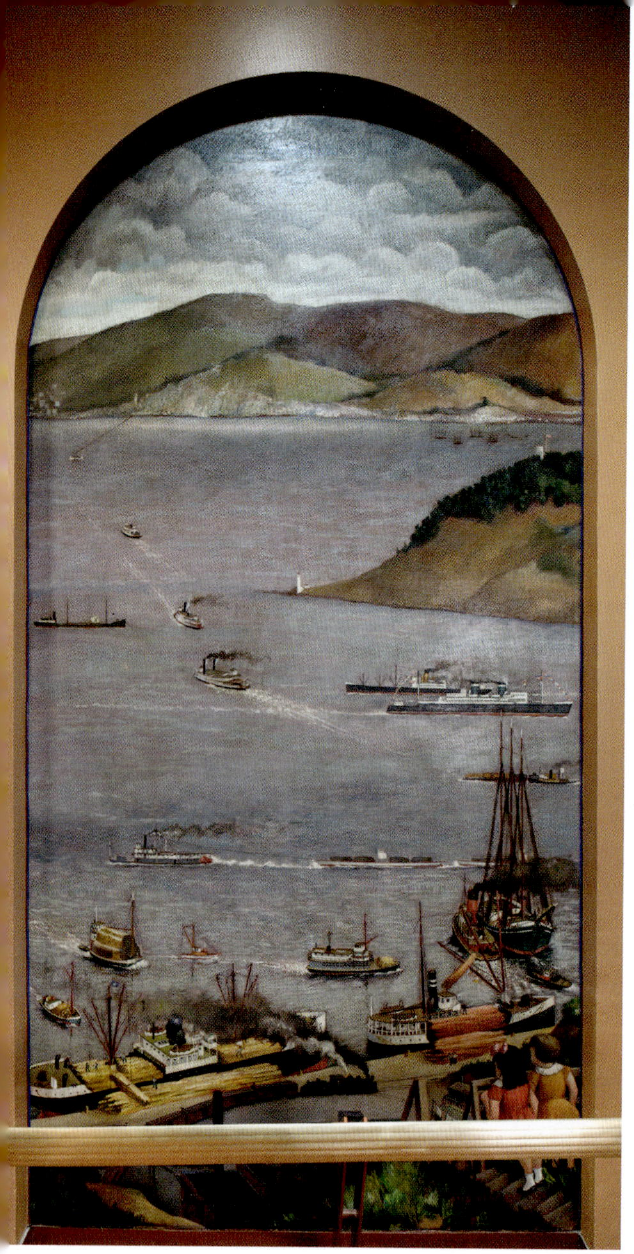

Plate 29. *San Francisco Bay*, Otis Oldfield. Courtesy of the San Francisco Arts Commission.

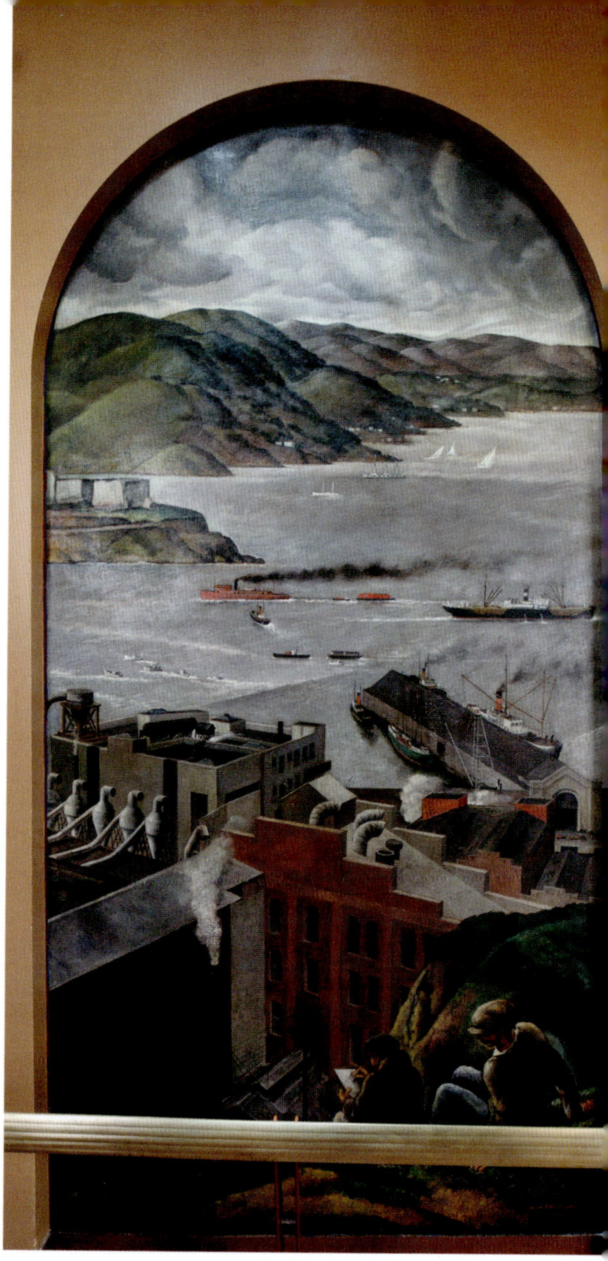

Plate 30. *San Francisco Bay North*, José Moya del Pino. Courtesy of the San Francisco Arts Commission.

Otis Oldfield's *San Francisco Bay* (plate 29) presents what one would see looking east from this spot on Telegraph Hill. The elevator lobby was reserved for those who were painting with oil on canvas, all of whom were assigned cityscapes or landscapes.

José Moya del Pino's *San Francisco Bay North* (plate 30), which is opposite Oldfield's cityscape, presents the view looking northwest from Telegraph Hill.

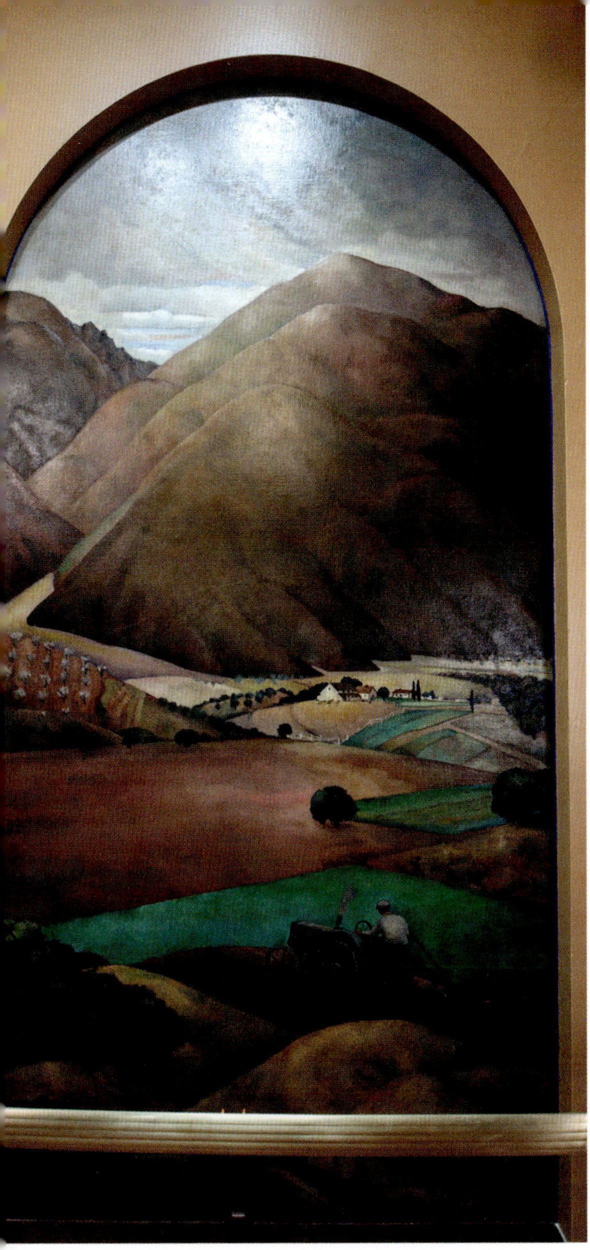

Plate 31. *Bay Area Hills*, Rinaldo Cuneo. Courtesy of the San Francisco Arts Commission.

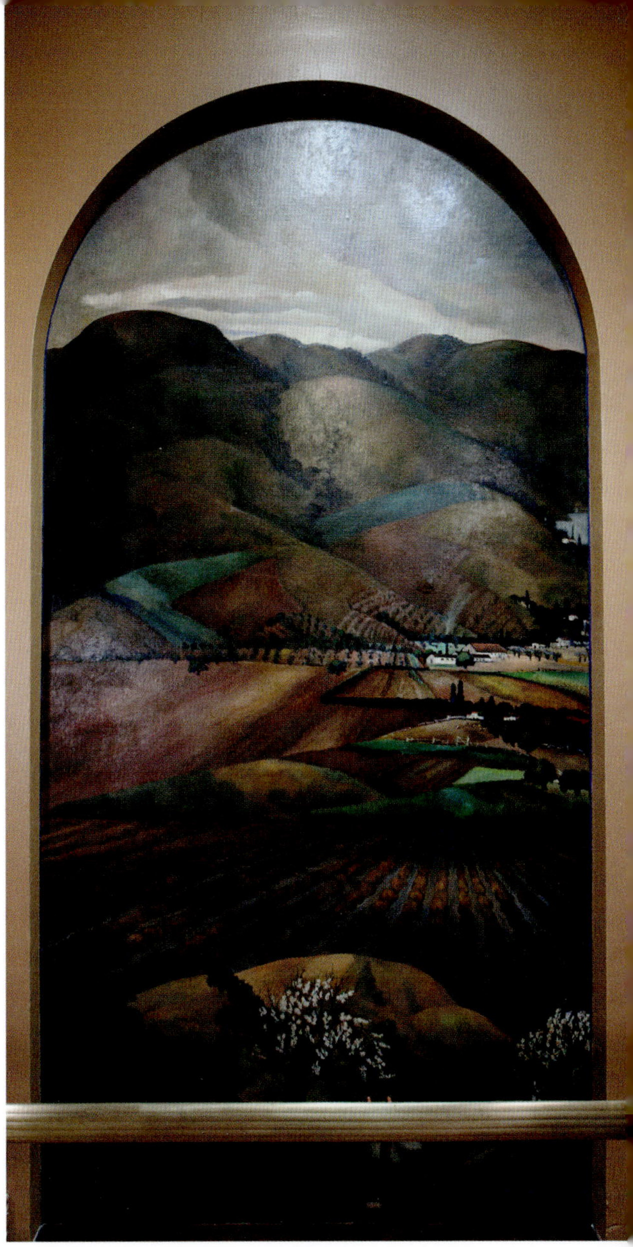

Plate 32. *Bay Area Hills*, Rinaldo Cuneo. Courtesy of the San Francisco Arts Commission.

Rinaldo Cuneo's murals, *Bay Area Hills*, present landscapes. The one pictured in plate 31 is of the Santa Clara valley and hills, at the southern end of San Francisco Bay. It is on the east side of the elevator lobby. Plate 32 is Cuneo's depiction of the East Bay hills, which is on the west side of the elevator lobby. Mount Diablo, in the center of plate 32, is about twenty-nine miles from San Francisco and is visible from high spots in the city.

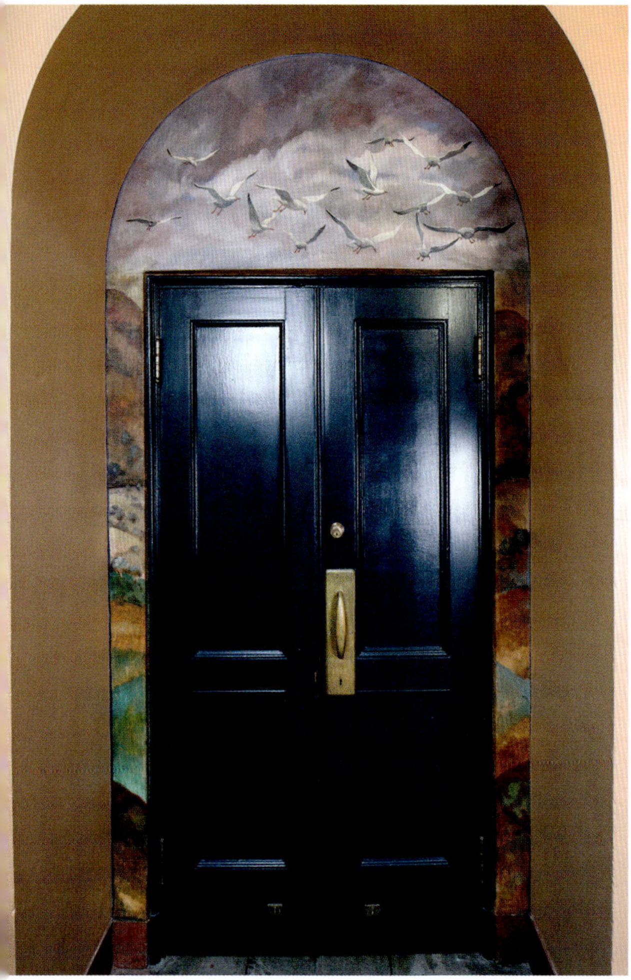

Plate 33. *Seabirds* (gulls), Otis Oldfield. Courtesy of the San Francisco Arts Commission.

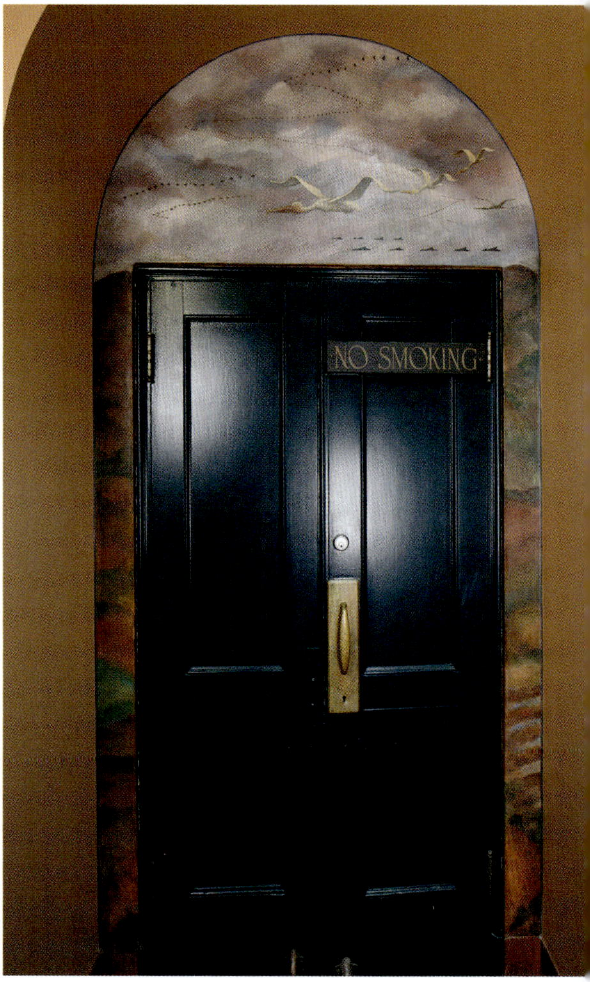

Plate 34. *Seabirds* (pelicans), Otis Oldfield. Courtesy of the San Francisco Arts Commission.

Oldfield also decorated the areas over the elevator lobby doors with seabirds, gulls on the left and pelicans on the right as one faces them, with a Bay Area map in the center, around the elevator floor indicator (see plates 33, 34, 35).

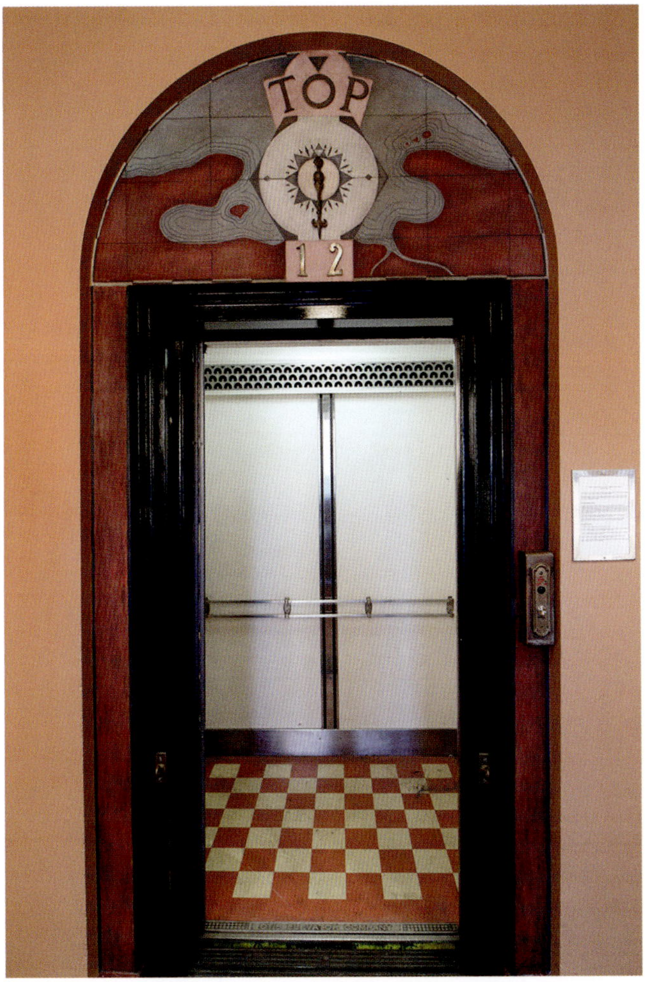

Plate 35. *Bay Area Map*, Otis Oldfield. Courtesy of the San Francisco Arts Commission.

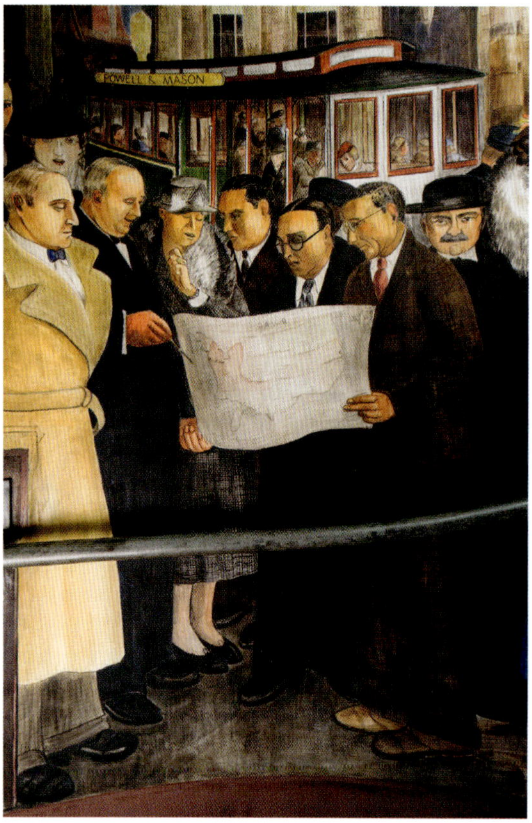

Plate 36A. *Powell Street*, Lucien Labaudt. Courtesy of the San Francisco Arts Commission.

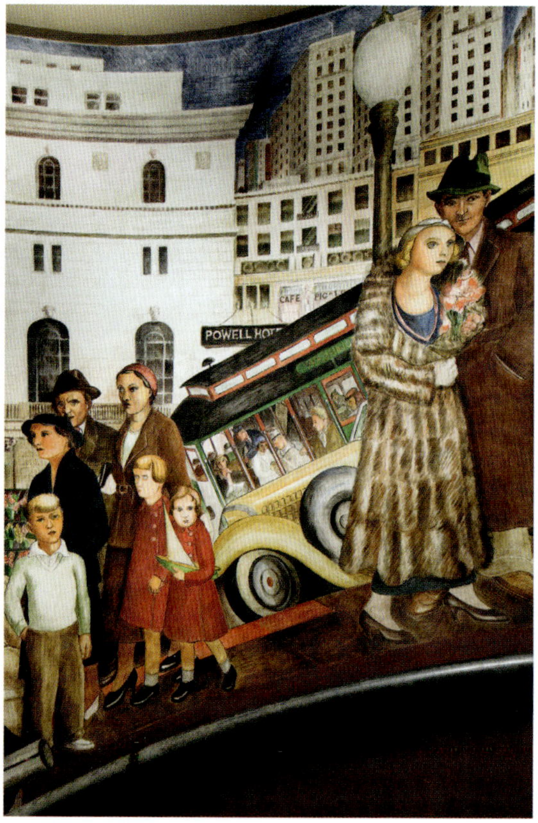

Plate 36B. *Powell Street*, Lucien Labaudt. Courtesy of the San Francisco Arts Commission.

Lucien Labaudt's *Powell Street* (plates 36A–I) covers both sides of the curving stairway between the first and second floors. He depicted Powell Street, a part of the central business district, as it rose from Market Street to the top of Nob Hill, passing fashionable stores and hotels. He included many identifiable people and buildings. This scene, on one's left when entering, is based on a photograph of participants in the December 8 meeting that launched the PWAP, but Labaudt moved the group from Washington, D.C., to the foot of Powell Street, in front of the cable car turntable.

Plates 36A–E show the images on one's left when climbing the stairs.

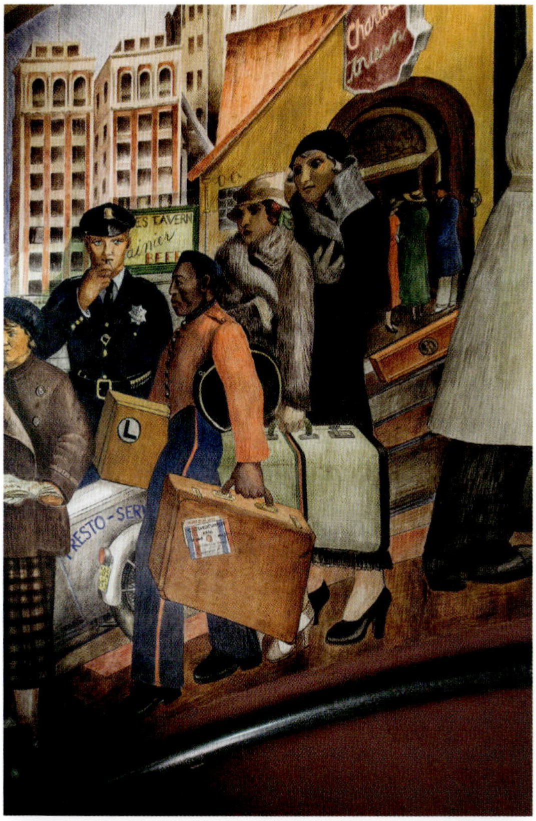

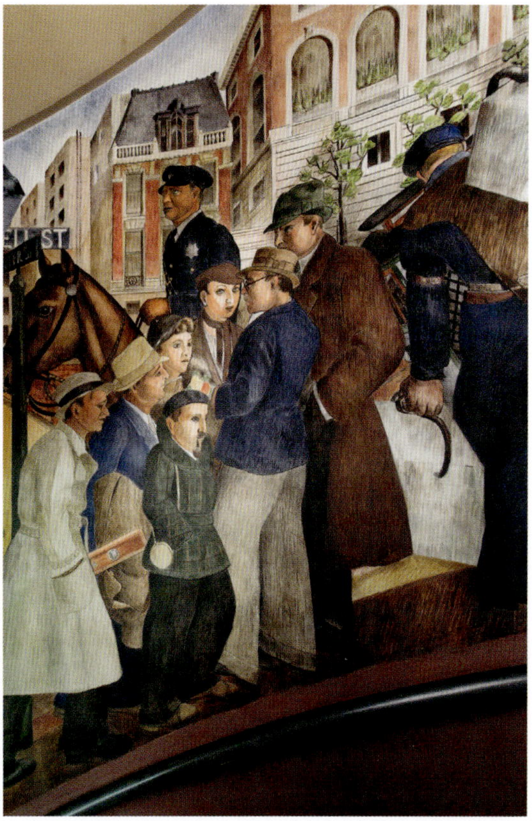

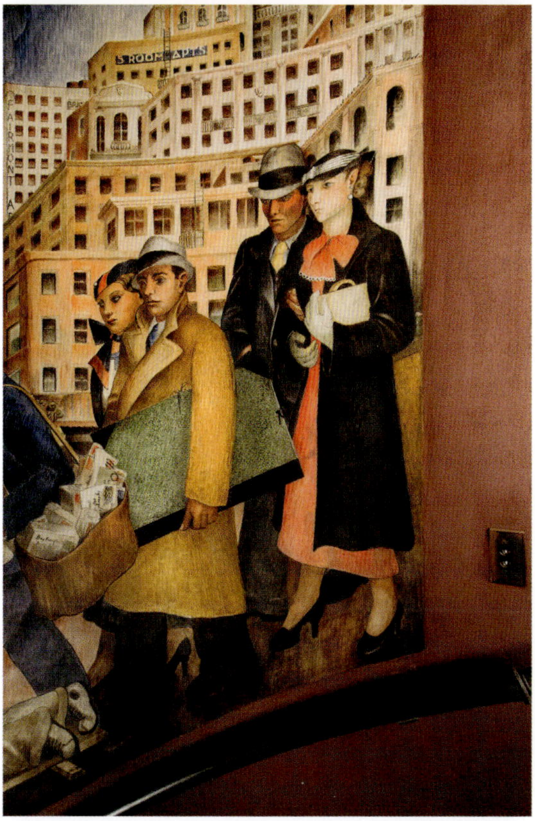

Plate 36C. (above, left) *Powell Street*, Lucien Labaudt. Courtesy of the San Francisco Arts Commission.

Plate 36D. (above, right) *Powell Street*, Lucien Labaudt. Courtesy of the San Francisco Arts Commission.

Plate 36E. (left) *Powell Street*, Lucien Labaudt. Courtesy of the San Francisco Arts Commission.

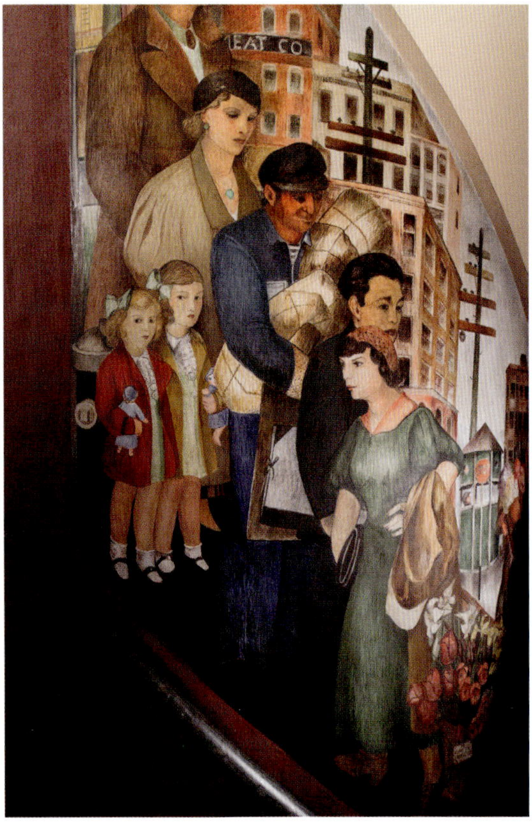

Plate 36F. *Powell Street*, Lucien Labaudt. Courtesy of the San Francisco Arts Commission.

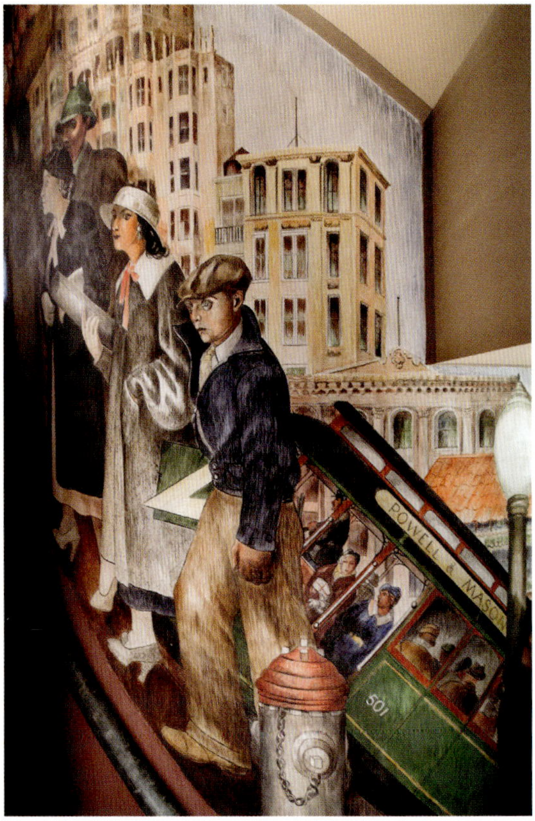

Plate 36G. *Powell Street*, Lucien Labaudt. Courtesy of the San Francisco Arts Commission.

Plates 36F–I show the images on one's left when descending.

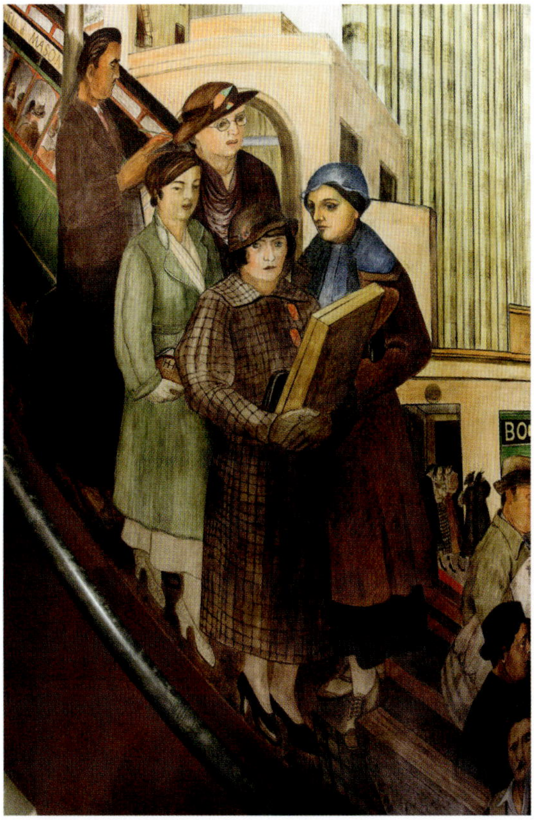

Plate 36H. *Powell Street*, Lucien Labaudt. Courtesy of the San Francisco Arts Commission.

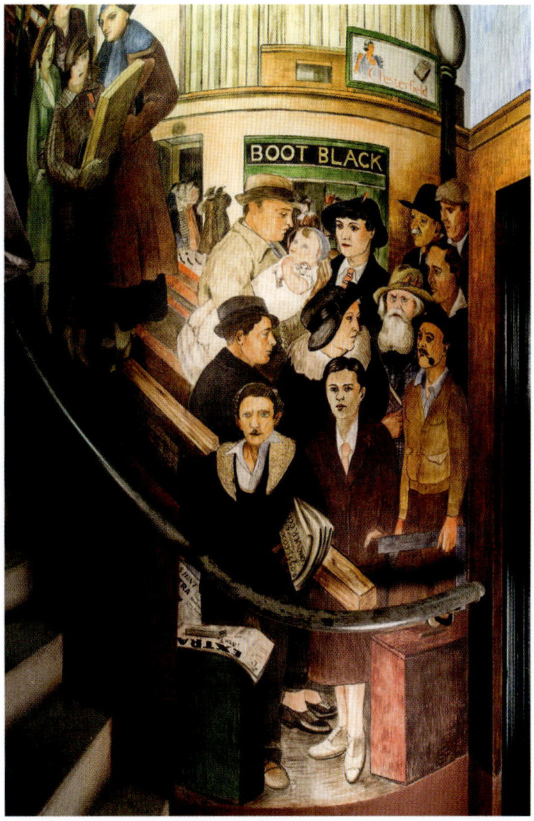

Plate 36I. *Powell Street*, Lucien Labaudt. Courtesy of the San Francisco Arts Commission.

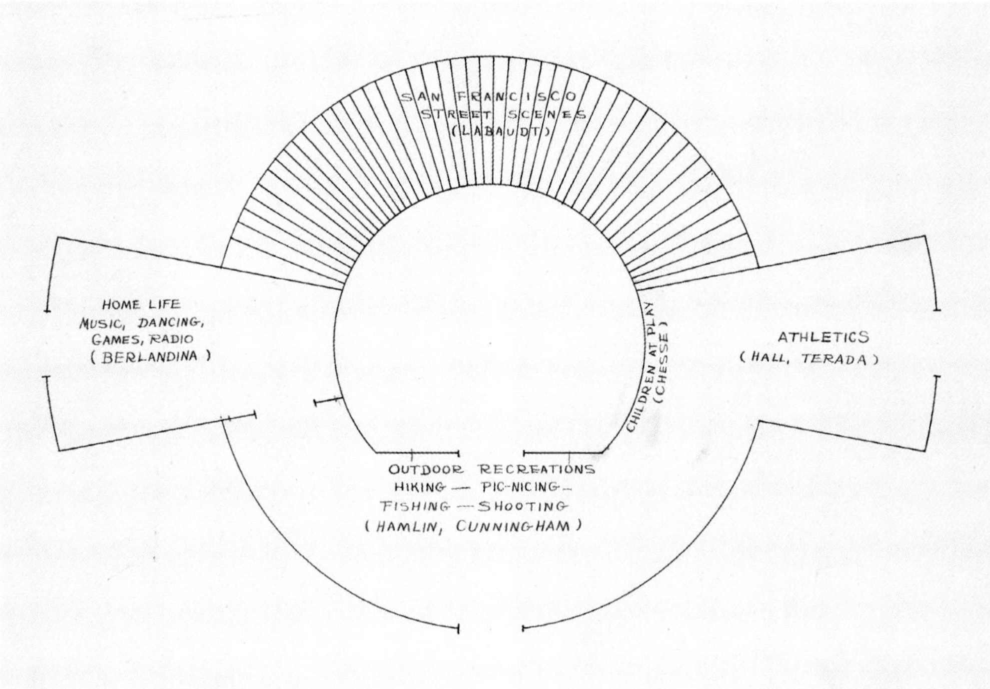

Figure 3.2. Original sketch for the stairs and second floor. (Source: Unknown artist, *Coit Tower, Floor Plan for the Murals [Second Floor]*, black ink on paper, 18½ x 27 in. [470 x 686 mm], December 1933, Federal Art Project, FA9513.1, Courtesy of Fine Arts Museums of San Francisco.)

Figure 3.2 is the original sketch for the stairs and second floor. As the sketch makes clear, most of those working in this area had to deal with curved walls for part or all of their mural.

The second floor presents recreation and home life. Ralph Chessé's *Children at Play* (plate 37) is on one's right as one comes to the top of the stairs. The curved walls presented challenges for the muralists and also for modern photographers.

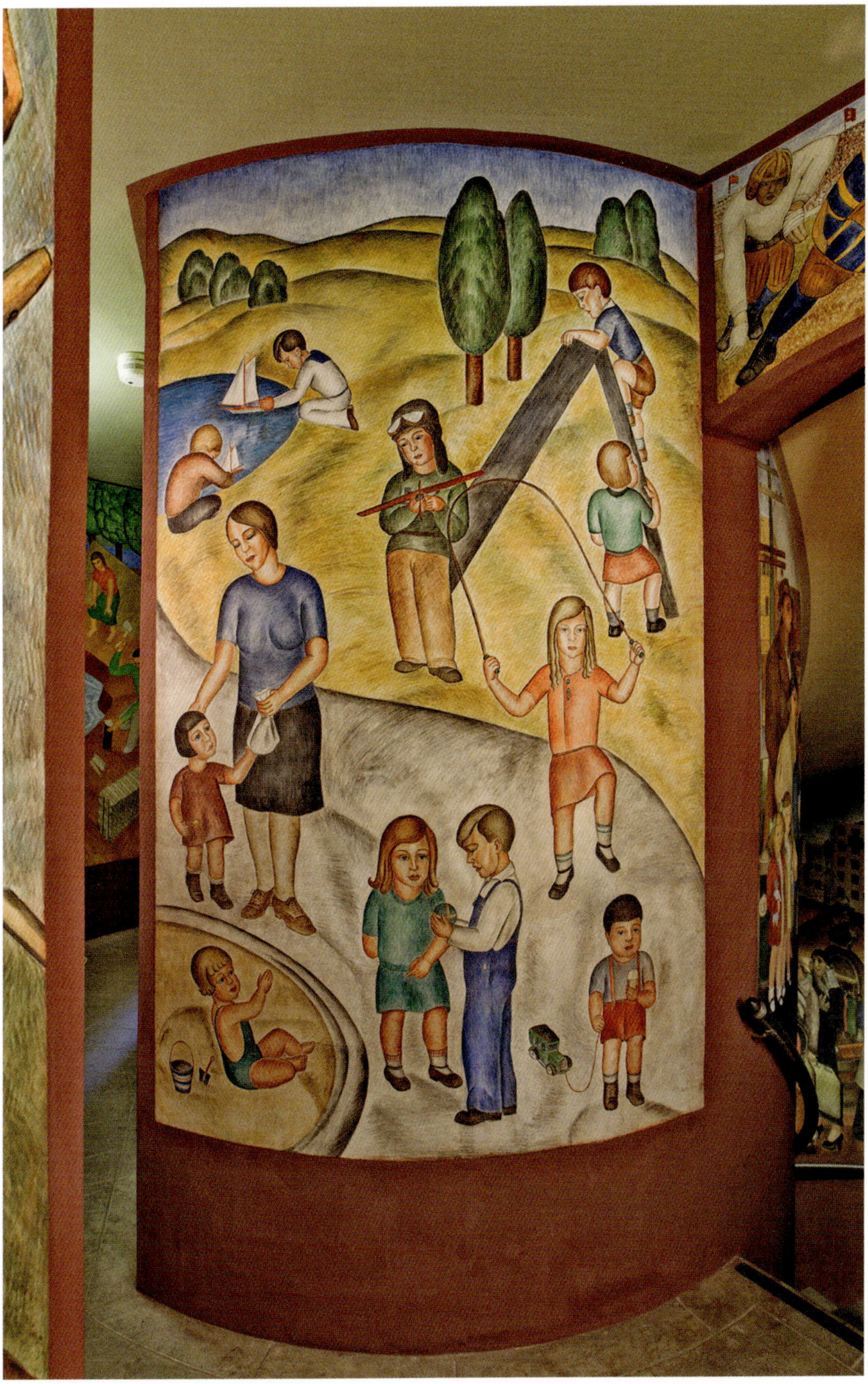

Plate 37. *Children at Play*, Ralph Chessé. Courtesy of the San Francisco Arts Commission.

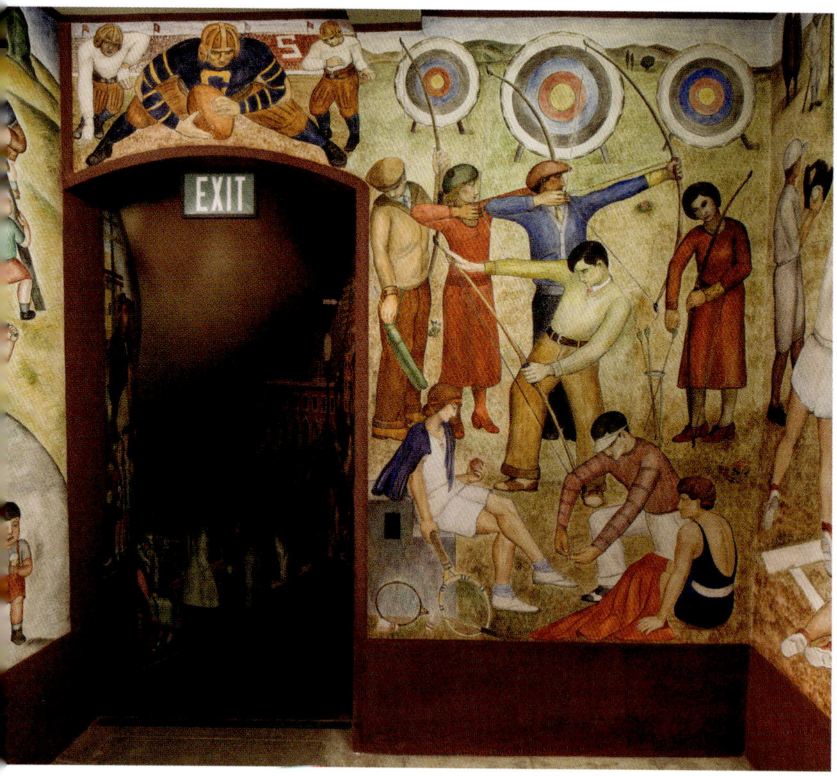

Plate 38A. *Collegiate Sports*, Parker Hall. Courtesy of the San Francisco Arts Commission.

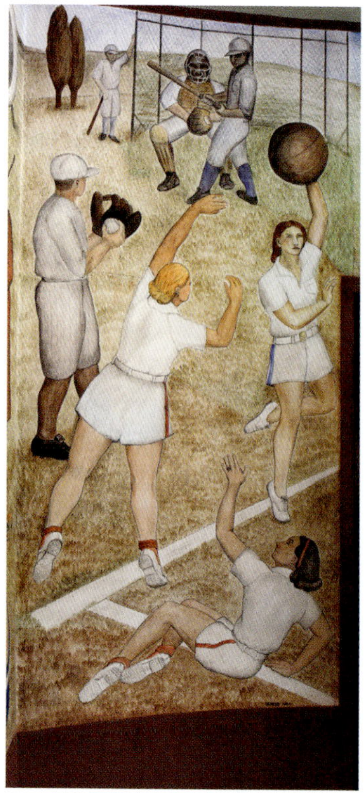

Plate 38B. *Collegiate Sports*, Parker Hall. Courtesy of the San Francisco Arts Commission.

The murals by Parker Hall and Takeo Edward Terada are in an alcove opposite Chessé's mural. Parker Hall's *Collegiate Sports* (plates 38A–B) included a depiction of the annual Big Game between the University of California, Berkeley, and Stanford, along with a variety of other collegiate sports for both men and women.

Takeo Edward Terada's *Sports*, (plates 39A–B) opposite Hall's mural, also includes both men's and women's athletics. In 1933–1934 there were polo matches in both San Francisco and San Mateo County, south of San Francisco.

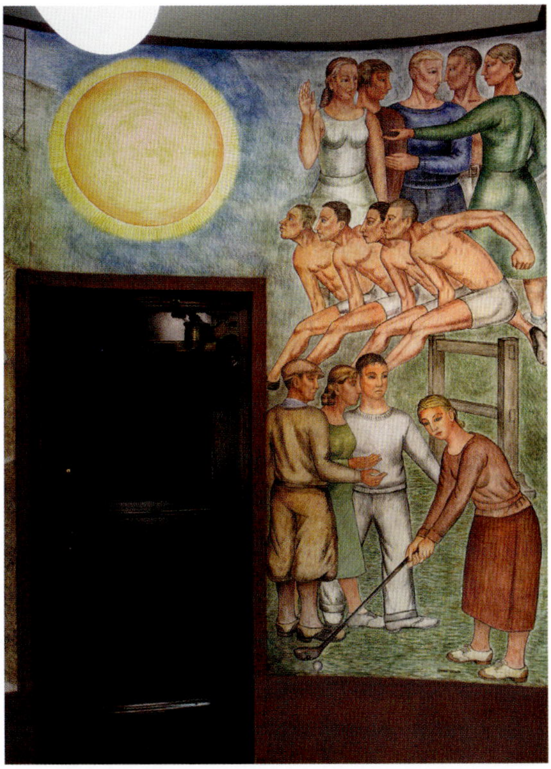

Plate 39A. *Sports*, Takeo Edward Terada. Courtesy of the San Francisco Arts Commission.

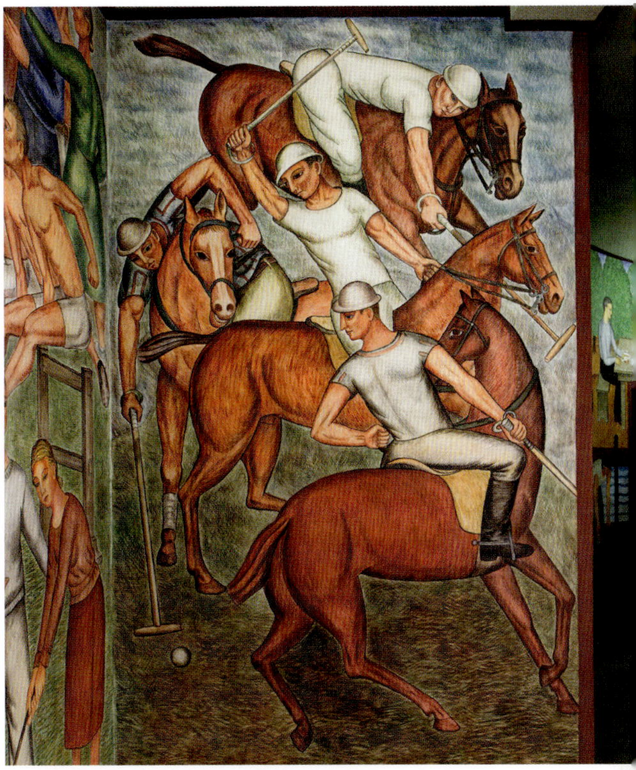

Plate 39B. *Sports*, Takeo Edward Terada. Courtesy of the San Francisco Arts Commission.

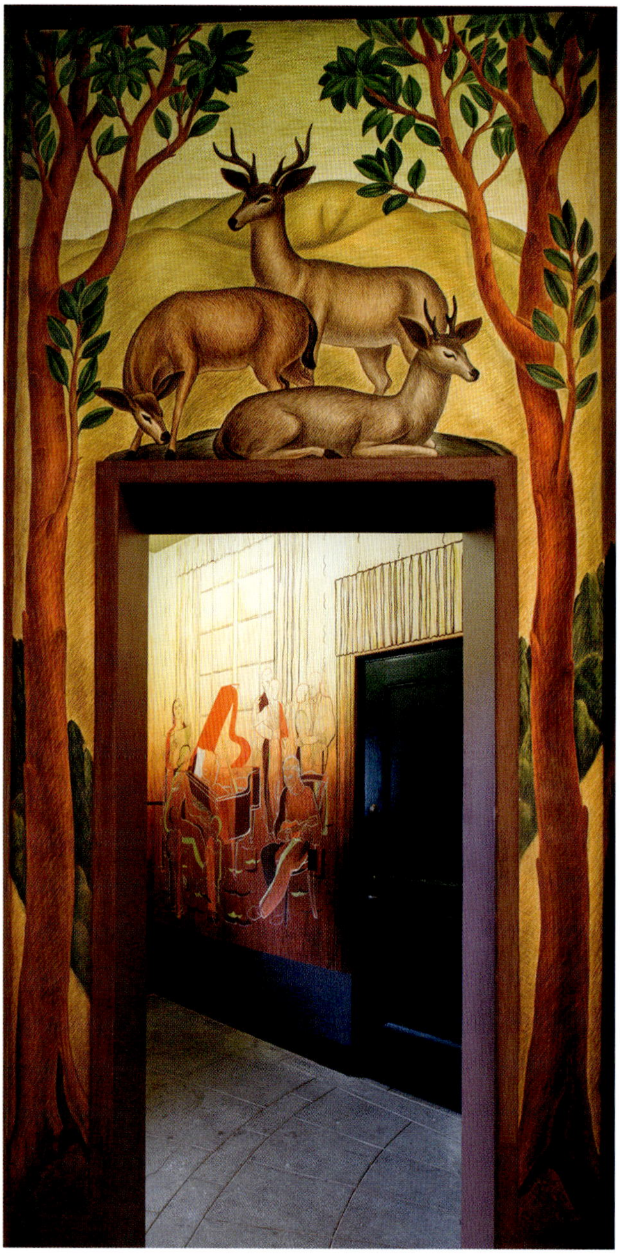

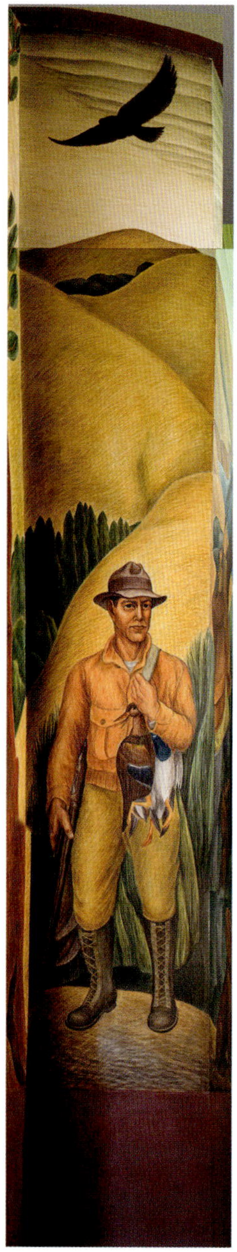

Plate 40A. (above, left) *Hunting in California*, Edith Hamlin. Courtesy of the San Francisco Arts Commission.

Plate 40B. (above, right) *Hunting in California*, Edith Hamlin. Courtesy of the San Francisco Arts Commission.

Edith Hamlin's *Hunting in California* (plates 40A–C) is on three walls, the flat wall around the elevator door, a curved wall to its left, and the flat wall over the entrance to the room at the end of the hallway. The first, on the left, is a bucolic scene, but the other two depict hunting.

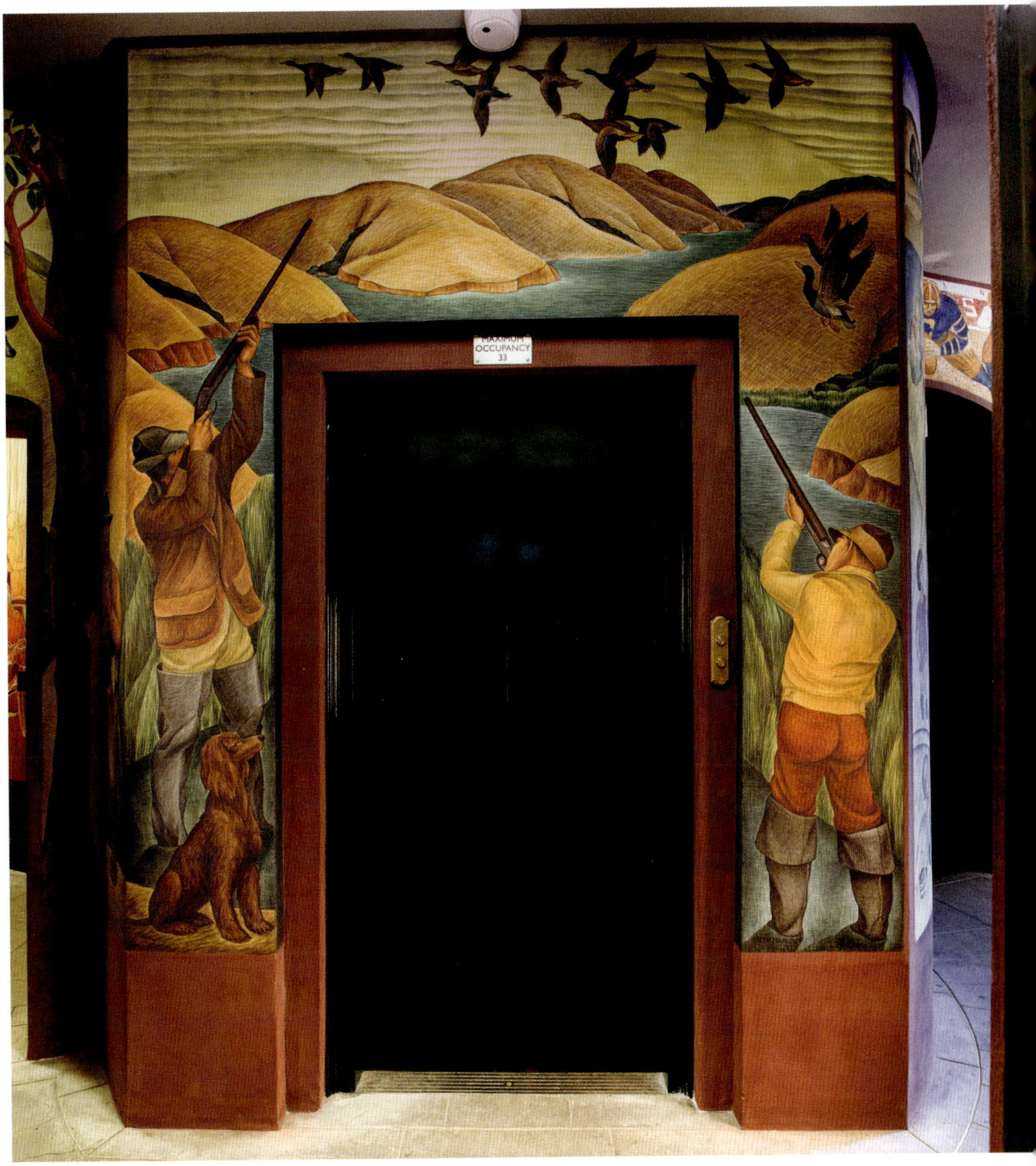

Plate 40C. *Hunting in California*, Edith Hamlin. Courtesy of the San Francisco Arts Commission.

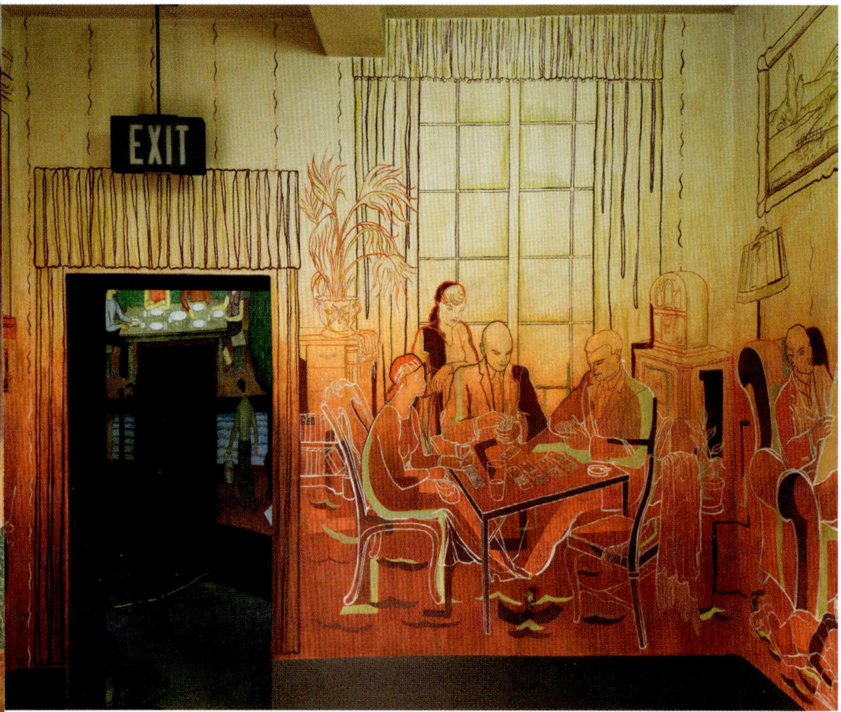

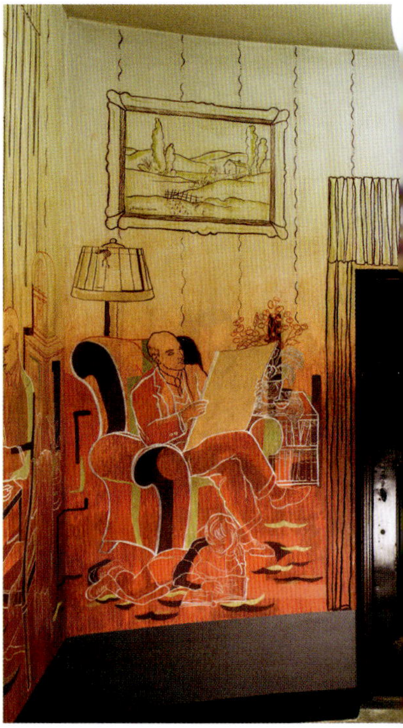

Jane Berlandina's *Home Life* (plates 42A–D) presents an upper-class home. One family member is modeled on her husband, Henry Temple Howard. While this may reflect Berlandina's home life as a member of the Howard family of architects and artists,[1] it is a far cry from the homeless people and May Day marchers in the mural of her brother-in-law, John Langley Howard. Like those who worked with oil on canvas for the lobby, Berlandina had a separate room for her egg tempera mural, which also departed from the others in its palette and style.

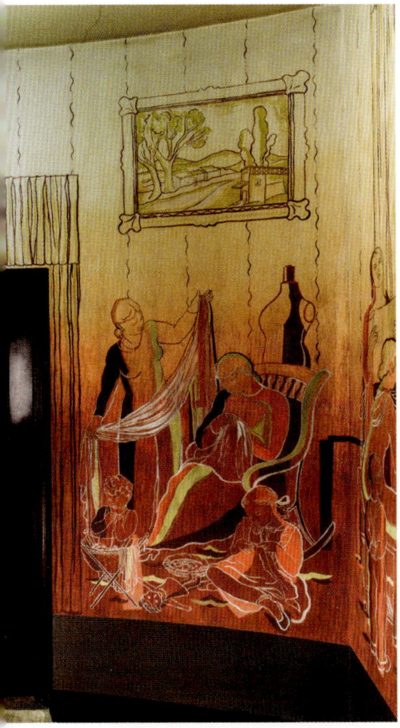

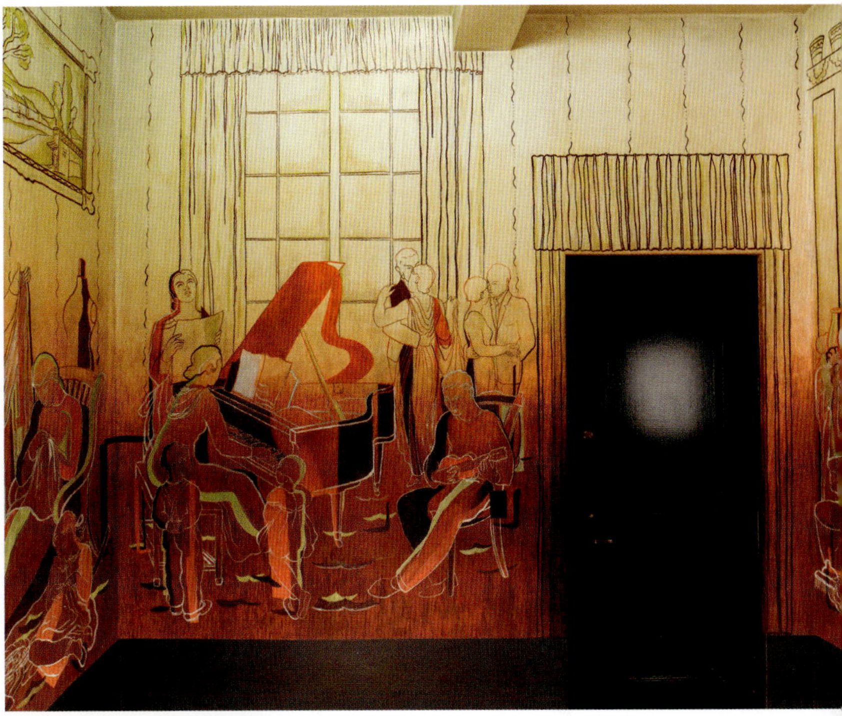

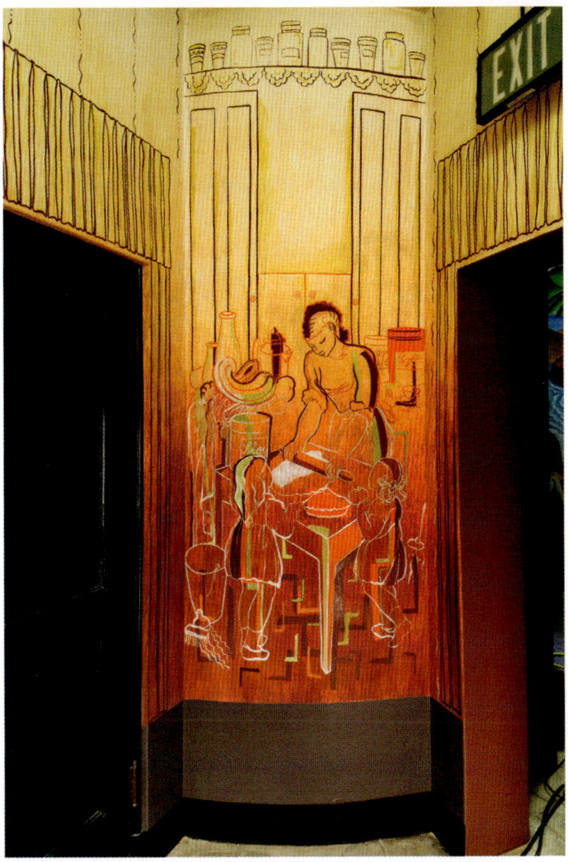

Plate 42A. (above, left) *Home Life*, Jane Berlandina. Courtesy of the San Francisco Arts Commission.

Plate 42B. (above, center) *Home Life*, Jane Berlandina. Courtesy of the San Francisco Arts Commission.

Plate 42C. (above, right) *Home Life*, Jane Berlandina. Courtesy of the San Francisco Arts Commission.

Plate 42D. (left) *Home Life*, Jane Berlandina. Courtesy of the San Francisco Arts Commission.

4

Political Controversy, 1934

References to the New Deal in several Coit Tower murals provoked no criticism, but there was a significant reaction to overt leftist imagery in a few murals. John Langley Howard depicted worker militancy, contrasted wealth with poverty, and presented the *Western Worker*, local newspaper of the Communist Party. Victor Arnautoff put two Communist publications on his newsstand and presented a man being robbed in the Financial District. Bernard Zakheim included the *Western Worker* among his many newspapers, included leftist authors on his bookshelves, and showed a man reaching for Marx's *Das Kapital*. And Clifford Wight placed a hammer and sickle over one of the west windows.

Those four artists were a small minority, but their imagery generated a major controversy given the prominent place in local and national politics of Communist Party activism and an intense local red scare. Junius Cravens, a local art critic, tagged the hysterical outbursts about subversive symbolism in the murals as a "tempest in the Coit Memorial Tower teapot."[1] The tempest had consequences, though. Administrators of subsequent New Deal art programs closely supervised federal art projects nationwide in order to avoid being condemned for expressing leftist sympathies, and some later art historians have unduly emphasized the controversy in writing about the Coit Tower murals.

The Park Commission had initially scheduled Coit Tower for a grand opening on July 1, 1934. However, other events preoccupied civic leaders throughout May, June, and July. A strike by Pacific Coast dockworkers began on May 9, and other maritime unions soon struck with issues of their own, shutting down the San Francisco waterfront and producing a ripple effect in other parts of the city's economy. A battle between police and strikers on July 5 left two dead and more than a hundred injured.

The police violence and subsequent deployment of the National Guard to protect strikebreakers precipitated a general strike in San Francisco, shutting down much of the city on July 16–19. A citywide red scare began in May when corporate leaders accused some strike leaders of being Communists, and the red scare escalated dramatically during the general strike as anonymous vigilantes burst into offices of left organizations, smashed furniture and machines, beat those found inside, and quickly departed. Police then arrived to arrest those just beaten.[2] The red scare had significant consequences for some Coit Tower artists and their murals.

Some, perhaps many, of the Coit Tower artists may have sympathized with the striking workers on the waterfront, but they had no opportunity to refer to the strike in their artwork. Two-thirds of the artists had completed their murals by April 28, before the strikes began on May 9. Since the fresco muralists painted from the top down, all of those who had not finished by April 28 were working on details in the lower third or lower quarter of their murals when the strikes began. Nonetheless, consistent with the prevalent mood in 1934 and quite apart from the strikes, a few of the Coit Tower artists incorporated into their murals overt leftist imagery or provocative images of militant labor. Those details, in the context of the citywide red scare, acquired greater significance than they might otherwise have had.

All the artists had presented detailed scaled drawings of their proposed murals for approval in December and January. Most kept quite close to their approved sketches as they added details. As Ralph Chessé later recalled, "The artist improvised and elaborated as he went along." Zakheim, for example, showed in his drawing that half of his library mural would depict people reading newspapers, but he selected the headlines day by day, based on what caught his eye in the press the day before. His headlines are of events from mid-February to late March 1934. Arnautoff's drawing showed a large number of people around a newsstand, but he added a robbery when filling in the details. John Langley Howard made the most changes as he developed his mural; he later remembered that he had not consulted anyone about his changes.[3]

Arnautoff's newsstand holds a wide range of mainstream newspapers and magazines but also two Communist publications, the *Daily Worker* and *New Masses*. Zakheim's library includes books by Soviet and leftist authors. He later recalled that he'd been given a list by Kenneth Rexroth. Among Zakheim's newspapers is a February headline from the *Western Worker*, the semiweekly newspaper of the Communist Party in the western states; the paper's banner included a small hammer-and-sickle logo. In the center of Zakheim's mural, a man modeled on John Langley Howard reaches for a copy of Marx's *Das Kapital*. Zakheim's mural had been completed in early April, well before the beginning of the city's red

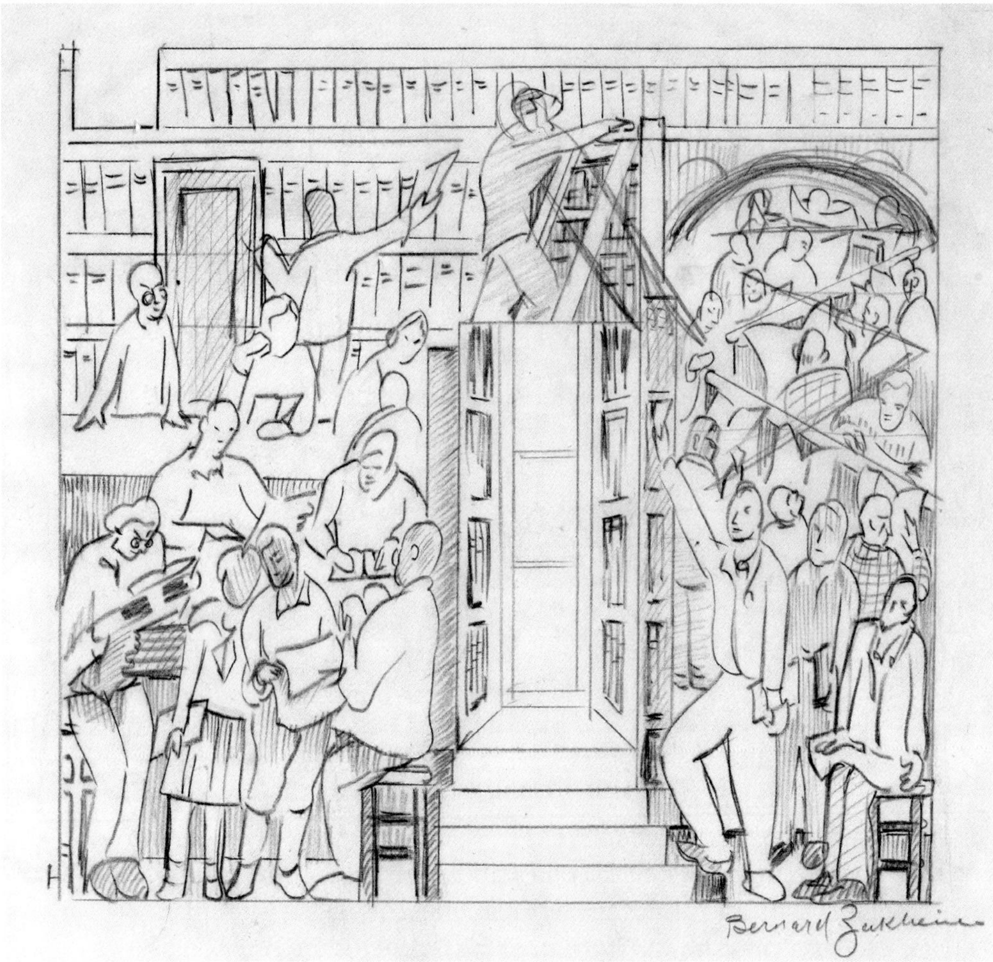

Figure 4.1. Zakheim's initial sketch for his mural showed people reading newspapers, a man reaching for a book on the right, and other library patrons on the left. Compare this sketch with the final mural (plate 14). (Source: Bernard Baruch Zakheim, *Coit Tower, Study for the Mural: Library*, December 1933, graphite on Japanese paper, 15 x 12 in. [381 x 305 mm], Federal Art Project, FA9503, photograph by Randy Dodson, courtesy of the Fine Arts Museums of San Francisco.)

scare, when he and others might not have realized the potential problems that could arise from the appearance of Communist publications.[4]

Howard's dramatic depiction of unemployment and poverty also included a copy of the *Western Worker*, held by one of the May Day demonstrators. The center of his mural contrasted homeless victims of the Depression with wealthy Californians. The workers' demonstration did not appear in his approved drawing; some of the homeless people may have been vaguely suggested. He later explained, "I was definitely trying

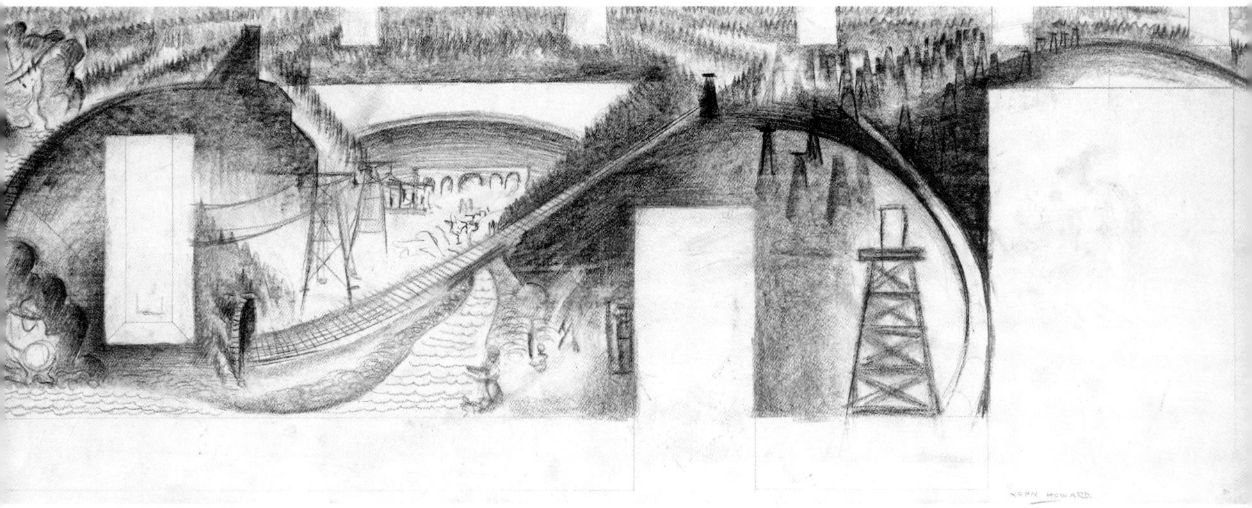

Figure 4.2. John Langley Howard's sketch, showing the basic pattern for the center of his mural, included someone panning for gold in a different location than in his final mural, and suggestions of a few other people, but did not include the May Day demonstration. Compare with his final mural (plate 25). (Source: John Langley Howard, *Coit Tower, Study for the Mural: California Industrial Scenes [Hydro Electric Power]*, December 1933, graphite and charcoal on illustration board, 11½ x 31¼ in. [292 x 794 mm], Federal Art Project, L43-12-19, photograph by Randy Dodson, courtesy of the Fine Arts Museums of San Francisco.)

to bring to the consciousness of people who were comparatively well off the conditions and the state of mind of people who were not so well off."[5]

All those details might have escaped notice had it not been for Clifford Wight's prominent hammer and sickle, certain to attract attention even without the fraught context of mid-1934.

Late in the project, a decision was made to include the areas above the east, south, and west windows, but those areas were considered so minor that the artists—Wight for the east and west windows, Dean for the south—had not been required to submit sketches for approval. Wight's sketches for the east windows survive, depicting agricultural symbols. Dean painted the area above the south windows, but there is no record of what he placed there. For the west windows, as one faces them, on the left Wight placed a dollar and the motto, "In God We Trust," which he intended to symbolize rugged individualism. Over the center window he painted the most prominent symbol of the New Deal, the blue eagle of the National Recovery Administration, which several other artists also included in their murals, in the center of a suspension bridge. (Construction of the Golden Gate Bridge was visible from that window.) On the right side, as one faces the window, he put a hammer and sickle and the motto "Workers of the World Unite."[6]

Figure 4.3 and 4.4 captions:

Figure 4.3. (right) Wight's symbols over the west windows; the photo is dated August 8, 1934, the day after the Art Commission voted to remove everything above all three sets of windows. The hammer and sickle is on the right. (Source: Photo AAC-1523, San Francisco History Center, San Francisco Public Library.)

Figure 4.4. (below) Wight's hammer and sickle. (Source: "Murals in Coit Tower with Communist Flavor, Telegraph Hill," Fang family *San Francisco Examiner* Photograph Archive Negative Files, BANC PIC 2006.029—NNEG box 40, courtesy Bancroft Library, University of California, Berkeley.)

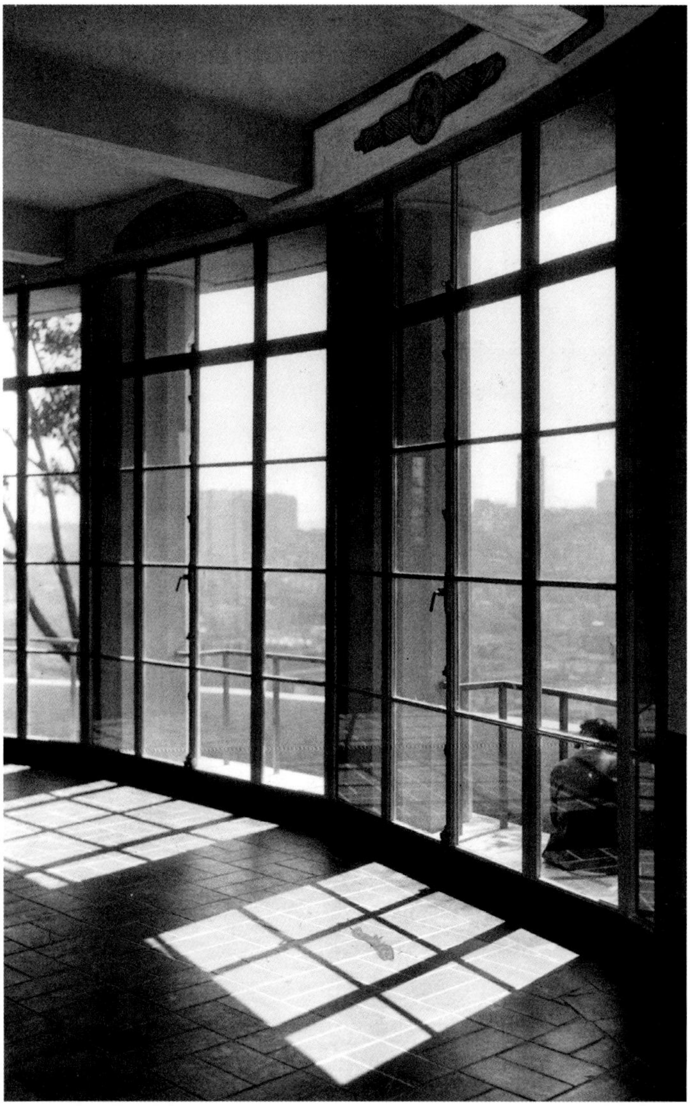

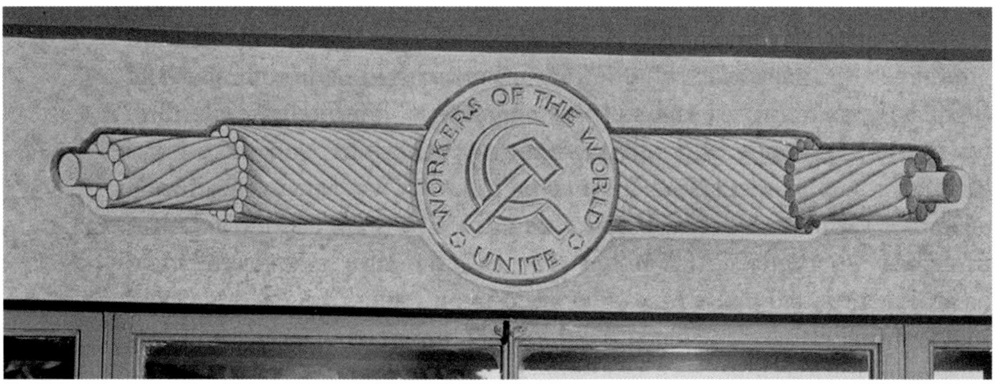

Though one might read his symbols as suggesting that the New Deal was a bridge from "rugged individualism" to socialism, Wight later argued that in depicting "the contemporary American Scene," the "paramount issue" is "social change," and "for this reason I made a representation of this historical fact by means of three symbols[—]the first depicting the Capitalism of 'Rugged Individualism,' the second 'The New Deal' which has superceded [*sic*] the first, and in the third panel, Communism another alternative which exists in the current American Scene." He insisted, "This symbol is in no way an exhortation or propaganda, but a simple statement of an existing condition as evidenced by the fact that there is in this country today an officially recognized Communist Party." Wight also explained, "There was no attempt made to conceal the sketches which were pinned up a couple of days before the painting was begun. They were seen by the artists working at the Tower at that time, including the 'Technical Director & Art Chief' of the project, none of whom made any objection to them."[7]

In his memoirs published thirty-nine years later, Arnautoff recalled that as technical director for the entire project, "At times I approached colleagues, inquiring how their work was developing," but he seems to have understood his role as advisory, not supervisory. His memoirs present this account of his reaction to Wight's hammer and sickle:

> Wight was painting an area above three windows and the fresco fell into three parts, united by a common theme. This theme seemed too risky to some, inasmuch as a hammer and sickle were represented in one part.
>
> I asked Clifford, "You're not afraid of an uproar?"
>
> "What uproar?" he replied, surprised.
>
> "I somehow feel there'll be some unpleasantness."
>
> "Really?"
>
> I viewed the outlines of the still uncompleted hammer and sickle and said, "that's like waving a red flag in front of a bull."
>
> Wight gave a mischievous wink and said, "Very much so. But I'm an optimist. Don't we live in the land of the free, as the newspapers tell us a hundred times a day? Can't I, then, freely express my thoughts and feelings?"
>
> "But you must know freedom in America is understood in a special way."
>
> Wight's eyes blazed in anger. "So be it. I'm not afraid of anything, not even a scandal."[8]

Wight succeeded in creating a scandal. Arthur Brown Jr., the architect of Coit Tower, had been hesitant about the murals from the beginning. When he saw Wight's hammer and sickle during what he described as "a casual visit to Coit Tower" on Saturday, June 23, he denounced it the following Monday in a letter to Herbert Fleishhacker, a member of the Art

Commission and president of the Park Commission. Fleishhacker told Heil to deal with the situation. All the murals then received close scrutiny.[9]

On Thursday, June 28, Heil telegraphed Bruce to inform him that "some artists have at the last minute incorporated in their murals details such as newspaper headlines and certain symbols which might be interpreted as communistic propaganda." In fact, all had been in place for weeks at that point. Heil continued: "Tower not open to public yet but th[r]ough reporters knowledge of these things has come to the editors of influential newspapers who have warned us that they would take hostile attitude towards whole project unless those details be removed." The response from Forbes Watson, Bruce's assistant in Washington, on Friday, June 29, was prompt and clear: the murals should be completed "according to the approved designs without additions"—but, of course, there had been no approved designs for the areas over the three windows or for the specific details in all the murals.[10] Howard, Wight, and Zakheim were directed to make changes in their murals, but the orders to Howard and Zakheim were soon dropped. Wight refused.[11]

The park department, almost certainly on orders from Fleishhacker, locked the tower the last week of June and canceled the official opening date of July 1. The windows were whitewashed to prevent anyone from seeing inside.[12]

On July 2, several of the artists gathered in front of the tower to protest what they understood as an attack on artistic freedom analogous to the destruction of the Rivera mural in February. A statement by the Artists and Writers Union executive committee declared, "We have stationed pickets at the tower to prevent the Art Commission and the PWAP from disfiguring or destroying either Mr. Wight's mural or the works of any other artists in the tower," and that the executive committee "stands behind" Wight "in his refusal to alter his work." Among those appearing in photographs in that day's *San Francisco Call-Bulletin* are Frede Vidar, George Harris, and Rinaldo Cuneo. Shirley Staschen and Julia Rogers, Zakheim's assistants, are also pictured, standing forlornly in front of the locked Coit Tower doors, heads in their hands, sadly staring down at a sign that in large black letters states simply, "CLOSED."[13]

On July 3, Lewis Hobart, president of the Art Commission, replied to the union's statement with his own declaration that the artists "were given great latitude in their designs and conceptions but that does not give them the liberty to exceed the commission's views upon what should be exploited as their personal views in opposition to the generally accepted tradition of national Americanism." Hobart was consciously or unconsciously echoing Edward Bruce's late-January letter to all PWAP artists: "It is time that all of us forget ourselves and our individual interests and personal preferences for the sake of a great cause."[14]

Also on July 3, the *San Francisco Chronicle* printed a photo of Zakheim's mural with the headline "IS THIS RED PROPAGANDA?" and sub-headline "Murals on Coit Shaft Hint Plot for Red Cause." The article explained, "Perspiration has begun to bead the brows of members of the Park Commission and Art Commission, who are sore put to decide whether the daubings on the interior of the Coit Memorial Tower are art or whether they are merely grotesque rebellion of starved souls against the existing order." The article failed to mention Wight's hammer and sickle and instead focused on Zakheim's mural, describing it as "showing a lot of emaciated intelligentsia in a reading room perusing radical books and literature."[15]

On July 3, however, most San Franciscans, especially the city's business and civic elite, were focused on more momentous events. Late that afternoon, waterfront employers, backed by most corporations in the city and with major police protection, attempted to open the strike-bound port using strikebreakers. The striking unions and their supporters presented strong resistance, but both of those efforts lasted just a short time that afternoon. July 4 was a holiday; both sides rested and prepared. July 5 was a day of bloody conflict, culminating in the deaths of two workers, killed by police, and injuries, some serious, to a hundred people, including ten police and seven bystanders. The governor immediately mobilized the National Guard and sent them to the waterfront with tanks, machine guns, and snipers to protect the strikebreaking operations. Both sides of the longshore and maritime strikes escalated their rhetoric and actions. The San Francisco Labor Council moved toward a general strike—a protest strike by all the city's unions. The city's business and civic leaders loudly accused Communists of fomenting revolution, and some of them convinced themselves that revolution was already under way.[16]

Also on July 5, the *San Francisco Examiner* published a photograph superimposing Wight's hammer and sickle over Zakheim's depiction of a man reaching for *Das Kapital*, as if both were part of the same painting. The headline read, "Soviet Symbol in Tower" above the composite photo, and the caption below it read, "Here is the painting in the Coit Memorial Tower that has caused a bitter dispute between artists and the Art Commission." The article falsely stated, "The Government, which employed the artists, has demanded its removal because of the Communist emblem, the hammer and sickle, which appear above." The article was filled with other misinformation as well, describing the hammer and sickle as "above a large window on the south side of the tower" and "the emblem is in the form of painting [*sic*] surmounted by a seal, with the hammer and sickle in the center." The article accurately quoted a telegram from Bruce, on June 29, addressed to all PWAP artists in District 15: "Unless the painting were removed, San Francisco artists would 'seriously jeopardize' their chances to receive more Federal funds."[17]

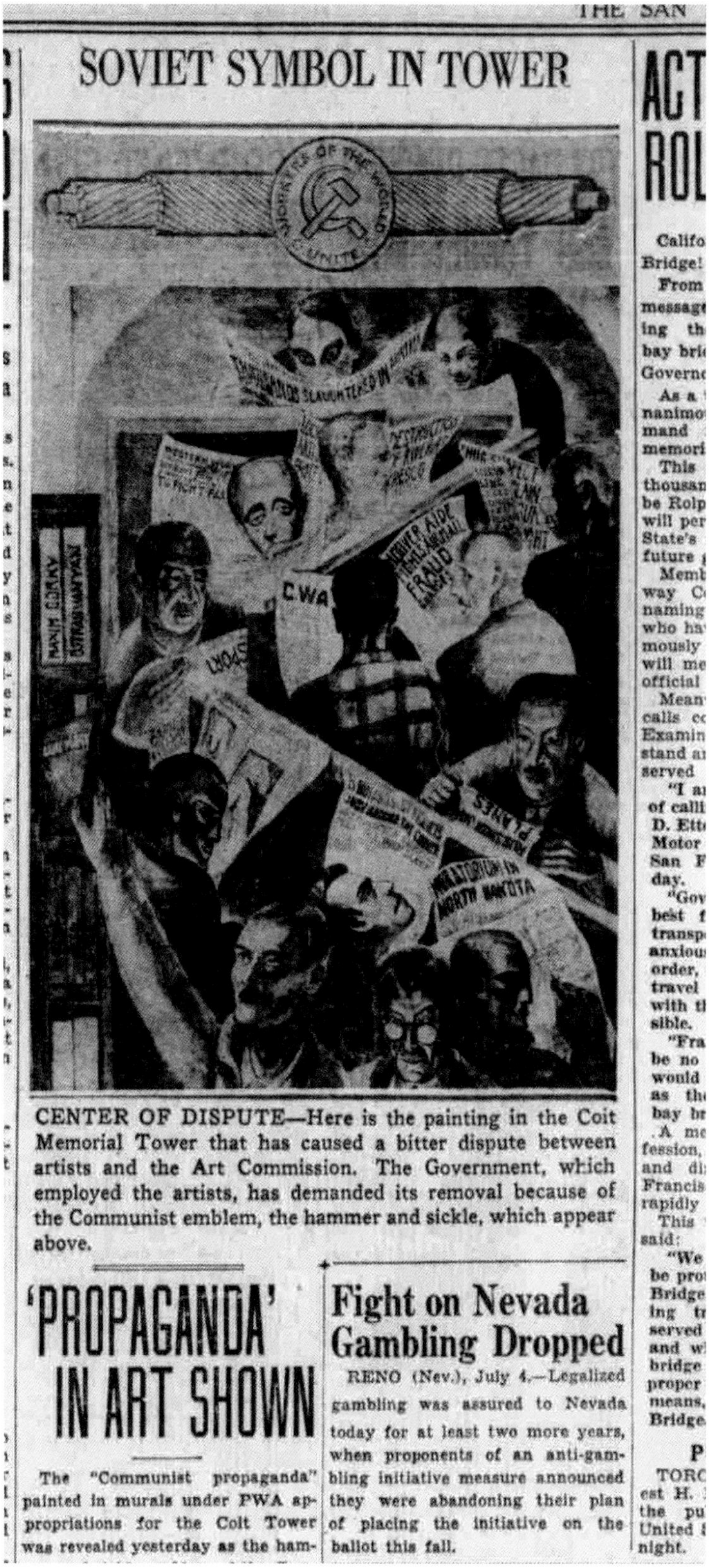

THE SAN

SOVIET SYMBOL IN TOWER

CENTER OF DISPUTE—Here is the painting in the Coit Memorial Tower that has caused a bitter dispute between artists and the Art Commission. The Government, which employed the artists, has demanded its removal because of the Communist emblem, the hammer and sickle, which appear above.

'PROPAGANDA' IN ART SHOWN

The "Communist propaganda" painted in murals under PWA appropriations for the Coit Tower was revealed yesterday as the ham-

Fight on Nevada Gambling Dropped

RENO (Nev.), July 4.—Legalized gambling was assured to Nevada today for at least two more years, when proponents of an anti-gambling initiative measure announced they were abandoning their plan of placing the initiative on the ballot this fall.

Figure 4.5. The *San Francisco Examiner* superimposed Wight's hammer and sickle over Zakheim's depiction of a man reaching for Marx's *Das Kapital*. (Source: *San Francisco Examiner*, July 5, 1934, p. 7, courtesy ProQuest Historical Newspapers.)

Joseph Danysh, a gallery owner, was featuring a one-man show of Zakheim's work at the time the doctored photo appeared in the *Examiner*. Danysh later recalled that Zakheim came to him and wanted to sue the paper for a million dollars, but a lawyer quickly explained that they could not prove that they had been damaged by the photo. Nonetheless, Danysh and the lawyer went to an *Examiner* editor, explained that the photo was of two different works, and asked for a retraction. In response, "The editor just laughed at us" and said, "The young man's scissors slipped . . . this could happen any time." Next Danysh and Zakheim wrote a letter to all the city's Jewish organizations, explaining what had been done to Zakheim, printed up hundreds of copies, took the copies to show to the editor, and again asked for a retraction. Instead, the editor offered to have a glowing and prominent article about the exhibition in Danysh's gallery. That was done on July 17.[18]

On July 7, Junius Cravens, art critic for the *San Francisco News*—the most liberal of the city's four daily papers—provided a detailed description of Wight's three symbols, although he admitted that he had not seen them himself and was reporting based on "rumor." The rumor was largely accurate. Cravens wrote:

> Over the central window he stretched a bridge, at the center of which is a circle containing the Blue Eagle of the NRA. Over the right-hand window [on the left as one faces the window] he stretched a segment of chain; in the circle, in this case, appears the legend, "In God We Trust"—symbolizing the American dollar, or, I presume, capitalism. Over the left-hand window he placed a section of woven cable and a circle framing a hammer, a sickle, and the legend, "United Workers of the World," in short, Communism.

Cravens was wrong about the legend, as his source had apparently not studied the writing carefully.[19]

Although Cravens pooh-poohed the whole thing with his "tempest in the Coit Memorial Tower teapot" comment, he also jocularly added, "At least three of the 25 or 30 artists . . . had seen red," and "The naughty boys had indulged in a little Communist propaganda, and at the expense of the U.S. government." He attributed it to the influence of Rivera: "the god of many American fresco painters, particularly those who careen larboard [port, or left], so to speak. In their eagerness to follow in his brush strokes, they not only lean over toward the extreme left, but also backward." Although Cravens specified that he had not been able to view the murals, he also described Howard's May Day marchers with the *Western Worker* in hand and Zakheim's library reading room, "in which radical books and newspapers are rampant."[20]

A sympathetic description of Wight's symbols appeared three weeks later, on July 29, in the *New York Times*. The article mentioned Zakheim's newspapers and books and stated, incorrectly, that Howard's mural contained "several questionable periodicals." The reporter, identified only as a special correspondent, seems to have interviewed Wight or had access to Wight's account of the situation, given the reporter's quotations in describing the symbols: the symbols portrayed "three stages of social and political development." The article continued: "For the first he chose figures representative 'of the rugged individualism stage of American capitalism,' and thus the first panel contains an American dollar, among other things, with the words, 'In God We Trust' and 'E Pluribus Unum.' Indicative of the New Deal, the second space contains a Blue Eagle, with the [NRA] slogan, 'We Do Our Part.' But in the third he chose to paint the Soviet hammer and sickle, with the words, 'Workers of the World Unite.'" Noting that the work had been branded as "Bolshevik propaganda" and a "Red plot," the article claimed, again suggesting an interview with Wight or someone close to him, "It does not seem that the artist had any but a purely objective, impersonal intent."[21]

Cravens concluded his July 7 article by noting that the regional committee of the PWAP "finds itself in the position of the teacher in the schoolroom—plenty of authority but no control over the naughty boys. At this writing, all hands seem about to appeal to Washington to settle the dispute. Alas, poor Washington."[22]

"Poor Washington" was slow to act. Edward Bruce—not in Washington but vacationing in Vermont—was still seeking information on July 9, when he wrote to Harold Mack, his friend, who was vacationing in Oregon. A key member of Heil's advisory committee, Mack had taken an active interest in the work at Coit Tower. "I understand," Bruce wrote, "that some of the artists engaged on that project introduced a lot of communistic propaganda in their pictures." He assured Mack, "I am not for or against communistic propaganda of this kind, but I am against their trying to put something over by introducing it in pictures in Government buildings and paid for by Government funds when it was not in the original designs approved by the committee." He asked Mack to gather more information and offer advice.[23]

Before Bruce could receive Mack's reply, the city was plunged into the general strike, July 16–19. Much of the city shut down for those four days. From July 16 through the end of July, vigilante groups roamed the region, smashing the offices of left organizations and beating those inside. Fleishhacker, like other civic leaders, was preoccupied with the crisis on the waterfront. Marvin McIntyre, President Roosevelt's secretary, considered Fleishhacker a "friend" of the administration and asked him on July 17 to help cool things down. The Park Commission did not meet between June 14 and July 23.[24]

Mack's handwritten reply to Bruce was dated July 16, the first day of the general strike:

> Visited San Francisco for a couple of weeks & found a "tempest in a tea pot" over the Coit Tower. Too bad so many people take themselves seriously. It seems Clifford Wight who used to be Rivera's assistant was asked to paint a small formal decoration over the window at Coit Tower. It was only an unimportant detail and no preliminary sketches were asked for as it amounted to nothing. He painted three symbols one the symbol of money, one symbol of the N.R.A. and one the Communist symbol, hammer & sickle perfectly formal, but totally unnecessary. Brown the architect who has been looking for trouble saw it, got the newspapers to attack it and the Art Commission to refuse to accept it etc. So the Tower remains closed & 3600 square feet of fine painting are condemned because of two square feet of symbols. Of course it's all rot. The artist was Stupid & so is everyone else to make a fuss over it but hysteria is here & it is better not to stir up controversy now. Artist refuses to remove it[.] Other artists back him up. Art Commission Edgar Walter etc. refuse to pass it & Park Commission, Fleishhacker wont open it. If its removed artists raise hell[;] if it isnt newspapers do the same. You settle it.[25]

Bruce did settle it. He informed Mack in a letter on July 27: "Re the Coit Tower tempest in a teapot over the Communistic symbols, I agree with you that it is a silly business, and I have suggested to them that the best way to clean it up is to destroy the Wight painting. A smart aleck situation like that gives me a pain in the neck." The same day, Bruce wrote to Edward Rowan, his assistant, in Washington: "I hope they don't fool around with this socialistic thing any longer" and that they "wipe the damn painting out of the Tower!"[26] Though Bruce was clearly upset by the situation, his letters suggest that he left the final decision to Heil and the Art Commission.

Though the union had put a picket line around the tower to protect the works inside on July 2, the police soon closed the access road to the top of Telegraph Hill, supposedly to prevent waterfront strikers from using the hill as a vantage point, but in the process preventing further picketing of the tower.[27]

Though the executive committee of the Artists and Writers Union supported Wight, a large majority of the Coit Tower artists ultimately did not, including several who had protested on July 2. On July 30, the day after the *New York Times* article, sixteen of the master artists announced, "We wish to go on record as being opposed to the use of this symbol which is unimportant artistically and which has no place in the subject matter assigned." Wight's refusal to remove his "Communist symbol," they continued, "has categorized us in the public opinion as supporting the doctrines for which this symbol stands. That is not so." They requested the immediate removal of "the offending work" so that "in fairness to the artists concerned and to the public the Coit Tower may be opened." Nine master artists did not sign. Berlandina, Dean, and Howard were out of town. Six refused: Arnautoff, Cunningham, Olmsted, Stackpole, Zakheim, and, of course, Wight.[28]

Throughout July, the city was caught up in the longshore and maritime strikes, general strike, and red scare—the hysteria mentioned by both Mack and the union. The striking longshore and maritime unions returned to work on July 31. By then, some civic leaders had begun to criticize what Judge Sylvain Lazarus, on July 24, termed the "public hysteria."[29] During that time, the Art Commission did not meet, perhaps because, as Mack put it, they didn't want to stir up controversy.

On August 1, the day after the strikers returned to work, a special committee of the Art Commission met at Coit Tower. The committee included Edgar Walter, a prominent sculptor and faculty member at the CSFA who had taught several of the Coit Tower muralists. There is no record of the committee's discussion, only its conclusion, which echoed the statements of the sixteen master artists that Wight's symbol was "unimportant artistically and . . . has no place in the subject matter assigned." Walter's committee similarly, and unanimously, recommended, "for artistic reasons, in order to conform with the major motive of the general scheme, that the three panels over the west, south, and east windows in the main floor be removed, and the same background as contained in the adjacent frescos be continued and substituted therefor[e]." On August 7, the full commission unanimously accepted that recommendation and asked the Park Commission to carry out those changes "for the adornment and beautification of the interior of Coit Tower."[30]

The committee and the commission chose to frame their decision in terms of artistic values rather than political censorship. There is no record of Dean's work over the south windows, but Wight, over the east windows, put line drawings of an ear of corn, a head of grain, and the head of a cow flanked by what seem to be two heads of sheep.[31] Given that all the other artwork on both floors was in full color and was representational rather than symbolic, Wight's drawings over both east and west windows were, in fact, out of conformity with "the general scheme." However, it seems highly unlikely any issue would have arisen if the drawings over the west windows had been as politically innocuous as those over the east windows. So, though the Art Commission left a public record that explained its decision as being based on artistic values, everyone understood that the decision was an act of political censorship, just as Nelson Rockefeller's action four months before had been an act of political censorship. For Coit Tower, however, the act was initiated by public officials who likely agreed with the sixteen artists that limiting the freedom of expression of one artist was necessary both to make available the work of all the other artists and, perhaps more importantly, to avoid undermining the New Deal's great experiment in democratizing art. Artists themselves understand that working on commission rarely involves complete freedom of expression.

The changes were soon completed, probably by park department personnel. Apparently, the frescoes over the windows were broken out, replastered, and painted.[32] Probably at the same time, the *Western Worker* banner in Howard's mural was painted over, and the hammer and sickle in the *Western Worker* banner in Zakheim's mural may have been blurred. There was no mention of those changes in the Art Commission's minutes, and those changes could not be justified on other than political grounds.

The tower remained closed on August 11, when Junius Cravens, writing in the *San Francisco News*, likened Wight to the dog in the manger, keeping the public from viewing the work of the other artists for "an ulterior rather than for an essential purpose" and correctly specified that a majority of the artists "have turned against him." Cravens also voiced a concern about public arts policy that had been raised by both local and federal authorities: "The hopes for future federal support seems [*sic*] to be pretty thoroughly blasted—thanks to Mr. Wight." The August issue of *California Arts and Architecture* raised similar issues, condemning as "public enemies" any tax-funded artists who presented "Communist propaganda." By then the controversy had gone nationwide, covered not only in newspapers throughout California but also in New York and elsewhere.[33]

Many years later, Arnautoff's memoirs recorded Wight's final words to him: "You turned out to be right, Mister Arnautoff. I teased the bulls too much."[34]

The tower was still closed in September, when Arnautoff wrote an article for the San Francisco Art Association's *Bulletin*. In it, he expressed his frustration and that of the other artists over the continued closure of the tower:

> I wonder why the Coit Tower is closed! So far as I know, the symbols . . . responsible for this, have been removed. . . . Tourists come and go. . . . They cannot even peer through the windows because the windows are whitewashed! I wonder why the windows have been white-washed—to protect the frescos from sun-stroke? . . . I wonder why the roof that has been leaking all last winter has not been fixed during the summer! I do not wonder what will happen to the frescos next winter when the rain will go right through the ceiling and the water will run all over the

paintings. I do not wonder because I do know that the paintings will be ruined. Who will be responsible for the lost Art? I guess the rain![35]

The reason for the repeated delays in the public opening of the tower may have been as mundane as the inability of the Park Commission to achieve a quorum anytime between July 23 and September 19. On July 23 the commission had met and received a request from Arthur Brown Jr. to appropriate funds to repair the roof of Coit Tower, but the minutes show no other mention of Coit Tower at that meeting. When the commission next convened on September 19, the commissioners approved plans to open the tower in October and authorized twenty-five dollars to repair the roof.[36]

The tower finally opened to the public on October 12, 1934. Everything above the large windows was gone. No hammer and sickle was visible anywhere. There were no other changes. The *San Francisco Chronicle* reported that first-day visitors to the tower "staggered away in a daze" from the "frescoes that packed every inch of wall space."[37]

In 1982 Karal Ann Marling's *Wall-to-Wall America: A Cultural History of Post-Office Murals in the Great Depression* presented the significant effect that the Coit Tower controversy had for later New Deal art policy. Marling's book focuses on post office murals, but she began with the controversy over the Coit Tower murals, which she considered key for understanding important aspects in the later history of the Treasury Section art program. "Bruce," she wrote, "was furious with all concerned," and "no program with which Edward Bruce was [later] associated would tolerate such slack supervision procedures that courted such dismaying surprises. *The Coit Tower mess taught the Treasury negative lessons it was not likely to forget* [emphasis added]." She described Bruce's later administration of the Treasury Section as requiring that approval for all projects had to proceed "along an exceedingly constricted path." She called it a "strategy of avoidance" intended "to nip controversy in the bud and to stifle adverse publicity." Under Bruce's supervision, the Treasury Section required artists to submit detailed, full-size sketches at every step of their project, all of which had to pass muster in Washington. The files of the Treasury Section contain myriad examples of the way Bruce's staff scrutinized every detail, excluded anything likely to cause controversy, and required revised drawings before giving final permission to proceed with painting.[38]

A few of the muralists and painters who created the Coit Tower murals did sympathize with the left, but San Francisco Communists did not conspire to cover the walls of Coit Tower with leftist symbols. Though Clifford Wight was undoubtedly a "smart aleck" leftist who indulged himself by "teasing the bulls," Mack was certainly correct in his assessment of the controversy as "a tempest in a teapot cooked up by the newspapers." However, there was a lesson there for artists: as John Langley Howard later reflected, "Trying to be a propagandist in murals is not feasible."[39] Further, the legacy of that political controversy reappeared throughout later New Deal art programs nationwide as administrators closely supervised federal art projects to avoid such future controversies. And the controversy has continued to dominate the approach of most subsequent art historians.

5

Contemporary Reactions

Although first-day visitors to the murals in Coit Tower may have "staggered away in a daze," the *San Francisco Chronicle* reported that some visitors reacted with "pained perplexity" or complained about "the sardonic touch to many of the scenes, the bitter twist to some of the painted faces." The artists who attended the opening enjoyed pointing out where they appeared on the walls, but the reporter was bothered by the "bitter irony struck out at the onlookers from the city life scenes by Victor Arnautoff" and the "tense, drawn, terrible faces of workmen in Howard's mural." One visitor pronounced an entirely negative verdict: "To me it is unpleasant. I'd hate to have such pictures around me or even be where they are for more than an hour or so."[1]

Contemporary art critics, in contrast, uniformly judged the murals successful and praised them with enthusiasm. They especially recognized four aspects as significant: the influence of Diego Rivera and the Mexican mural movement, the high degree of cooperation among a large number of artists, the overall size and scale of the project, and the use of fresco as a medium. Subsequent art historians have agreed.

Two detailed accounts of the murals appeared in the national press before the tower was opened to the public. Both critics presented mural-by-mural descriptions and photographs of individual murals, suggesting that they had access to the building during the time it remained closed to the public. The first, by Nadia Lavrova, appeared in the *Christian Science Monitor* on August 1, 1934. Formerly arts editor for the *San Francisco Examiner*, Lavrova had become a freelance writer for national publications. Her title, "Forty-Six Artists—One Palette," provides her overall evaluation of the collaborative nature of the project. "It was thought that a group work by a number of artists, reputed to be temperamental individualists, might present a problem," she noted, adding, "Apprehension was expressed that so many artists, including conservatives and moderns, literalists and symbolists, might produce a motley ensemble." However, she declared, the artists, "all doing contiguous mural painting, developed so fine an attitude of harmony that it is reflected in the completed series of frescoes.... Today astonishment is expressed that there is such an impression of unity for the whole." And she quoted Stackpole: "'We all worked under happy and ideal conditions, in perfect harmony.'"[2]

By the time she was writing, Lavrova would likely have been familiar with accounts of PWAP accomplishments in other parts of the country, since the end of the PWAP was marked by exhibitions in Washington and New York and articles in national publications. She specified that Coit Tower included three types of murals: fresco, oil on canvas, and egg tempera, but she emphasized that nearly all the Coit Tower murals were frescoes and, as such, the Coit Tower murals were unique in the country—"by far the largest group of frescoes found anywhere in the United States." Her statement is borne out in the final report of the PWAP; in it, only Region 15 listed frescoes separately from oil and tempera murals, and Region 15 reported a total of thirty-eight frescoes.[3] Lavrova apparently had access to such records, for she cited forty frescos from Region 15 and "three or four . . . in the rest of the country."

Lavrova surveyed the history of fresco painting and provided a detailed explanation of the technique for creating fresco murals. She specified that the Coit Tower artists included women, who "for the first time in history" (she meant all of human history) were working in fresco as well as men. She added that, for all the artists, "their 'helpers,' among whom there were several young girls, learned to do fresco work on a large scale, and acquired a great deal more experience than if they had spent that time studying at an art school."[4]

Lavrova emphasized the influence of Rivera and other Mexican muralists on both the technique and content of the Coit Tower muralists: "Their paintings draw their inspiration from the contemporary age and give to their frescoes a social content." She described how Rivera's influence had led to "a California school of fresco painting," and declared that, besides the harmony among the artists, "there is another feature that distinguishes the Coit Memorial Tower undertaking from other fine art produced under the PWAP auspices in every part of the country. It has afforded a splendid means of expression to artists who comprise the informal, unofficial, but easily recognizable San Francisco school of fresco painting."[5]

Lavrova obviously had full access to the closed tower, for she led her readers through the murals, wall by wall, floor by floor, noting each artist and each subject. She gave special attention to those by Albro ("a young artist, she yet holds the distinction of being the first California woman ever to take up the painting of frescoes"), Arnautoff (whose mural has "all the elements that go toward making an outstanding fresco: rhythm and movement, achieved by a contrast of light and dark patterns, by varying the intensity of colors and by a clever handling of masses, which lead the eye from one end of the painting to the other"), and Scheuer ("a gifted young artist's first important fresco"). Labaudt's mural, Lavrova said, "shows much sly humor and reflects this artist's feeling for color and decorative effects." Berlandina's mural, Lavrova thought, indicated the influence of "the French school" and was "the least influenced by the new California movement." Lavrova's article included black-and-white photographs of the murals by Albro, Arnautoff, Oldfield, Berlandina, and Wight, thereby including examples of each medium (fresco, oil on canvas, egg tempera) and of a rural scene, an urban scene, a cityscape, an abstract, and one of the tall figures.

Among all the murals, Lavrova failed to mention only one—that of Olmsted; perhaps she didn't notice it above the entrance door. She said not one word about Wight's hammer and sickle or the controversy. She closed her survey of the individual murals by quoting Heil: "'There is no reason why Coit Memorial Tower with its mural paintings should not stand 500 or 1000 years from now, a monument to this epoch and to the artists who worked in it.'"[6]

Although Lavrova produced the first article in a national publication that surveyed all the murals, Evelyn Seeley likely reached the largest number of readers nationwide. Her long, illustrated article "A Frescoed Tower Clangs Shut amid Gasps," appeared in the August 25 issue of *Literary Digest*, one of the most influential general publications at the time. Seeley, a frequent contributor to national journals, opened her article with an account of the controversy before turning her attention to the art. Like Lavrova, she was likely familiar with the various published summaries of PWAP work that had appeared in national publications; she described the Coit Tower project as "an accomplishment generally considered one of the greatest produced under the PWAP."[7]

Seeley agreed with Lavrova that the project "proved, to the amazement of both artists and public, that several dozen artists can work together effectively and harmoniously" and that the extensive use of fresco made the project "unique." Noting that "in most cities one can count the fresco-painters on one hand," she attributed the large number in San Francisco both to the influence of Rivera and "the tendency of local artists to trek down to Mexico to work for him" and to Boynton's pioneering fresco works in the area and his teaching of the technique.[8]

Seeley obviously had access to the closed tower, for, like Lavrova, she took her readers on a tour of the murals, beginning with the giant eyes over the entrance to the elevator lobby. Like Lavrova, she complimented the tall figures by Wight and Dean. Seeley described Albro's mural as the "richest and most vivid" and also singled out for special praise the murals by Arnautoff, Boynton, Labaudt, Stackpole, Terada, and Vidar. Seeley concluded that the artists "have presented California as powerful and productive, its machines as well-oiled, its fields and orchards bountiful, its people—happy in the sun. They have left out of the picture, as some realists have mentioned, such aspects as the Mooney case, or strikes, or lynchings."[9] (There had been a recent lynching in San Jose.)

The critique by Junius Cravens, the art critic for the *San Francisco News*, did not appear until October 20, eight days after the official opening of the tower. He began by noting the context for the murals:

> The whole project was begun amid confusion and uncertainty, and it continued so to the end; uncertainty of the time to be allowed—of how long the pay would continue; no time really to think out their problems. "Rush" was the keynote; a fitting inspiration, surely, to interpret the American scene, since the inception was so typically American. . . . the artists were at a disadvantage from the start.

Given that, he concluded, "the tower decorators have done remarkably fine work. . . . Even the worst mural faults are of minor importance as compared to the merits of the job as a whole." He described Wight's four tall figures as "superb," Arnautoff's mural as "outstanding" and "finely executed," and Cunningham's mural as having "most successfully achieved rhythmic decorative pattern on a very difficult wall." Cravens called out the murals by Cuneo, Moya del Pino, Oldfield, and Langdon as "notable," and he described Howard's depiction of hydraulic power as "the outstanding artistic achievement of the lot."[10]

There was a similar outpouring of critical praise for the results of the PWAP more generally. Bruce proclaimed the PWAP to have been "the first completely democratic art movement in history," and added, "A great republic has accepted the artist as a useful member of society and his work as a valuable asset to the State." On April 24, 1934, President and Mrs. Roosevelt opened an exhibition at the Corcoran Gallery in Washington, D.C., that included some five hundred works of art produced by PWAP artists from across the country. The exhibition included six large oil-on-canvas murals, but other murals were represented only by small black-and-white photographs. The photos included details from seven of the Coit Tower murals. Three thousand people attended the opening day, including cabinet members and ambassadors. Edward Alden Jewell reported in the *New York Times* that a "very gratifying aspect of the exhibition is its inclusion of so much meritorious or conspicuously good work by artists as yet unknown." President and Mrs. Roosevelt selected thirty-two easel paintings for the White House, including one of the Golden Gate Bridge by Ray Strong. Another exhibition of PWAP artworks opened at the Museum of Modern Art in New York in September and brought similar acclaim.[11]

In early 1935, Forbes Watson, technical director for the PWAP and chief assistant to Bruce, summarized the accomplishments of PWAP: 3,749 artists had been employed to produce 3,821 easel paintings in oil, 1,075 etchings, 2,938 watercolors, and 706 murals. Watson stated that the Treasury Section of Painting and Sculpture (created in October 1934) "would not have come into being except for the success of the P.W.A.P." Watson, like Bruce the previous April, emphasized that the PWAP had been "the first time that painting and sculpture have been brought to the people of the country under any but precious auspices, at one extreme, and uplifting auspices, at the other." Among the many PWAP projects, Watson selected five photographs to include in his article, including one of Cuneo's murals at Coit Tower.[12]

Three decades after completion of the murals, in 1964, Dorothy Puccinelli Cravath, who did a large mural project at the Mother's Building at the San Francisco Zoo, a project that began with the PWAP and concluded with the WPA/FAP, and who was centrally involved in a restoration at Coit Tower in the 1960s, reflected on the significance of the New Deal art programs:

> I think it was terrifically important because it gave a great many artists the subsidy that they needed to make a real start. And it also was important because it educated the public. People began to think that possibly walls of buildings needed murals or could stand murals, and it hadn't occurred to them before. I think most of the American public felt that all real painting had been done in the Renaissance and stopped there. After the WPA they observed that it could be done.[13]

6

Later Controversies

Despite the praise that art critics showered on the Coit Tower murals in 1934, some local naysayers continued to find them objectionable. In the years to come, the murals survived all the disparagement, even a demand by a park commissioner that two of them be destroyed and another altered. Other threats to the murals came from carelessness, vandalism, and neglect, to the point that in 2012 San Franciscans voted to limit commercial activities at the tower and direct that income from concessions be used to maintain the building and its murals.

In the immediate aftermath of the events of 1934, disgruntled members of the public continued to denigrate the murals. One exchange in mid-1935, carried out through letters in the *San Francisco Chronicle*, began when one person wanted them destroyed, calling them "atrocious" and "eyesores," painted by "novices." Ray Boynton wrote in defense of the murals, only to provoke a response from another member of the public who claimed, "The very fact that there is a continuous controversy about the Coit tower murals would show that there is something wrong with them. . . . The next generation will have these daubs painted out."[1] The notion that "continuous controversy" justified destruction appeared much later, in the controversy over Arnautoff's murals at George Washington High School.

By 1935 the red scare of mid-1934 had died down. However, some business leaders in San Francisco, along with such patriotic groups as the American Legion, continued to accuse longshore and maritime union leaders of being Communists. In the late 1930s, accusations of Communist influence in unions and in New Deal programs intensified at the national level. In 1938 the House of Representatives created the Special Committee on Un-American Activities (HUAC). That committee endorsed the claim that San Francisco longshore union leader Harry Bridges was a Communist and also argued that New Deal projects, especially the WPA's Federal Writers Project and Theater Project, were infested with Communists. Both of those programs were terminated. In 1939 the San Francisco press prominently covered an Immigration Service hearing to determine whether Bridges was a Communist and should be deported. After the hearing officer found in Bridges's favor, a new and highly publicized FBI investigation of Bridges began almost immediately, producing a new hearing in mid-1941. The years 1939–1941 also mark the duration of the Molotov-Ribbentrop Pact (a nonaggression treaty between Nazi Germany and the Soviet Union), which also contributed to the rise of anti-Communist rhetoric. Federal authorities sought to strip the citizenship of William Schneiderman, the head of the Communist Party in California, and the California legislature approved a new law to remove the CP from the state ballot.[2]

At the same time as these increased attacks on the CP, local anxiety was also rising because of the wars against the Axis powers raging in Europe and Asia and the possibility that the United States might be pulled into war. Once again, the Coit Tower murals were branded as unpatriotic, Communist propaganda. On June 5, 1941, Leo Sullivan, a band leader and San Jose resident, wrote a furious letter to San Francisco mayor Angelo Rossi. Calling himself a San Francisco taxpayer, Sullivan claimed that he had just visited Coit Tower, where, he said, he had been "greatly shocked at the glaring propaganda that screams 'Communism' from its walls." He demanded that something be done about "the radical propaganda." Rossi appointed a committee consisting of three members of the Art Commission's Committee on Painting and Sculpture, chaired by Spencer Macky (head of the California School of Fine Arts), and one member of the Park Commission, John J. Lermen, a lawyer. After the four visited Coit Tower, the press reported that the Art Commission members "took the murals very placidly . . . but not Commissioner Lermen." On June 14 the Art Commission tried to rid itself of the issue by unanimously accepting Macky's committee's recommendation that "any changes, alterations or removals should come from the Park Commission, the duly designated custodians of the Coit Tower."[3]

The controversy was thoroughly aired in the city's press in mid-July. The central figure was Lermen. Describing him as "spluttering with rage," the *Chronicle* quoted him as saying that some of the murals were "objectionable . . . awful, terrible, and Communistic . . . definitely calculated to arouse class hatred at a time when the Nation's crying need is for unity." Lermen called Howard's mural "terrible and awful" and claimed that the May Day marchers "epitomize hatred. . . . One can see murder in their hearts." He also attacked Zakheim's library for including "non-patriotic volumes." By contrast, Otterino Ronchi, an artist, associate editor of the local Italian-language newspaper, and president of the Art Commission, found nothing objectionable in the murals: "Art is supposed to hold a mirror to life and if some men don't like their work, it's the artist's job to paint it." The *Chronicle* also printed a copy of Zakheim's mural with the caption: "Here's a Sample. This mural by Bernard Zakheim is among those which have brought down a storm of disapproval on Coit Memorial Tower's art."[4]

On July 25, Ralph Stackpole entered the fray, stating:

> The Coit tower murals are dated: dated 1934. The national disaster was in 1929 and anyone with a memory can recall the struggle and effort to get out of that mess. . . . [The] work in Coit tower was a little part of the recovery effort. . . . Among 25 artists, as among 25 other people, there were differences in beliefs and ideas. . . . If some ardent artist read Carl [*sic*] Marx, can you blame him? It was in 1934, and artists, like everyone else, search for better conditions. . . . If a little current-thought-of-the-time is in the Coit murals, a little Marx in the library scene, some sternness in the strikers' faces . . . they should not be condemned by some hothead now. . . . I think the honorable Park Commissioner should forget the idea of having them removed. Prejudices grow; they might even grow to the actual point of having the murals destroyed. Then next would come the books.

Stackpole's words were an unmistakable reference to the burning of books (and art) in Nazi Germany. A few months later, he became the first person from the Pacific Coast to serve on the U.S. Commission of Fine Arts.[5]

The press also noted that the city attorney, John J. O'Toole, "had a slight headache . . . trying to determine to whom the murals actually belong," whether to the city or the federal government, an issue not resolved until federal legislation in 1949. O'Toole finally issued a ruling that avoided the ownership issue. Instead, he specified that Coit Tower was "undoubtedly" within the jurisdiction of the Park Commission but cited the city's charter as specifying, "No existing work of art in the possession of the City and County shall be removed, relocated, or altered in any way, without the approval of the [Art] Commission," and therefore any change in the murals requited "joint action" of both commissions.[6]

On August 28, the Park Commission voted unanimously to adopt a long resolution stating the "opinion" of the park commissioners that the murals by Howard and Zakheim and the part of Arnautoff's mural depicting a robbery were "objectionable . . . calculated, as well as designed, to create and arouse class hatred"; that "the impression sought to be created by said murals, namely, that class hatred rules this community, is false and a libel upon the people of the City"; and that "it becomes our patriotic duty to remove these murals without delay." The resolution concluded with a request that the Art Commission approve "the removal of said murals."[7]

The Art Commission did not meet until October 10, and the minutes of that meeting fail to mention Coit Tower, not even to note receipt of the resolution from the Park Commission. Nor did the minutes of any subsequent Art Commission meeting take note of that resolution or the controversy.[8] After the Japanese attack on Pearl Harbor on December 7, 1941, civil defense became the overriding issue for San Francisco's civic leaders. Commissioner Lermen's complaints about seven-year-old murals fomenting class hatred were forgotten, at least for a time.

The World War II years brought an influx of people to San Francisco and many visitors to Coit Tower. The popularity of the views from the tower and the New Deal–era murals on its walls continued to attract many visitors in the late 1940s and early 1950s, the Cold War era. The Cold War brought renewed attacks on anyone or anything that could be linked to the Communist Party. Amid concern over the expansion of Soviet control in Eastern Europe and revelations of Soviet espionage in the United States during World War II, HUAC added to such fears with hearings about Communist influence in Hollywood and elsewhere. Senator Joseph McCarthy was so prominent in this new red scare that "McCarthyism" became a new noun.[9] Those years also brought an attack on one of the city's other large New Deal art projects, the murals by Anton Refregier at the Rincon Annex post office (see chapter 9). Not surprisingly, some San Franciscans again complained about "Communist propaganda" at Coit Tower; for example, a letter to the editor of the *San Francisco Examiner* on September 23, 1953: "My husband and I and our eastern visitors were completely aghast and astounded to see the obviously Communistic paintings surrounding the entire wall in the Tower. . . . It was certainly unbelievable to us as four decent Americans that such Communistic works would be permitted to remain in such a public and popular place."[10] A similar letter to the editor came a week later: "It is always shocking to me to find that the Communist propaganda in the Coit Tower murals still survives." However, in 1953, even in the midst of McCarthyism, San Francisco's public officials took no notice, perhaps because they had just gone through an extended defense of the Refregier murals.

Challenges to the murals of more mundane varieties also grew. Leaks in the roof, already a problem when the original artists were at work, continued despite repeated repairs, producing efflorescence on some murals.[11] There was little or no supervision of visitors, who carelessly brushed against the murals as they walked past. Some carved their initials into the murals or otherwise vandalized them. In 1957 one proposal for dealing with the vandalism was to cover all the murals with redwood and

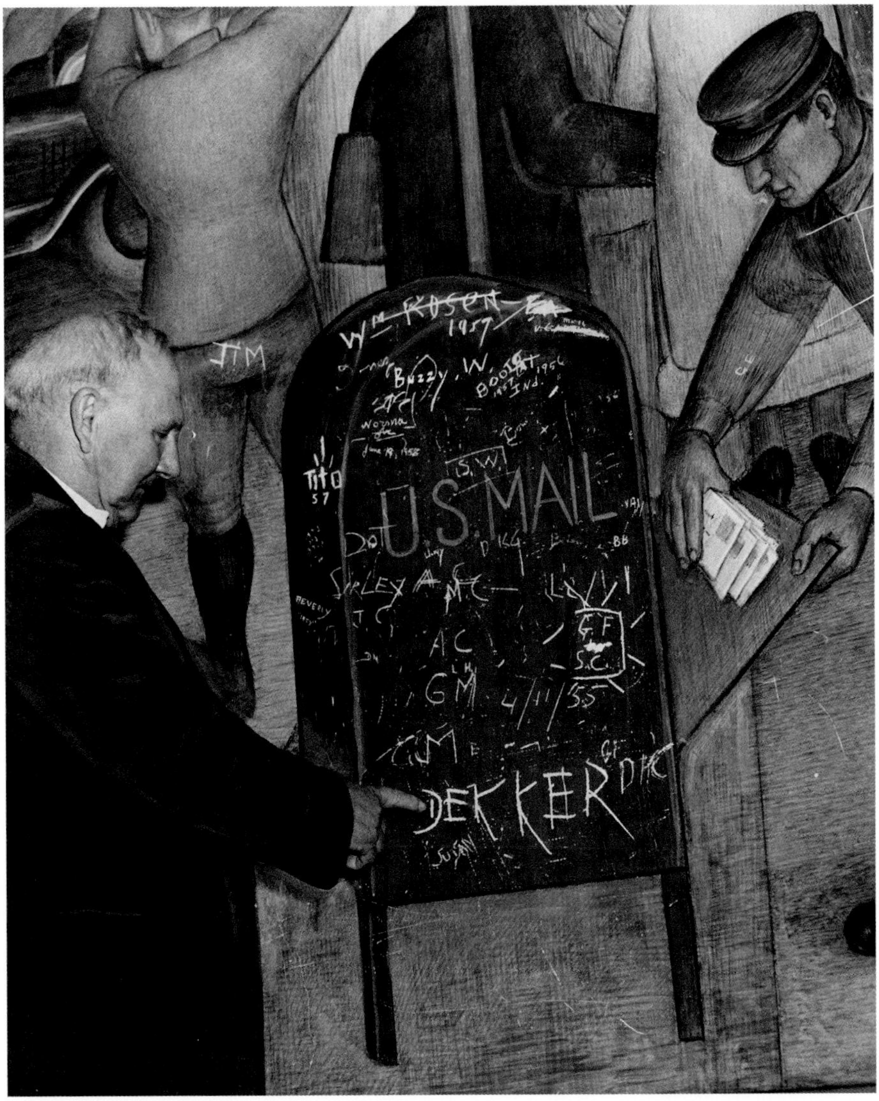

Figure 6.1. Charles Weber, Coit Tower maintenance man, points to vandalism of Arnautoff's mural in 1957. (Source: Photo AAC-1522, courtesy of San Francisco History Center, San Francisco Public Library.)

aluminum panels. By the late 1950s vandalism had become so severe that the first-floor murals were closed off, allowing visitors access only to the elevator lobby. (Taking the elevator to the top of the tower was and continues to be highly popular with tourists, creating a significant revenue stream for the park department.) Protection for the ground-floor murals was accomplished, ironically, by bolting door hinges and latches directly into some of the murals. The door at the bottom of the staircase closed off the second floor.[12]

In 1961 some restoration was undertaken, led by Dorothy Puccinelli Cravath, who had produced major murals under the PWAP and the WPA/FAP. Arnautoff, Scheuer, and Zakheim all restored their own work. Scheuer took advantage of the opportunity to place the name of the *Chronicle* on the newspaper in her mural; in 1934 she had understood that she was not to identify any actual publication. The ground floor was again opened to the public. In 1975 another restoration project was commissioned by the city, led this time by Emmy Lou Packard, a major artist and former assistant to Diego Rivera. She cleaned and repaired all the murals on both floors after extensive research and consultation. Guard ropes were installed to prevent visitors from getting too close to the ground-floor murals—and, ironically, some of the fixtures holding the guard ropes were attached with screws driven into the murals![13]

In 1988–1989 Anne Rosenthal, a professional art conservator, led an assessment of the murals and concluded, "The amount of damage is, collectively, extensive and alarming." Her assessment was followed by a major project to conserve, repair, and fully document all the murals, which was completed in 1992. An improved barrier system was installed to protect the ground-floor frescoes from visitor contact. Brass plates and plexiglass panels were installed to protect vulnerable areas. Access to the second floor was and continues to be limited because of insufficient space to install barriers and lack of a person posted there to guide visitors and protect the murals.[14]

By the time the 1992 restoration was completed, the Coit Tower murals had long since achieved a unique place in the city. Any controversy over the content had likewise long since disappeared, along with the headlines generated by HUAC or McCarthy. In 1984 the board of supervisors designated the building as San Francisco Landmark #165. Chiori Santiago, in a magazine article about the 1992 restoration, described Coit Tower and its murals as "our Statue of Liberty, our Parthenon, our Sistine Chapel. It's as much a portrait of another era as those world-class monuments."[15]

A very different sort of political controversy swirled around the murals and the tower itself in 2011–2012, not about the subject matter of the murals, but instead about how the city could best care for them. Deferred maintenance as well as the age of the building had resulted in significant water damage in and around the murals. In addition, lead-based paint was flaking from the ceilings, asbestos insulation had to be removed, and some structural problems needed repairs. Calls for action came from a variety of concerned individuals, including Richard Rothman, who regularly led tours of the murals for City Guides (the city's official docent program, conducted by volunteers organized though the San Francisco Public Library); Ruth Zakheim Gottstein, daughter of the Coit Tower muralist Bernard

Zakheim and publisher of her sister's book on the murals; and Kevin Starr, former state librarian and author of highly regarded books on California history. The problems had developed despite the considerable amount of funds that came to the city's Recreation and Parks Department through the concessions at the tower; 90 percent of the charge to ride the elevator to the viewing areas at the top, some $500,000 annually, went directly to the Parks Department, plus an additional $150,000 annually from the Parks Department's portion of the concessionaire's sales receipts from the Coit Tower gift shop.[16]

Then, in November 2011, the Parks Department announced that they were seeking a new concessionaire, one that would be willing to offer private cocktail parties and seated dinners in the tower. The lede in *SF Business Times* was, "Coit Tower is up for grabs."[17]

That news sparked another effort to protect the murals. The key person was Jon Golinger, an attorney and president of the Telegraph Hill Dwellers, the neighborhood association whose territory includes Coit Tower. Golinger took the lead in forming the Protect Coit Tower Committee, which, on December 7, 2011, filed the necessary paperwork with the city's Department of Elections to initiate a ballot proposition to define a new city policy:

> It shall be the policy of the People of the City and County of San Francisco to protect Coit Tower and preserve the historic murals inside Coit Tower by strictly limiting commercial activities and private events at Coit Tower and by prioritizing the funds received by the City from any concession operations at Coit Tower for preserving the Coit Tower murals, protecting and maintaining the Coit Tower building, and beautifying Pioneer Park around Coit Tower.

Golinger's group was drawing upon a rarely used and apparently unique provision in the city charter to use the initiative process for a declaration of policy.[18]

The Protect Coit Tower Committee quickly collected 16,000 signatures, far more than the required 9,702, to put Proposition B on the ballot for the June 2012 primary election. The petition drive brought national attention to the issue, including coverage by the *PBS News Hour*, *New York Times*, and *Los Angeles Times*, as well as media outlets in the city. The *New York Times* article, in early February 2012, was titled "Tower for Rent, with Million-Dollar Views" and led with an account of a gathering in a North Beach art gallery that featured six poets lyrically praising Coit Tower and other participants angrily denouncing what they saw as the increasing privatization of the city's public parks, a concern that extended to Parks Department efforts to raise funds by charging for many park features that had previously been open to the public without charge. Proposition B was endorsed by the Sierra Club, the Coalition for San Francisco Neighborhoods, the San Francisco Democratic Party, several neighborhood organizations, and groups opposed to privatization. Descendants of several of the Coit Tower muralists gathered at Coit Tower to show their support for the ballot campaign.[19]

Proposition B drew strong opposition from the Recreation and Parks Department, the Parks Alliance (a nonprofit closely aligned with the Parks Department), both daily papers, the union representing park employees, the chamber of commerce, the Building Owners and Managers Association, and the Alliance for Jobs and Sustainable Growth, a political action committee for business interests. Golinger later reflected, "The opposition to the initiative was significant. It was led by Phil Ginsburg [head of the Recreation and Parks Department]. . . . They spent over $60,000 on TV ads and doorhangers opposing the measure and secured strongly worded opposition editorials from both the Chronicle and Examiner."[20]

Turnout in the primary election was low, less than a third of registered voters. Of the 145,105 voters who cast ballots, 94 percent took a position on Proposition B, more than voted in the primary for the U.S. Senate and significantly more than voted in the uncontested Democratic presidential primary. Despite the barrage of campaign material opposed to the measure, 53 percent voted in favor.[21] On election night, at the Prop. B victory party in North Beach, Golinger presented Ruth Zakheim Gottstein with a symbolic "check" from the City of San Francisco to fund the murals' restoration.

A major renovation and restoration project took place in 2012–2014, at an estimated cost of $1.7 million, most of which came as a onetime item in the city budget. Conservators, again led by Anne Rosenthal, took cross-sections and scrapings of the walls to determine the original colors of the walls and ceilings on the first floor. They discovered that the original ceiling color, from 1934, was "mushroom," a light gray-buff, which, Rosenthal told me, leaves the standard of whiteness within the frescoes where it should be so that the frescoes are the brightest, not the ceiling or the surrounding walls. That restoration also recreated the original red stripe at the top and sides of the murals, which frames and balances the murals. The walls of the elevator lobby were also returned to their original "pumpkin-like" color, balancing the cool tones of the landscapes. (The photos in chapter 3 show these restored colors.) The new concessionaire did a major renovation of the concessions area. The reopening was a gala event, with a jazz band and a speech by the mayor. Several children or grandchildren of the muralists attended.[22]

Coit Tower with its murals had been designated as a city landmark in 1984 and was added to the National Register of Historic Places in 2008;

the National Register nomination was significantly amended in 2017 to correct factual errors in the original nomination, add new information, and elevate Coit Tower's status from that of state-level importance to "national historic significance" due to the murals' influence on subsequent New Deal programs and public art across the United States. The tower and the murals are currently moving toward designation as a National Historic Landmark.[23]

7

Subsequent Perspectives on the Coit Tower Murals

Serious attention to New Deal art was slow to revive after World War II and the end of the New Deal programs. After World War II, figurative art became passé as many artists, art schools, and art critics focused instead on abstract expressionism. "In most histories of twentieth-century American art," Jonathan Harris explained in 1993, New Deal art projects "are mentioned briefly (if at all) and disparaged simultaneously." He asked, "What pattern or trajectory does the paradigmatic history of American art follow that necessitated this virtual elision of a decade of art and artists?" His answer: "Predominant accounts of American art have been concerned primarily with the development and success of abstract art and artists." This pattern, he concluded, "constitutes a logical (and, of course, *ideological*) repression of a social and political conjuncture."[1]

Harris may have been correct in his critique of some, even many, general histories of American art, but he was too quick to dismiss the interest of all art historians in New Deal art. To be certain, as Martin R. Kalfatovic's exhaustive bibliography (1994), makes clear, the few publications dealing with New Deal art in the late 1940s and 1950s tended to have been memoirs or discussions of the Index of American Design rather than analytical in nature. However, scholarly interest in New Deal art began to revive in 1961 with an exhibition of New Deal art at the Smolin Gallery in New York.[2] Art historians' interest in New Deal art accelerated in the mid-1960s with efforts by the Archives of American Art (AAA) to collect the papers and oral histories of participants and with a major exhibition at the Washington Gallery of Modern Art. This renewed interest extended to the Coit Tower artists. Between 1964 and 1967, the AAA conducted oral history interviews with nine of the Coit Tower artists and three assistants: Albro and Hall, Cunningham, Chessé, Hebe Daum

Stackpole (an assistant, who later married Ralph Stackpole's son, Peter), George Gaethke (an assistant), Hesthal, Moya del Pino, Oldfield, Scheuer, Shirley Staschen Triest (an assistant), and Zakheim. There were later oral history interviews with John and Mary Howard in 1991 and Shirley Staschen Triest in 1996.

Francis V. O'Connor also began to focus the attention of art historians and historians on New Deal art. In 1966, at the University of Maryland, he organized the first comprehensive exhibition of New Deal art programs and authored the catalog *Federal Art Patronage, 1933 to 1943* (1966). In 1967–1968 he led a research project funded by the National Endowment for the Arts on the federal patronage of art during the New Deal, leading to three books: *Federal Support for the Visual Arts: The New Deal and Now* (1969), *New Deal Art Projects: An Anthology of Memoirs* (1972), and *Art for the Millions: Essays from the 1930s by Artists and Administrators of the WPA Federal Art Project* (1973).[3]

The first book-length academic history of New Deal art also came in 1973: Richard McKinzie's *The New Deal for Artists*, an overview of the various federal programs. He focused his treatment of the Coit Tower murals almost entirely on what he called "the most publicized clash" between artists and federal administrators, referring to the controversy over Wight's hammer and sickle. McKinzie briefly mentioned the controversies over other murals and provided black-and-white photographs of Zakheim's full mural and a close-up of the newspaper headlines. Of Arnautoff's mural, McKinzie said only that it had been "criticized for its unpleasant details" and provided photographs of the newsstand and robbery. McKinzie said nothing about the other murals.[4] Several of the subsequent studies of New Deal art that referred to the Coit Tower murals tended to follow McKinzie's lead: they focused on the controversy and said little about the other murals or the project as a whole.

In the mid-1970s an exhibition at the de Saisset Art Gallery and Museum at Santa Clara University attracted significant attention to New Deal art in California, including the Coit Tower murals. That project began when Francis O'Connor visited that gallery in 1971 as part of his research on New Deal art. His visit prompted research by the de Saisset staff that led to a grant from the National Endowment for the Humanities in 1975, an exhibition that year, and a book, *New Deal Art: California*, in 1976. The project included videotaped interviews with Chessé and Zakheim, a videotaped tour of the Coit Tower murals by O'Connor, photographs of all the murals, short videos on New Deal art in California, and a list of all then-known New Deal art sites in the state, organized by artists and community.[5]

In his videotaped tour of the murals, O'Connor explained the fresco technique and discussed most of the murals. He emphasized that all the murals deal with working people, with the ground floor showing people at work and the upper floor showing working people at leisure. He suggested that the artists were not showing the "traumatized society of 1934" but instead "an idealized society," one of "health, vigor, vitality." This, he suggested, expressed the aspirations of the "young artists" at Coit Tower and "the ideal of the New Deal." However, the videotape was apparently never edited into a final document.[6]

In late 1975, after the de Saisset exhibition closed, Masha Zakheim Jewett, who taught English and humanities at San Francisco City College, published her first account of the Coit Tower murals, a long article in the magazine section of the *San Francisco Sunday Examiner and Chronicle*. She explained in the letter accompanying the article, "For a long time now, my father has been asking me to tell the story of the murals." She did so, one mural at a time, with information about each mural and muralist, some gained from interviews with the artists or with her father. She gave a brief account of the controversy over Wight's hammer and sickle but focused on presenting all the murals.[7]

The de Saisset exhibition also led to several publications. Steven Gelber, a faculty member in the history department at Santa Clara University, organized a book about the exhibition and contributed the major essay. The de Saisset exhibition likely inspired a special edition of *City of San Francisco*, a short-lived magazine published by Eleanor and Francis Ford Coppola and edited by Warren Hinckle, who reveled in the role of journalistic gadfly. The special issue, in February 1976, was titled "When Art Was Fun and Fabulous: The Treasures of the WPA: The Forgotten Great Public Art of the Bay Area." It included many photographs of Bay Area New Deal art of all varieties, reminiscences by some of the participants, and accounts of the Coit Tower controversy.[8]

In that special edition, Gelber drew upon his research to present an article on "The Irony of San Francisco's 'Commie Art.'" Gelber confirms that Hinckle wanted to call it "San Francisco's 'Commie Art,'" but Gelber objected because that title had nothing to do with his thesis. The final title was a compromise. Gelber began with his thesis: "The public art of the New Deal is conspicuously apolitical. . . . The public art of the New Deal reflected the traditional democratic-capitalist values of the New Deal itself." Given that, he declared it to be "one of the great ironies" that the "single greatest influence" on New Deal art in Northern California was Diego Rivera. And, he noted, a small group "not only accepted Rivera's style, they also accepted his politics," and he presented the controversy over Wight's hammer and sickle. However, Gelber was clear: the few who added radical imagery to their Coit Tower murals "in no way represented . . . the political ideology of the vast majority."[9] In 1979 Gelber published an article on California's New Deal murals in *California History*, journal of the California Historical Society. As with his earlier magazine article, Gelber's journal article gave significant attention to the Coit Tower murals, briefly discussed the controversy, and, much like O'Connor, concluded that most of California's New Deal muralists "refrained from painting images of contemporary problems because they believed that art should be inspiring for people. Having faith that the New Deal would revive the system that had operated so well in the past, they preferred to paint the world as it should be or as it should have been, not as it was. . . . [They] covered California's walls with visions of liberal imagination rather than radical anger."[10]

Masha Zakheim Jewett's *Coit Tower, San Francisco: Its History and Art,* the only book devoted entirely to the murals, appeared in 1983. She interviewed as many of the surviving artists as she could and incorporated biographical details about each into her book. Her book included photos of all the murals. A revised and expanded version was published in 2009. Her book addressed the controversy, especially the composite photograph from the *San Francisco Examiner*.[11] Coming on the fiftieth anniversary of the creation of the PWAP, Zakheim's book may have led to press attention to the Coit Tower murals, as that year also saw interviews with some of the artists in the *Oakland Tribune* and *San Francisco Examiner*.[12]

The Coit Tower murals received detailed coverage in Belisario R. Contreras's *Tradition and Innovation in New Deal Art* (1983).[13] Contreras devoted much of his chapter on the PWAP to an extensive treatment of the Coit Tower murals. His work makes clear that, like O'Connor, he spent time at Coit Tower studying all the murals. (That seems not to have been the case with some treatments by other art historians.) Contreras noted the controversy over Clifford Wight's hammer and sickle, but he also paid significant attention to all the murals:

> Although some unexpected radicalism appeared in the Coit Tower project, the murals also revealed that this group of twenty-five artists had carefully developed an iconography of the American scene that was relevant for PWAP throughout the country. In fact, this broad conceptual scheme—running the gamut from realism to abstraction—was to be used by artists in subsequent New Deal art programs. The Coit Tower project shows a contemporary America, reflecting agricultural, industrial, and urban themes. . . . The Coit Tower Artists Group carefully organized subject matter, mural scale, and color palette so that each work related to the other.

Contreras noted two exceptions: Moya del Pino's use of bird's-eye perspective and Berlandina's abstract work, and he described the latter as "in the manner of the French painter Raoul Dufy," with whom Berlandina had studied.

Contreras included six black-and-white photographs of the Coit Tower murals, three of them showing work in progress and three presenting parts of completed murals.[14] He also walked his readers through each mural, giving special attention to those by Arnautoff, Boynton, Labaudt, and Zakheim.

Contreras said of Arnautoff: "The realistic style and technique of Arnautoff's work is representative of the majority of the Coit Tower muralists. The influence of Diego Rivera's brilliant color, simple modeling, and refined brushwork is seen in Arnautoff's mural. His handling of complex, monumental groups in the foreground, contrasted with the deep perspective in the background, is strikingly reminiscent of Rivera's Detroit frescoes." Contreras drew further conclusions about Arnautoff's mural:

> The theme of social consciousness pervades, as it does in the work of the other muralists. People from all walks of life dominate the human drama. . . . A public newsstand stocked with radical publications, such as the *New Masses* and the *Daily Worker*, protests the economic shortcomings of the capitalist system. A magazine stand promotes *Screen Play*, a popular magazine of the era, with Hollywood actress Mae West on its cover. A theater marquee advertises Charlie Chaplin's film *City Lights*, another expression of the popular culture of the period. Roosevelt's "forgotten man" [a theme Roosevelt had developed] is implied by the portrait of Charlie Chaplin on the marquee, a popular cult figure outside of the "System" who managed to survive.[15]

Contreras gave significant attention to Zakheim's mural of the library. In comparing Arnautoff's mural with that of Zakheim, Contreras concluded that Zakheim's mural, "articulates a stronger note of social protest. . . . Blazing headlines reveal the scandals of the Republican administration and the riots in Austria, the results of the excesses of capitalism. Solutions to the exploitation of the masses are proposed: a reader takes Karl Marx's *Das Kapital* off of a library shelf." Contreras continued: "Zakheim not only disparages the conservatism of San Francisco's Art Commission but criticizes the destruction of Rivera's Rockefeller Center mural in New York. . . . Zakheim reflects the incisive drawing and strong coloring of Mexican muralist José Clemente Orozco; the mood of social protest is emphasized even more by Zakheim through the use of constricted placement of figures in the composition."[16]

Contreras's book surveyed the entire field of New Deal art. In discussing later developments, he sometimes returned to the Coit Tower murals. In discussing PWAP easel paintings, for example, he noted, "Not unlike what had occurred in the Coit Tower project when Jane Berlandina composed an abstract work, other artists also painted themes that are experimental and abstract in style." In introducing some of the Treasury Section projects in major federal office buildings in Washington, D.C., Contreras again referred to the Coit Tower precedent: "Similar to the Coit Tower cooperative venture, the Post Office and Justice Department programs were designated as a single project, and a select group of artists were assigned mural spaces—to paint broad phases of the American scene." In explaining the transition from the PWAP to the WPA/FAP, Contreras even cited a plaintive letter from eleven-year-old Ruth Zakheim to Edward Bruce, explaining that her father had completed his Coit Tower mural and now "he needs the money so badly."[17]

Contreras concluded his survey of the Coit Tower murals by noting their relation to later New Deal art: "The broad iconography used by the Coit Tower project under PWAP reappeared in WPA/FAP, revealing the following elements: social realism, Mexican influences, regionalism, social protest, social consciousness, and avant-garde." Though noting that these themes were common in paintings done under the WPA/FAP, Contreras also pointed to an exception: "The sort of social protest that had been painted by PWAP muralists Clifford Wight and Bernard Zakheim in Coit Tower—explicit and strident in tone—no longer seemed to interest the WPA/FAP artists. Their work pointed to the optimism and confidence that had been generated by the New Deal recovery programs."[18] However, Contreras might have added that several Coit Tower murals, especially those by Albro, Boynton, Labaudt, Scheuer, Stackpole, and Vidar, might also be seen as expressing "the optimism and confidence generated by the New Deal."

Also in the early 1980s, two scholarly works appeared that dealt with the post office murals commissioned by the Treasury Section. Such attention to those murals, and not to the murals created under the PWAP or WPA/FAP, is not surprising in that the records for the post office murals had become easily available in the National Archives, whereas those of the PWAP and WPA/FAP were more scattered. As previously discussed, Karal Ann Marling, in *Wall-to-Wall America*, saw the Coit Tower controversy as the source of Edward Bruce's later stringent oversight of all Treasury Section artwork.[19] The other early scholarly work on post office murals, *Democratic Vistas: Post Offices and Public Art in the New Deal*, by Marlene Park and Gerald E. Markowitz, a collaboration between an art historian and a historian, appeared in 1984. Park and Markowitz never referred to the Coit Tower murals, but some of their generalizations about New Deal art are relevant for understanding the significance of the Coit Tower murals. The two coauthors echoed Edward Bruce: "The New Deal sought to change the relationship between the artist and society by democratizing art and culture. . . . The projects were a uniquely American blend, combining an elitist belief in the value of high culture and the democratic ideal that everyone in the society could and should be the beneficiary of such efforts."[20] The Coit Tower murals exemplify these goals: works of art, including some by leading artists of the area, in a location where anyone could walk in and study them without charge.

Though Francis V. O'Connor had conducted a videotaped tour of the Coit Tower murals in the mid-1970s, he did not write about them at any length until 1986, in an essay published as part of a major retrospective on Diego Rivera. Opening his essay with a color photo of part of Arnautoff's mural at Coit Tower, O'Connor first discussed the nature of influence in art history, surveyed Rivera's influence on two nationally prominent artists during the 1930s, and then turned to Rivera's influence on New Deal muralists. "By 1934," O'Connor wrote, "Rivera had virtually single-handedly forged a strong mural tradition. He was the best, and certainly the most famous, muralist in the Americas, and his walls had become the standard against which those who aspired to be muralists were judged (or judged themselves). Rivera was the role model both stylistically and ideologically. This is very clear indeed at Coit Tower." "It is not surprising," O'Connor then noted, that "those who had either worked with or were inspired to emulate Diego Rivera produced some of the more competent early murals created under New Deal patronage. Nowhere is this more explicitly the case than at Coit Tower in San Francisco." He illustrated his essay with the map of the main floor from Zakheim's book and with one color and five black-and-white photos of Coit Tower murals, those by Arnautoff, Stackpole, Labaudt, and Zakheim.[21]

A somewhat revised version of O'Connor's essay, focused specifically on the Coit Tower murals, appeared in the 2009 edition of Zakheim's book on Coit Tower. In that version of his essay, O'Connor drew upon his wide acquaintance with New Deal art to describe the Coit Tower project as "a mural environment that can be ranked with the finest wall paintings created on the government's subsequent art programs." He also expanded on the significance of the group nature of the Coit Tower murals, a topic first developed by Lavrova:

> Most murals are painted by individuals; large groups of muralists working in unison are rare in the history of American art. . . . What happened at Coit Tower in 1934 under PWAP, while not unprecedented—was not usual. Later, especially in New York, groups of muralists shared large-scale work spaces provided by the WPA/FAP, but it was seldom that more than two or three were working on walls at the same time.[22]

O'Connor noted the relation of Stackpole's mural on industry to Rivera's Detroit murals and those he had done in San Francisco. O'Connor also pointed out that the center section of Albro's mural, depicting fruit trees, "directly 'quotes'" Rivera's mural for the Stern family home. O'Connor concluded that Labaudt had "successfully managed the almost impossible problems of scale and perspective posed by the peculiar site."[23]

In both versions of his essay, O'Connor specified, "Of all the Rivera-influenced murals in the Tower, certainly *City Life* by Arnautoff is the most successful in assimilating all of the aspects of the master's style." O'Connor then described nine ways in which Arnautoff's mural reflects "the master's style." Among the nine aspects of Arnautoff's mural that reflect the priorities of Rivera, O'Connor identified the relation of the content of the mural to "the exterior world." He noted how Arnautoff's, Stackpole's, and Albro's murals are oriented both to one another and to the "external world":

> The Arnautoff mural . . . faces out the window toward the actual intersection, eight blocks to the south, of Washington and Montgomery streets which are depicted in the mural. The other murals along the south outer walls of the rotunda, depicting a department store, banks, lawyers, stock brokers, scientists, a library, and a newspaper office, all relate to the significance of this crossroads of the city's economic life. A similar situational direction determines the placement of the other major walls and their related panels. Thus Stackpole's mural of local industries on the west wall overlooks the expanse of the city and its waterfront which lies to the west, and Albro's agricultural mural faces east in the general direction of California's fertile interior.[24]

O'Connor did not mention, but it is worth noting, that Stackpole's mural, part of which depicts a cannery, overlooks what was, in the early twentieth century, the largest fruit and vegetable cannery in the world.

In his 1986 version of the essay, O'Connor specified, "Coit Tower is the only mural site in the country that displays so varied a range of walls painted in the style and spirit of Rivera."[25] He was more effusive in 2009 and returned to a theme he had first developed in his videotaped tour of the murals in the mid-1970s:

> Overall the Coit Tower murals cannot escape their turbulent era, and stand as evidence that lasting art is produced in periods when the country's creative culture is inspired by a common ideology. In the early 1930s, this consisted of a desire to celebrate an ideal view of the "American Scene" with which to alleviate the practical and moral effects of the Great Depression by showing what the nation was once and could be again. On the other hand, the idealism of the Social Realists expounded a vision of social and economic revival and justice that would hopefully prevent future Depressions. So the murals at Coit Tower overall represent a rare and brilliantly achieved example of painting in the spirit of Diego Rivera—as well as an intelligently balanced encyclopedia of subject matter typical of the 1930s major national and social ideals.[26]

In 1987 the Coit Tower murals became the subject of a stage play titled *Mind's Eye: Paint and Politics—The Coit Tower Murals and the '34 Strike*, by Stacey McNutt, presented at a community center's theater in San Francisco and likely inspired by the publication in 1983 of interviews with some of the original artists. In the play, a film crew interviews Lydia Borelli, a surviving assistant (a fictional figure), whose interview leads to flashbacks of her talking with Clifford Wight, Victor Arnautoff, John Langley Howard, Walter Heil (identified as head of the Art Commission), and a few others about the controversy over Wight's hammer and sickle. An early scene, identified as taking place during the longshore strike, has Wight showing his sketches. Later scenes, also set inside the tower but in early and mid-July, feature the characters discussing whether or not Wight's symbol should be destroyed. Wight argues that the artists should join the longshoremen. (Scenes set inside the tower in July are clearly fictional, since the tower was locked all that month.) Toward the end of the play, Arnautoff passes out leaflets during the general strike. The review in the *Chronicle* described the play as "admirable if somewhat awkward" and "inelegant."[27]

Scholarly interest in the murals continued into the 1990s. Peter Selz briefly addressed the Coit Tower murals in an essay that deals with international influences on California modernism. He described the murals as the "first and most important achievement" of the PWAP and focused especially on Rivera's influence on the muralists. Arnautoff's mural, Selz said, is "closely related in its composition to Rivera's murals at Mexico's National Palace," where Arnautoff had been an assistant to Rivera. Selz also noted that "the striking workers" in Howard's mural "have their source in Rivera's paintings. The bold modeling of figures and the chromatic scheme of subdued earth colors is clearly indebted to Rivera's work." He concluded his essay by saying, "The frescoes in the tower embody Rivera's belief that the new mural art could help in the revolutionary struggle to create a more equitable social and political system."[28]

Political activism was front and center in the interpretation of the Coit Tower murals offered by Anthony Lee, an art historian, in his *Painting on the Left: Diego Rivera, Radical Politics, and San Francisco's Public Murals* (1999). Lee's thesis is, first, that the murals at Coit Tower represented a concerted and coordinated effort by San Francisco Communists led by Zakheim and Arnautoff and that several of the other Coit Tower artists belonged to an "organized Communist group," and, second, that several of the muralists depicted—or consciously chose not to depict—strike events in their murals.[29] Neither part of this thesis stands up to careful examination.

Regarding the first part of Lee's thesis—his claim that Zakheim was a Communist Party member—is not in dispute, although in 1934 Zakheim sometimes denied his membership.[30] Lee, however, asserts that Arnautoff, too, was a party activist in the 1920s and later. In fact, Soviet and FBI sources agree that Arnautoff did not join the party until 1937–1938. He was born in Ukraine in 1896, served as an officer in the Imperial Russian Cavalry during World War I, and then was a cavalry officer in the White (anti-Bolshevik) Siberian Army during the Russian Civil War. Because of his White Army service, he could not return home. He studied at the CSFA in the mid-1920s; another White Army veteran later assured an FBI agent that Arnautoff was anti-Communist in the 1920s. Arnautoff then worked as an assistant to Rivera in Mexico, especially in Cuernavaca and at the National Palace, during a time when Rivera had been expelled from the Mexican CP—that is, a time when a CP member would likely have been discouraged, if not barred, from associating with Rivera. Arnautoff did keep informed about life in the Soviet Union while at the CSFA, and he and Rivera discussed politics at length. He was clearly interested in the CP as of early 1934, as witness his inclusion of two CP publications in his mural, but in his autobiography he attributed his radicalization and eventual CP membership to the violent police actions against the strikers in July 1934 and to the Spanish Civil War, both of which occurred *after* he had completed his mural at Coit Tower.[31]

Lee devotes considerable attention to the fresco mural Arnautoff created during late 1931 and early 1932 on the wall of his studio in San Francisco's art colony. In that mural, Arnautoff depicted twenty-two young artists from that neighborhood. Lee claims that the mural depicted an "organized group of Communist artists" and "the loose core of a leftist agitprop group."[32] The only citation he offers for this statement is a list of the names of some of the artists. Nowhere does Lee provide evidence for his assertion that the artists depicted in Arnautoff's mural were Communists or even an organized group. In my reading of the oral histories of many of those artists and my research on the CP in the 1920s and early 1930s, I found no evidence for such a claim, although my research found that several of them—perhaps all of them—were involved with the Art Center on Montgomery Street. Oral histories and press notices make clear that gallery members held a variety of political views. Three of those in the mural, including Arnautoff, were former officers in the White Siberian Army.[33]

Instead, Arnautoff's studio mural is better understood as a bid for public attention and new commissions. He had returned from Mexico in April 1931, held a one-man show at the Art Center in July (which received a highly favorable review in the press), and then opened his studio in February so that the public could see his mural—that is, he was demonstrating his skill at large-scale fresco painting. He even posed for a newspaper photograph with the mural—another bid for publicity and commissions. It seems highly unlikely that any "organized group" of Communists in early 1931, a time when the local CP was in significant disarray, would have splashed their names and faces across a newspaper.[34]

As evidence for Arnautoff's politics, Lee notes the inclusion in his Coit Tower mural of "the soldier waving a red flag." In fact, it is not a soldier but a traffic squad officer. At that time, San Francisco traffic squad officers wore brown uniforms and routinely used red flags to direct traffic; the officer in Arnautoff's mural is directing traffic away from men working around an open manhole.[35]

In support of his assertion that there was an organized Communist group among the Coit Tower muralists, Lee recounts an episode from Zakheim's oral history involving a meeting with Herbert Fleishhacker and some members of Heil's advisory committee. Zakheim recalled, "I was told that I was to lead the idea that they were going to collect the artists to come into the Coit Tower." Lee interpreted Zakheim's comments this way: "The radicals, who had publicized themselves collectively" through Arnautoff's mural (an unproven and unsupported assertion) "were now being gathered as a unit for a single mural project, with Zakheim . . . nominated as their spokesman" (yet another unproven and unsupported assertion resting atop the original one).[36] Of the twenty-two artists in Arnautoff's studio mural, only four in addition to Arnautoff painted at Coit Tower: Maxine Albro, Ben Cunningham, Harold Mallette Dean, and Parker Hall. No one has suggested that those four included any obvious political content in their murals, although Albro and Cunningham were later involved with the Artists and Writers Union. A survey of the thirteen oral histories by the Coit Tower artists and assistants, as well as subsequent newspaper interviews of Chessé and Hamlin, yields *not one* that even suggests Zakheim was the group's leader. Three of the oral histories point to Stackpole as the chief advisor to Heil in the recruitment and selection of the artists, and two mention Harold Mack in that regard. That so many of those selected had connections to the CSFA also points to Stackpole's influence and not that of Zakheim, who had only a limited connection to the CSFA.[37]

In the second part of his thesis, Lee claims that the muralists were all still at Coit Tower while the strike was in progress on the docks below them: "From Telegraph Hill, all of them had clear sight lines to the waterfront below, where picket lines ran from one pier to the next, and between July 3 and 5 they could see the bloody hand-to-hand battles between strikers, scabs, the National Guard, and city police." This could not have happened. First, the large majority of artists had completed their work before April 28, nearly two weeks before the strike began. Second, while it is possible to see parts of the northern waterfront from Telegraph Hill, the major conflicts with police, on May 28 and 30 and on July 3 and 5, all took place on or near the southern waterfront, one to two miles away from Telegraph Hill. Even if there were no multistory buildings between Coit Tower and the southern waterfront, it would have been impossible to make out the details of those events from Coit Tower without high-powered binoculars. Third, there were never battles between the strikers and the National Guard, which did not arrive in the city until late on July 5, after the major conflicts of that day. Finally, and most importantly, as already noted, by July 1, all of the artists had completed their work and the tower had been locked; soon after, police blocked all access to the top of Telegraph Hill.[38]

As a central part of his thesis, Lee also claims that some of the muralists consciously chose either to depict the strike in their murals or to ignore it. For example, "When Jose Moya del Pino and Otis Oldfield painted their panels of the bay and harbor . . . their decision not to include a mass of picketers was an omission of great significance, an ideological choice." *Both men completed their murals months before the strike began on May 9.* All three were featured in a newspaper article in mid-February, including a photograph of Oldfield's mural, mistakenly attributed to Del Pino. Oldfield was similarly photographed a few weeks later, with his mural nearly complete (see fig. 7.1).[39]

Lee finds only one clear example of a muralist choosing to depict strike events: Hesthal's painting of the waterfront and a locomotive. Lee says, "The waterfront behind the ship crane has been interrupted in midair, the docks are virtually empty, the workers at left have halted traffic and are pulling spikes from the tracks (one spike is held by a figure closest to us), and the signalman has nothing to do but sit and smoke—all because of Bridges's union and the strike longshoremen." However, Hesthal's painting closely follows his sketch done in December, more than five months before the strike began, and he, too, had completed his mural before the strike began. Further, a close examination indicates that the workers in Hesthal's mural are pulling weeds not spikes.[40]

Although Lee attributes to Zakheim the central role in leading the Communists among the artists, he found only one reference to the strike in Zakheim's mural: "the hint of Bridges in a headline about the 'Slaughter in Australia'."[41] (Harry Bridges, the controversial chair of the longshoremen's strike committee, had been born in Australia.) Lee misread the headline, which actually is "Slaughter in Austria." Located at the top of the mural and therefore among the first Zakheim painted, that headline refers to the civil strife in Austria in mid-February between Engelbert Dollfuss's regime and the left. Zakheim was paid for fifteen and a half weeks; he had finished in late March or early April, more than a month before the strike began.[42]

In other errors, Lee cited Cravens's mistaken version of the slogan that Wight placed around his hammer and sickle—"United Workers of the

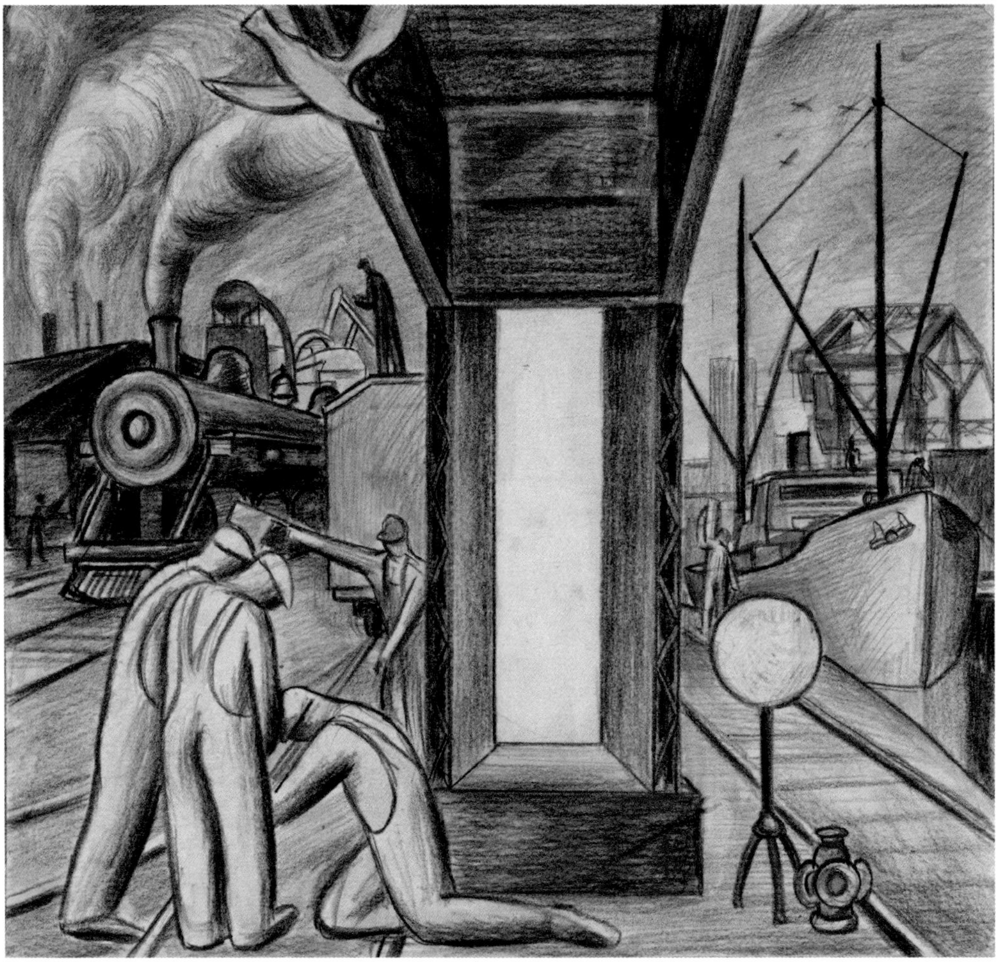

Figure 7.1. Hesthal's original sketch, from December 1933, is substantially the same as his final mural (see plate 21). (Source: William Jurgen Hesthal, *Sketch for Mural Railroad and Shipping, Coit Tower*, December 1933, graphite and colored pencil on paper, 9 5/16 x 10 1/16 in. [237 x 255 mm], Federal Art Project, L43.12.14, photograph by Randy Dodson, courtesy of the Fine Arts Museums of San Francisco.)

World"—rather than the accurate version available in several sources. Lee claimed that the crumpled newspaper at the feet of the man at the right edge of Howard's mural was the *Western Worker*; in fact, there is no banner on that paper, and the headlines indicate that it is not the *Western Worker*.[43]

Though Zakheim acknowledged that he was a Communist Party member at the time, I have found no statement by him that there were other party members at Coit Tower or that Communists consciously sought to inject party propaganda into the murals. John Langley Howard, whom Zakheim painted reaching for Marx's *Das Kapital*, considered that part of Zakheim's mural a prank rather than a political statement. Victor

Arnautoff was not a CP member in 1934. Clifford Wight, the artist who painted the controversial hammer and sickle was most probably not a party member at that time. He had worked closely with Rivera during the years when Rivera had been expelled by the Mexican Communist Party; if Wight were a CP member, he would have been expected to shun Rivera.

Shirley Staschen was an assistant to Bernard Zakheim at Coit Tower. While they were working there, Zakheim invited her to his house to meet two Communist organizers from New York. Staschen recalled, "We were supposed to have a really core group there" to accelerate organizing among artists and writers, because, as she put it, "signing up people for party work hadn't been flourishing in the bay area." But Staschen was the *only one* who showed up other than Zakheim, Kenneth Rexroth, and the two organizers—whom Staschen described as "almost scary with the amount of energy and lack of humor."[44] No other artists were present, which suggests that *none* of the other Coit Tower muralists were party members—indeed, Staschen's account suggests that the party's only members among San Francisco artists and writers may have been Zakheim and Rexroth. Rexroth's lengthy memoir says nothing about the Coit Tower artists or murals. The other three Coit Tower muralists who painted Communist publications or symbols in their murals—Wight, Howard, and Arnautoff—likely agreed with the party on particular issues but were not committed ideologues or disciplined party members when they painted their murals at Coit Tower.

In 1935 Coit Tower figured prominently in the call for an American Artists' Congress. The impetus for that organization came from New York, led by Alexander Trachtenberg, a CP functionary; CP members were always prominent in the organization, especially in the leadership. Although the call for the congress explicitly mentioned Coit Tower as the site of "suppression, censorship or actual destruction of art," the only San Francisco artists who signed were Zakheim and Howard (Howard was then living in New Mexico) and two sculptors who had not been involved at Coit Tower.[45]

Though seriously flawed, Lee's claims continue to inform the analysis of many subsequent art historians.

Apart from the conclusions of art critics and art historians, some of the Coit Tower murals are in contemporary use as icons or teaching aids. Howard's protest marchers have recently appeared on two book covers dealing with the 1930s, and Stackpole's food-processing workers have appeared on the cover of a California history survey. Roosevelt University in Chicago has a Center for New Deal Studies that includes study of New Deal art; in introducing content analysis of New Deal art to students, the Roosevelt University program uses Arnautoff's mural at Coit Tower as "an excellent example of the American Scene."[46]

Coit Tower is San Francisco Landmark #165 and California Historical Landmark #91, and it was added to the National Register of Historic Places (#07001468) in 2007. In 2020 Judge Charles Breyer, of the Federal District Court for Northern California, arranged for high-resolution photographs of the Coit Tower murals to be placed in the courtrooms of the district court in San Francisco.[47]

Historians of American art concur that the Coit Tower murals provide striking examples of the influence of Diego Rivera, specifically, and of the Mexican muralists more generally. The murals present a remarkable example of close cooperation among a large number of artists, who were working at the same time and in close quarters, and a nationally prominent example of the use of fresco, a technique that was relatively rare at the time. The murals provide the most prominent example of the PWAP, the precursor of all the New Deal art programs, and they prefigure and exemplify the major themes of subsequent New Deal art. The Coit Tower murals include examples of the wide range of themes, styles, and techniques to be found in other New Deal art, but at Coit Tower *they all exist in one place*. In 2020 Andrew Hemingway, in an essay about the PWAP, described the Coit Tower murals as "arguably the project's greatest accomplishment," and said, "In the whole span of New Deal art patronage, it was unparalleled in its ambitious model of collective labor."[48]

8

Legacies

In 1964 Maxine Albro looked back on her experience at Coit Tower: "I think that it gave all of us a tremendous boost because we were offered these nice, big walls which isn't a very usual thing. That certainly must have been quite a feat to accomplish for many of us who hadn't worked on big walls and had only worked on canvas, easel." She added that "the opportunity to design and to work in a group" was "wonderful." The Coit Tower experience did give her "a tremendous boost," as she later did a large mosaic mural at what was then San Francisco State College and had several private commissions for fresco murals in residences.[1] The Coit Tower project and the PWAP experience more generally had significant legacies both for the individual artists and for the city and the region.

Later Murals by the Coit Tower Artists

For most of the Coit Tower artists, their work there proved a training ground in fresco specifically and in the creation of large, public murals more generally. The Coit Tower mural project also elevated the professional reputations of most of the participating artists.

Ten of the twenty-five master artists and one assistant artist from the Coit Tower project subsequently received commissions for WPA/FAP projects. As work relief, the WPA/FAP projects were designed to benefit local artists, and nearly all of those projects were in San Francisco. Those eleven Coit Tower veterans carried out seventeen such work-relief projects that created fifty-two murals and four sculptures. The large majority have been recognized as historic in one way or another. In addition, Ben Cunningham later served as supervisor for mural painting for the Northern California WPA/FAP.[2] Though all were work-relief projects, it is nonetheless clear that project sponsors preferred experienced lead artists and assistant artists for these projects. Coit Tower veterans obviously fit that preference.

Three of the Coit Tower veterans stand out for the extent of their later work—they might be thought of as San Francisco's equivalents to Mexico's *Los Tres Grandes*. With SERA funding, Victor Arnautoff did a large fresco mural at the Protestant Chapel in the Presidio of San Francisco, and, with WPA/FAP funding, thirteen fresco murals at the new George Washington High School. Also with WPA/FAP funding, Lucien Labaudt created one large fresco mural at George Washington High School, twelve fresco murals at the Beach Chalet, and two large murals at the Golden Gate International Exposition. With SERA funding, Bernard Zakheim created two small fresco murals at a neighborhood health center and then, with WPA/FAP funding, two larger fresco projects at the University of California medical school in San Francisco. These SERA and WPA/FAP projects in San Francisco are discussed further below.[3]

Ten Coit Tower veterans also created thirty-two murals in federal buildings, through the Treasury Section program. Arnautoff received five post office commissions: College Station, Texas (no longer extant); Linden, Texas; Pacific Grove, California; Richmond, California (relocated to the Richmond Museum); and South San Francisco, California. Zakheim did post office murals in Mineola, Texas, and Rusk, Texas. Labaudt did two murals in what was then the federal courthouse and post office in Los Angeles. Suzanne Scheuer created post office murals in Berkeley, California, and Caldwell, Texas (now relocated to the Burleson County courthouse). George Harris did a post office mural in Woodland, California, and Ben Cunningham did one in the Ukiah, California, post office. Ray Boynton was the lead artist for fourteen murals in the Modesto, California, post office; Scheuer and Dean were assistants for some of those murals. Hamlin did post office murals in Tracy and Martinez, California. Moya del Pino created murals in the post offices of Redwood City and Lancaster, both in California, and in the Stockton, California, federal building. Stackpole, who was primarily a sculptor, carved a bas-relief mural for the Department of the Interior Building in Washington, D.C.[4]

In all, the Coit Tower artists created more than a hundred public murals through the New Deal arts programs. However, a listing of the many contributions by the Coit Tower artists to New Deal art projects does not exhaust the many legacies in San Francisco of the Coit Tower project specifically and the New Deal art projects more generally.

Other Murals Funded by PWAP

There were several other PWAP mural projects in the city, all with the same constrained calendar as Coit Tower. Three murals were commissioned at the new Roosevelt Junior High School (now Theodore Roosevelt Middle School). There, Nelson Poole, a CSFA faculty member, executed two large, and quite traditional, pastoral murals, *Harvest* and *Land*. George Wilson Walker created a more modernist mural titled *Education*, depicting students and student activities. Glenn Wessels completed four murals at Laguna Honda Hospital: *Air*, *Earth*, *Water*, and *The Professions*. David Park completed murals on *Art*, *Civilization*, and *Nature* at John Muir School, an elementary school.[5] The artwork at Roosevelt school is included in the city landmark documentation for that building.

The Mother's Building at the San Francisco Zoo has two PWAP projects, neither reflecting the American Scene. Helen, Esther, and Margaret Bruton, sisters, completed two mosaic murals, *Children and Their Animal Friends* and *St. Francis*, at either end of the loggia of that recently constructed building. Helen Bruton recalled that Herbert Fleishhacker, who had donated the building in which the murals were to be located, visited the sisters' studio to be certain the murals did not contain anything "offensive." Inside that building, Dorothy Puccinelli and Helen Forbes began work on a large mural, covering all four walls and depicting the story of Noah's ark. When PWAP funding ended on April 28, that mural was left incomplete. It was completed later, with WPA/FAP funds.[6] The art projects at the Mother's Building constitute the largest New Deal art project in the area completed entirely by woman artists, and may be the largest anywhere in the country. The artwork at the Mother's Building is included in the city landmark documentation for that building.

Coit Tower was not the only PWAP project in the city, but it was—and is—the one most easily available to the public and it received the most attention in the press, both local and national. Other PWAP murals were located in schools, a hospital, and a building at the zoo. Many New Deal art projects in San Francisco subsequent to the existence of the PWAP were also in schools or other locations not regularly open to the general public.[7] Given Coit Tower's location and the flood of press publicity it received, the Coit Tower murals immediately became the best-known New Deal art project in the city and, as such, had some influence—even a significant influence—on later mural projects and later public art projects that extended beyond the work of the Coit Tower veterans.

Murals Funded by the State Emergency Relief Agency

In addition to funding completion of the largest murals at Coit Tower, the State Emergency Relief Administration also paid Nelson Poole to complete his two murals at Roosevelt Junior High School.[8] SERA also commissioned two new projects by Coit Tower veterans.

Late in 1934, SERA commissioned Arnautoff to paint *Peacetime Activities of the Army*, a large mural, ten feet by thirty-five feet, at the Protestant Chapel (now the Interfaith Center) at the Presidio of San Francisco. Arnautoff painted a statue of Saint Francis, namesake of the Presidio, surrounded by vegetation, in the center, dividing the space into two equal parts. On the left as one faces the mural, Arnautoff presented the Presidio's history, beginning with a depiction of the First People that included the complex artistry of a man's fox-skin quiver and a woman making a basket. Moving clockwise, Arnautoff presented the meeting of the First People with Spanish colonizers; the much-romanticized love story between Concepción Argüello, daughter of the *comandante* of the Presidio, and Nikolai Rezanov, a Russian nobleman and explorer; the only surviving structure from the Spanish Presidio (which had become the Presidio Officers' Club by 1935); and the arrival of Americans—a mountain man, an army officer, and a settler. Arnautoff modeled the comandante after José Moya del Pino, another Coit Tower veteran who had been born in Spain. On the right side, Arnautoff depicted peacetime activities of the army as of 1934–1935, including aviation and radio communication just right of Saint Francis and supervision of the Civilian Conservation Corps, a New Deal agency for young men who worked with environmental projects in the center. For the latter, he showed army officers supervising CCC workers fighting a forest fire. In the upper right corner, he presented the Gatun Locks of the Panama Canal, designed and built by the Army Corps of Engineers; in the lower right corner, he showed the army's role in the design of the Golden Gate Bridge, then under construction. Arnautoff had eleven assistants, including four Coit Tower veterans: Suzanne Scheuer, Ben Cunningham, Edward Terada, and Parker Hall. Richard Ayer, another assistant, recalled that Arnautoff was a stickler for detail: "All of the flora [had to be] accurate and correct."[9]

SERA also funded two small fresco murals by Bernard Zakheim at the Alemany Emergency Hospital and Health Center, then part of the city's Department of Public Health. Titled *Community Spirit* and *Growth*, they are on two levels of the chimney of the fireplace in the building's waiting room. The upper one, *Community Spirit*, depicted the Alemany neighborhood; the lower one, *Growth*, presented an allegorical depiction of love, birth, and parenthood.[10]

Murals Funded by the Federal Art Project of the Works Progress Administration

With the creation of the Federal Art Project within the WPA, San Francisco city officials were quick to take advantage of those funds to commission murals in a number of city buildings, including Mission High School,

George Washington High School, the Beach Chalet, the new Aquatic Park Bathhouse (now the Maritime Museum), and San Francisco City Hall, and to complete the murals inside the Mother's Building at the zoo.

Mission High School

Edith Hamlin, a Coit Tower veteran, created two murals, each six feet by twenty-four feet, in the library of Mission High School, located across from Mission Dolores Park and a block south of the only surviving structure from Mission Dolores, formally Misión San Francisco de Asís, founded in 1776 by Spanish missionaries to convert the local Ohlone people to Christianity and train them in the ways of the Spanish colonizers. Hamlin depicted an idealized view of life at Mission Dolores. One mural, *Civilization through the Arts and Crafts as Taught to the Neophyte Indians,* depicts Spanish missionaries presiding over a scene where Indigenous women are spinning wool into yarn, weaving a blanket, and pounding corn into meal; two Indigenous people are playing a violin and cello; one is drawing; and others are making pottery. The other mural, *Mission San Francisco de Asis,* depicts a missionary supervising Indigenous people hauling lumber and unloading a basket of fish. Hamlin's approach, depicting the Spanish missionaries as the source of civilization for the First People, was fully in keeping with most historians' accounts at the time. Hamlin also created a third mural at the school, in a stairway, but it is no longer extant. Maynard Dixon, whose studio was near that of Hamlin, helped paint some of the faces. Hamlin and Dixon were later married and moved to Tucson, Arizona, where she continued to create large public murals.[11]

George Washington High School

George Washington High School (GWHS) has one of the largest collections of New Deal art in the city, all funded by WPA/FAP. Robert Boardman Howard, who had executed the exterior relief sculptures at Coit Tower (not funded by the New Deal), created three bas-relief sculptures over the main entrance to GWHS: Thomas Edison, symbolizing invention; George Washington, symbolizing statesmanship; and Walt Whitman, symbolizing literature. Howard was likely the sculptor of other exterior relief work at the school.[12]

Along the interior primary entry steps and hall of the main building, Victor Arnautoff, assisted by George Harris and Gordon Langdon, all veterans of Coit Tower, created four large murals, six smaller murals, three ceiling murals, and three banners, all *buon fresco,* on the life and era of George Washington. In several of the murals, Arnautoff embedded counter-narratives to the treatment of Washington and his times in the history textbooks of that day. The first mural chronologically, along the south side of the entry stairs, depicts Washington's early life as a surveyor and officer in the French and Indian War, but Arnautoff put Indigenous Americans in the center, surrounded by and resisting white colonists. Facing it is a mural on the origins of the American Revolution, showing the Boston Tea Party, the Boston Massacre, and the burning of tax stamps on the left as one faces it and, in the center, four working-class revolutionaries raising the new flag of stars and stripes. Washington appears in the upper right to take command. The other eleven murals are in the hall at the top of the entry stairs. Six smaller ones are in three alcoves that open off the main hall. Three of these small murals treat events of the Revolution: the winter at Valley Forge, the surrender at Yorktown, and Washington's farewell to his officers. The other three small murals depict Washington's life after the Revolution: saying good-bye to his aged mother, mediating as president between Hamilton and Jefferson, and attempting to create a national university. Three ceiling murals are symbolic, one showing Lady Liberty placing thirteen new stars in the firmament and the other two depicting the moon, Arnautoff's symbol of war, and the sun and a rainbow, his representation of peace.[13]

There are two large murals in the upper hall. One shows Washington as master of Mount Vernon, but Arnautoff put enslaved African Americans in the center, demonstrating that Washington's plantation was based on slave labor. Across from the Mount Vernon mural, Arnautoff tried to connect Washington and his era to the west by depicting Washington pointing the nation in that direction. In the center, he presented what he called "the march of the white race from the Atlantic to the Pacific": several pioneers in *grisaille* marching west past the body of a dead Indigenous American, symbolic of the deaths and displacement of the nation's First Peoples. Thus, Arnautoff incorporated into his treatment of the life and era of Washington the two great injustices of early U.S. history: slavery and the genocide and dispossession of Indigenous Americans.[14]

The library includes two large buon fresco murals and a small one over the entrance. The one over the entrance, by Gordon Langdon, depicts *Modern and Ancient Science*. Between them stands Mercury, Roman god of communication, who is manipulating a painted mechanism that is connected to an actual alarm bell and siren horns. Inside the library are two large murals. The one on the east wall, by Lucien Labaudt and titled *Advancement of Learning through the Printing Press*, is about books, with Johannes Gutenberg and an assistant in the center, printing books as Father Time looks on. The rest of Labaudt's mural depicts figures who appear in books, including such literary figures as Longfellow, Poe, and Whittier; representatives of science, including Franklin and Edison; surgeons, paleontologists, and individuals from history books, including John

Smith, Washington, Jefferson, and Junipero Serra. On the west wall of the library, Ralph Stackpole's *Contemporary Education*, depicts a 1930s high school, emphasizing the gendered nature of the curriculum, with young women on the left engaged in sewing, typing, and cooking, and young men on the right working with technological projects.[15]

A spectacular bas-relief frieze at the head of the athletic field—the largest and arguably the most impressive example of New Deal sculpture in the region—was created by Sargent Johnson, who identified as Black. In his *Athletics*, Johnson depicted a wide range of athletic activities with figures more than ten feet tall.[16]

Beach Chalet

The Beach Chalet, constructed in 1925 as a resting and changing place for bathers at Ocean Beach, also has a rich collection of New Deal art, all funded by the WPA/FAP. Lucien Labaudt, whose mural at Coit Tower stretches along both sides of the stairway, covered all the walls of the main room on the ground floor of the Beach Chalet with *San Francisco Scenes*, nine murals depicting contemporary outdoor city life, from the Embarcadero and Fisherman's Wharf to Ocean Beach and Golden Gate Park. As with his Coit Tower and GWHS murals, most faces are identifiable as actual persons. Labaudt also designed mosaic murals over the doorways, which were set by Primo Caredio. The staircase to the second floor features spectacular carvings of real and fanciful undersea life by Michael von Meyer.[17]

The Aquatic Park Bathhouse

The Aquatic Park recreational complex was built with city and WPA funds between 1936 and 1939. Its centerpiece is the Aquatic Park Bathhouse, now the Maritime Museum and now administered by the National Park Service. Designed by city architect William Mooser Jr. in the Streamline Moderne style, the building suggests a 1930s ocean liner. The building, inside and out, includes work by a number of important artists under the overall supervision of Hilaire Hiler. All the art is notable for its surrealist and abstract style, which contrasts with nearly all other New Deal artworks.[18]

Sargent Johnson created bas-relief sculptures of green slate around the main exterior entrance, and for the opposite (north) exterior wall, inside a portico, he designed ceramic tile murals featuring fish, a sea turtle, sailboats, and ocean currents. Mohammed Zyani, a mosaic artist from Morocco, assisted Johnson. Johnson also created a green ceramic bas-relief lintel for an upper-floor doorway.[19]

Murals by Hilaire Hiler cover all the walls of the main room. He was named the art director for the Aquatic Park project after only a brief residence in San Francisco and left the city soon after the project was complete. His abstract murals depict the mythical lost continents of Atlantis and Mu and feature a wide variety of marine life floating among building fragments. In a smaller room, Hiler created *The Prismatarium*, a mural on all the walls and ceiling. The ceiling is a color wheel composed of 180 distinct shades, representing Hiler's effort to reconceptualize the standard treatment of the three basic colors, and walls are painted in ten bands of gray progressing from very dark at the floor to light near the ceiling. In the women's lounge near the *Prismatarium*, Charles Nunemaker painted a mural titled *Sepia Seascape*. The third floor of the building features a mural by Richard Ayer that presents abstract images based on ship components, including actual rope and pipe. Beniamino Bufano was commissioned to do a series of sculptures for the building, but only *Seal* and *Toad* remain in place.[20]

Hampered by management problems and cost overruns, city officials leased the building to become an exclusive restaurant. Several of the artists objected to this privatization of a publicly funded space. Johnson simply walked away from his tile mural on the north portico, leaving it unfinished. Bufano is reputed to have carried off several of his works.[21]

University of California Medical School

Bernard Zakheim's Alemany Health Center murals brought him two mural projects at the University of California's medical school, now the University of California, San Francisco (UCSF). The first two, begun in 1935 with SERA funding, were completed in 1936 with WPA/FAP funding. Originally in Cole Hall, a large auditorium, one mural depicts *Superstitious Medicine*. The other, *Rational Medicine*, celebrates the accomplishments of modern medical science, and all of those depicted can be identified as members of the medical school faculty.[22]

Acclaim for those murals brought Zakheim a second commission at the medical school, also funded by WPA/FAP, in Toland Hall, a major lecture hall. There, in ten large murals, Zakheim depicted *The History of Medicine in California*. Like Arnautoff at the Presidio, Zakheim began his history with the First People, sympathetically depicting their medical practices. Unlike Hamlin at Mission High School, Zakheim depicted the arrival of the Spanish conquerors as a disaster for the First People rather than a blessing, including the high rate of death at the missions. Zakheim continued the history of California medicine through the Gold Rush and the late nineteenth century, presenting both high points and low. He made a point of acknowledging the first woman to graduate from the school. He also presented the school's accomplishments in the twentieth century, including the fight against bubonic plague in the early twentieth century and modern medical practices.[23] Parker Hall and Michael von Meyer carved the proscenium arch and the lectern in Toland Hall.[24]

San Francisco State College

Five artists, including two veterans of Coit Tower, created murals at the campus of San Francisco State College at Haight and Buchanan Streets in 1936–1937. Some of them worked there for more than a year, creating very large projects. Maxine Albro created a large mosaic mural over the entrance at Haight and Buchanan, depicting a fanciful jungle filled with exotic plants and animals, presumably conjured up by the imagination of a person reading a book in the center of the mural. Hebe Daum Stackpole, an assistant at Coit Tower, spent a year decorating the walls of a passageway between buildings, and John Gerrity created murals on all the walls of the Haight and Buchanan entrance. None of these works is extant. Jack Moxom did several murals over and around doors and windows, only one of which survives. Reuben Kadish, a surrealist from Southern California, created a mural titled *Alchemy*, which survives with good integrity. Recently restored, that mural is now a centerpiece for the Haight Street Art Center.[25]

Treasure Island, the Golden Gate International Exposition, and *Art in Action*

In the late 1930s, as China continued to resist invading Japanese forces and as Europe edged toward war, San Francisco artists produced a final burst of WPA/FAP–funded art for the Golden Gate International Exposition, which opened in February 1939. The exposition was held on Treasure Island, one of the most ambitious of the city's Depression-era undertakings. In partnership with several New Deal agencies, the city created an island north of Yerba Buena Island by dumping tons of crushed rock on shoals and then topping it with muck dredged from the bay and a layer of topsoil. Treasure Island was intended to become the city's airport, with facilities for planes to land and take off and also for Pan Am's China Clippers to land and take off on the waters of the bay. Before becoming an airport, however, Treasure Island was the site of the Golden Gate International Exposition, to celebrate the completion of the city's two great bridges, both of which received some funds through New Deal agencies, and the construction of Treasure Island itself, and especially to demonstrate not only that San Francisco had weathered the Depression but also that the city was poised to become the nation's gateway to the Pacific.[26]

WPA/FAP funds were used to commission artists to adorn the exposition buildings and grounds. The art and architecture of the exposition were intended to draw upon cultures that surround the Pacific. Though the resulting art is likely today to be dubbed Art Deco, at the time it was described as a fusion of Mayan, Cambodian, and other Pacific cultural influences. Some fifty painters and sculptors produced murals and sculptures for the buildings and grounds, including five who had created murals at Coit Tower, six who had created other PWAP projects, and many who had held previous WPA/FAP commissions. The Palace of Fine and Decorative Arts was intended to become a permanent part of the city's airport.[27]

Several Coit Tower veterans were unavailable due to Treasury Section commissions in 1938, when most of the artwork was being created, but Victor Arnautoff served on a planning committee. Ralph Stackpole and Lucien Labaudt created major works. Stackpole sculpted an 80-foot-high figure, *Pacifica*, the major symbol of the fair and the center of the Court of Pacifica. Labaudt created two large murals for the exterior of the California Pavilion. Several other Coit Tower veterans also contributed to the art of the exposition. Jane Berlandina painted two murals, one in the San Francisco Building and the other in the Brazil Building. José Moya del Pino also painted two murals, one for the California Building and one for the Hall of Religion. Frederick Olmsted sculpted five figures on the California Building. The Bruton sisters, also PWAP veterans, created a 144-foot-by-57-foot relief sculpture for the Court of Pacifica, hopefully titled *The Peacemakers*. Helen Forbes and Dorothy Puccinelli, the PWAP muralists at the Mother's Building, jointly created murals at one of the major open courts. Nelson Poole, another PWAP veteran, did two murals in the same court.[28]

Sargent Johnson was among the sculptors who created twenty figures for the Court of Pacifica, intended to represent the major races of the Pacific. Other WPA/FAP–funded work included several by Latino artists. Jo Mora, a painter and sculptor born in Uruguay, created a massive diorama titled *Discovery of the San Francisco Bay by Portola*. Another exposition building, Pacific House, included eight large maps by Miguel Covarrubias, born in Mexico, and a large relief map of the region by Antonio Sotomayor, who was born in Bolivia. Roberto Vallangca, a Filipino, created a *Fountain of Youth* mural. Most of the exhibits in the Federal Building celebrated the accomplishments of various New Deal agencies. There, Herman Volz supervised a large crew of WPA-paid artists who created two large murals, *The Conquering of the West by Land* and *The Conquering of the West by Water*.[29]

The exposition had the bad fortune to open in 1939, the year when Europe went to war. It had a financially disappointing year, so the organizers decided to try again in 1940 with some new features. Timothy Pflueger, the architect who had brought Rivera to the city in 1931, was primarily responsible for creating an exhibition called *Art in Action,* in which sixty-eight artists, most from the city and most paid by WPA/FAP, created art in public view. Pflueger was also the chief planner for the new campus of what is now City College of San Francisco, and he intended that some of the artworks created during *Art in Action* would be permanently placed on the new campus he was designing.[30]

To draw the maximum attention to this new feature, Pflueger recruited Diego Rivera to create a huge mural—twenty-two feet by seventy-four feet—designed to be moved later. Rivera was not eligible for pay from the WPA/FAP, but he agreed to work in return for his expenses, and Pflueger secured contributions for that purpose. Rivera created a sweeping synthesis of the art, religion, history, politics, and technology of the Americas. His title was *The Marriage of the Artistic Expression of the North and of the South on This Continent,* but it is now usually called *Pan American Unity.*

The left side of the mural depicts the Indigenous people of Mesoamerica, emphasizing their spiritual practices, and a contemporary Mexican sculptor carving Quetzalcoatl, the plumed serpent god, representing the continuity of Mexican spirituality. The right side depicts the development of technology in the United States. Rivera described the central section this way:

> In the center . . . there is a large figure—on one side it has the neck of Quetzalcoatl [and] elements from the Mexican Goddess of Earth and the God of Water. On the other side the figure is made of . . . the machine which makes fenders and parts for airplanes. On one side of this figure there is the northern culture, on the other the southern art, the art of the emotions. . . . From the South comes the plumed serpent, from the North the conveyor belt.[31]

In the lower left part of the central element, Rivera depicted "the great liberators—Washington, Jefferson, Hidalgo, Morelos, Bolivar, Lincoln, and John Brown." Opposite them he presented Stalin, Hitler, and Mussolini as three villains, in grisaille, with Charlie Chaplin's portrayal of "the great dictator" below them. To the left of the dictators, a fist arises from an American flag to restrain a hand with a swastika holding a knife. Below them are the victims of the wars then raging. Rivera also included images of himself and Frida Kahlo, who was with him in San Francisco.[32]

Rivera had help from several assistants, led by Emmy Lou Packard. The team included several women and artists of color, including Thelma Johnson Streat, Peter Lowe, and Miné Okubo, although only a few actually took part in the painting. Matthew Barnes, whose title at Coit Tower had been "mural coordinator" but who was in charge of the plastering, served as the primary plasterer for Rivera's mural. At one point during the project, Packard took Rivera to view the Coit Tower murals; she later recalled that he had been very impressed by the project, especially Arnautoff's mural.[33]

Pan American Unity was Rivera's last project outside of Mexico. It has been called the most important work of art ever created in San Francisco and one of the most important works of public art in the United States. Timothy Pflueger intended that it would be placed in the library he was planning for City College. Then the war intervened and all nonessential construction came to a halt. Pflueger died soon after. The library he had planned was never built. Rivera's mural was broken down, put into crates, and placed in storage until 1961, when it was reassembled and placed in the lobby of the theater building at City College.[34] It was recently removed, restored, and displayed at the San Francisco Museum of Modern Art before being removed for installation in a new building at City College.

Several other works created through *Art in Action* were later installed at City College, including a mosaic mural by Herman Volz, *Organic and Inorganic Science*, now on the north portico of the Science Hall, and Frederick Olmsted's bust of Leonardo da Vinci, on the east exterior of that building.[35]

Murals Funded by the Treasury Section of Fine Arts

PWAP and WPA/FAP art projects were work relief for artists and therefore employed local artists. Art projects for new federal buildings were supervised by the Treasury Section and were commissioned based on competitions open to artists nationwide. The New Deal built many new post offices, and almost every one of them, if not all, got a mural. Several San Francisco artists received commissions for post office murals elsewhere in the country. San Francisco, however, has only two projects that were funded through the Treasury Section. One was a set of bronze reliefs by Albert Stewart at the former federal mint.[36] The Rincon Annex post office is the site of the other Treasury Section project in the city. It is the largest New Deal art project by a single artist anywhere in the nation. The jury for the Rincon Annex project, which included Arnautoff, chose a New York artist, Anton Refregier. He began work in 1942, but the project was then put on hold until after the war. It thereby became the last New Deal art project, completed in 1948, six years after all New Deal art programs were phased out.[37]

Refregier's murals line the entire lobby of the Rincon Annex. There are twenty-seven separate murals, 2,574 square feet, presenting the history of Northern California, especially San Francisco. Refregier's politics were on the left, and, like Arnautoff and Zakheim, he began his history with a respectful portrayal of the First People. The first mural is called *A California Indian Creates*, which was contrary to a view then common that the Indigenous Californians were among the least advanced of those who lived in what became the United States. The next mural, of three Indigenous Californians in a tule-reed canoe, is based on one of the earliest European drawings of the Indigenous people of the area. Refregier gave two panels to early European explorers, the first of Sir Francis Drake, who had claimed the area for England in 1579. The other, of Spanish soldiers, was originally described as the first sight of the Bay by Spanish explorers; it was later retitled *Balboa's Discovery of the Pacific*. The next two panels present the arrival of Spanish missionaries and creation of Mission Dolores. Refregier's *Preaching and Farming at Mission Dolores* tells a different story than Hamlin's murals at Mission High School, although less explicitly than Zakheim's version at UCSF. In Refregier's mural, a rotund priest—Refregier was told to slim him down, but he remained quite hefty—is doing the preaching and a group of emaciated-looking Indigenous Californians are doing the hard work of farming.[38]

Others of Refregier's murals tell a more traditional story, including a small one on Fort Ross (the southernmost Russian settlement, ninety-some miles north of the city), one depicting the hardships of the overland trail to California, a large one of the Bear Flag Revolt, and one presenting the discovery of gold at Sutter's Mill. His depiction of an early newspaper office suggests, by the gun on the editor's hip, some of the intense competition among the city's newspapers and the level of violence in the city in the 1850s. His mural on mining ranges from an individual prospector with a pan to heavily capitalized deep shaft mining and the construction of elaborate water systems, by which time the miners had become wage-earning employees of large mining corporations. A small mural presents newcomers arriving by sea, the route taken by most. Another small mural depicts a group of men in a torchlight procession, and a larger one showed early settlers getting their mail. The largest mural shows the construction of the transcontinental railway and is focused entirely on the workers, mostly Chinese, and completely ignores the "Big Four," the partners in the Central Pacific Railway.

Another large mural about the 1850s shows the shooting death of a newspaper editor and vigilantes lynching the murderer. A small mural presenting Civil War riots is next to another small one showing an anti-Chinese riot, a reference to the Workingmen's Party of 1877. On the ground in that mural, Refregier placed a statement by Frank Roney, an early union organizer, that reads, "Attacks upon the Chinese I consider unreasonable and antagonistic to the principles of American Liberty."[39] The next mural depicts early twentieth-century San Francisco as a cultural center, with portraits of literary, artistic, and scientific figures, including Mark Twain, Robert Louis Stevenson, Luther Burbank, and, the largest of the group, Jack London.

The center of the north wall has four large murals, In chronological sequence, the first two present the destruction of the 1906 earthquake and subsequent reconstruction. The next two large murals reflect Refregier's left politics, beginning with his depiction of the Preparedness Day bombing of 1916, for which two labor organizers, Tom Mooney and Warren Billings, were convicted based on perjured testimony and imprisoned for more than twenty years. The next one presents the 1934 longshore and maritime strikes.[40]

The last two murals on the north wall again put workers in the center. The first presents the building of the Golden Gate Bridge, with the workers in the center and Joseph Strauss, the designer, in a corner. The next mural was designed after the war and depicts World War II shipbuilding, also emphasizing the workers.

The final mural, one of the largest, was also designed after the war. It is divided into three parts: the defeat of the Axis, Franklin D. Roosevelt's Four Freedoms, and the founding conference of the United Nations (UN) in San Francisco. The last features several delegates sitting around a table, each with a national flag. However, a Black man at the table has no flag in front of him, Refregier's way of drawing attention to the many people of the world, especially those in Africa, who had been colonized by European powers and had no voice at the UN conference. The political controversies that swirled around Refregier's murals, both at the time and later, are presented in the next chapter.

All in all, the New Deal arts programs created a rich collection of art in San Francisco's public buildings, including more than a hundred public murals, the largest amount of public art created in such a relatively short period of time in the city's history. Works by the Coit Tower artists account for roughly half of that total.

Murals Not Funded by New Deal Programs

The influence of Coit Tower specifically and the New Deal arts programs more generally extended beyond federally funded projects and reached many parts of the city, both in the 1930s and later. To be certain, it is often not possible to trace a direct line from either Coit Tower or the New Deal arts programs to other murals. However, if murals were being created in the 1930s, amid all the attention to the New Deal murals, there is likely a connection even if it is not possible to identify specific causation.

Even so, there are some direct connections in that some Coit Tower veterans received later mural commissions from individuals or companies.

In 1936 Arnautoff, Boynton, Hesthal, Langdon, Olmsted, and Stackpole were commissioned to create lunettes above three walls of the library at what was then the California School of Fine Arts. Moya del Pino was commissioned to do three murals in the Acme Brewery in San Francisco, which are still extant, and three large murals for the Biltmore Hotel in Santa Barbara. In 1935 Takeo Edward Terada returned to Japan, where he created two large murals, *Florida Kitchen* and *Cotton Club*, for bars in Tokyo. Between 1947 and 1952, Hamlin completed seven murals in Phoenix and Tucson, Arizona. In 1950, the San Francisco Chamber of Commerce commissioned Harris to create a twenty-seven-foot-long mural in their offices.[41]

Some of the other New Deal artists also received commissions from individuals or companies, notably Esther Bruton, who created a circus on all the walls of the Cirque Lounge in the Fairmont Hotel, one of the city's first cocktail lounges to open after the end of Prohibition. Timothy Pflueger designed the lounge, and, as was the case with so many of his buildings, he wanted top-quality artwork on the walls. Pflueger again picked Esther Bruton to create murals in a department store in Los Angeles. Helen Bruton did a mosaic mural for a building on the campus of the University of California, Berkeley. Soon after, she did bas-relief sculptures for post offices in Fresno and Merced and also received a private commission for mosaic murals in a San Francisco hotel. Years later, Margaret Bruton described the New Deal arts programs as "wonderful," adding, "They gave the artists a terrific boost."[42]

The Wider Influence of New Deal Murals

The creation of murals in the 1930s was not limited to those created with federal funding in government buildings and those created in such elite establishments as the Cirque Lounge. And Rivera's influence was strong not only among artists carrying out federal commissions but among other artists as well.

As Mark Dean Johnson points out in his "Uncovering Asian American Art in San Francisco, 1850–1940," a number of Asian American artists worked with Rivera during his two visits to San Francisco. Hideo Benjamin Noda, for example, worked as an assistant to Rivera at the California School of Fine Arts and later in New York; in 1937 he created a WPA/FAP mural at Piedmont High School, across the bay from San Francisco. Previous to her work during *Art in Action*, Miné Okubo had created fresco and mosaic murals at Fort Ord, south of San Francisco, and in the Servicemen's Hospitality House in Oakland. Johnson notes that Rivera's influence—and, one might add, the likely examples of Coit Tower and the other New Deal mural projects—led to the creation of a number of murals in Chinatown during the 1930s, including those by Nanying Stella Wong in the Fong Fong soda fountain in 1935, by David Chun in the Chinese Village nightclub in 1936, and by Dong Kingman at the Chinatown YMCA in 1941.[43]

However, as Nancy Dustin Wall Moure points out in her *California Art*, "The 1939 Golden Gate International Exposition on Treasure Island can be regarded as the ending point for mural painting in the 1930s. . . . After 1940 the impetus went out of the mural movement, and the few murals produced between 1945 and 1965 took on a completely different aesthetic." With the coming of World War II, the New Deal and its arts programs ended. After the war, social realism became passé as artists, art critics, and art schools embraced abstract expressionism. Susan Landauer, an art historian, has described this change in the California art scene: "Realist tendencies . . . gave way to a powerful tide of modernism that ultimately swept them off the stage entirely." The California School of Fine Arts, incubator of so many of the artists who created projects under New Deal auspices, was at the forefront of the new direction. Douglas MacAgy, the new director of the CSFA, covered up the school's Diego Rivera mural, brought in new faculty members, and introduced a new curriculum that was, in his words, "strictly contemporary." New Deal–style murals throughout the building were painted over. New faculty members, notably Clyfford Still and Richard Diebenkorn, were leading the way to a Bay Area version of abstract expressionism.[44] Public abstract art may sometimes have produced puzzled looks but was unlikely to provoke political controversy. Yet there was a political dimension to this new aesthetic. In 1950 the CIA, as part of its efforts to attract non-Communist artists and intellectuals to support the United States in the Cold War, covertly influenced and underwrote projects that promoted abstract expressionism.[45]

Social realism in public murals reappeared and began to thrive in San Francisco in the 1970s with a veritable explosion of murals in the city's Mission District, soon labeled Muralismo. There is a temptation to trace those murals to the influence of the New Deal murals, but there is only a very roundabout connection. In a recent unpublished study of Latina/Latino art in San Francisco, Carlos Cordova notes the lack of continuity from early San Francisco Latina/Latino artists to those in the 1930s and after but emphasizes the influence of the Mexican muralists, especially Rivera, on both the New Deal artists and the later Latina/Latino artists of the Mission District. For developments in the 1970s and after, Cordova focuses on the creation of such Mission District institutions as the Galería de la Raza in 1970 and on the influence of the Chicano mural movement at the United Farm Workers' center in Del Rey, California, followed by other murals in San Diego, Los Angeles, and elsewhere. In San Francisco, however, Cordova explains, the Chicano mural movement was "absorbed into a broader cultural vision that encompassed a pan-Latino sense of community." This led to the earliest community murals in San Francisco around 1970, painted on the walls of Latina/Latino community organizations. The early 1970s also saw the organization of *Las Mujeres Muralistas*, a cooperative of women artists who included not just Chicanas but women from other parts of Latin America. One of their earliest works was on a garage door in Balmy Alley, the beginning of that street's reputation as a location for Latina/Latino murals.[46]

After 1969, Emmy Lou Packard's studio in the Mission District became a gathering place for young artists in the neighborhood. She had been the chief assistant to Rivera at the Golden Gate International Exposition, and she continued to produce representational art, sometimes with a political message. In 1973–1974 she served as technical advisor to Jesús "Chuy" Campusano, Luis Cortázar, and Michael Rios as they were creating *Homage to Siqueiros*, a ninety-foot-long work at a Bank of America branch on Mission Street at Twenty-third, in the heart of the Mission District, a prominent early example of Muralismo. Appointed to the city's Visual Arts Committee of the Arts Commission, Packard used her position there to encourage emerging Latino/Latina artists. In 1976 she strongly supported Susan Cervantes's proposal for a mural at Precita Park, the beginning of Cervantes's long career as a muralist. Cervantes then created Precita Eyes, one of the few community mural art centers in the United States and a source of inspiration for many of the murals that now adorn the Misson District. In October 1984 a program titled "Una Noche con Diego Rivera" at the Galería de la Raza included not only a slide show of Rivera's work but also "a special ceremony in honor of Emmy Lou Packard."[47]

In 2024 the resurgence of interest in public murals that was awakened first in the Mission District has extended to much of the city, where representational murals, some exhibiting social realism, others more fanciful, some political, others completely apolitical, now grace the walls of public schools, businesses, and private residences.

The Coit Tower project and PWAP more generally had significant legacies for the artists and for the city and the region. They provided a significant demonstration of what contemporary art critic Nadia Lavrova called "the informal, unofficial, but easily recognizable San Francisco school of fresco painting,"[48] a palette and style that Coit Tower veterans took elsewhere in the city—to the Presidio Chapel, Mission High School, George Washington High School, the Beach Chalet, San Francisco State College, the University of California medical school—and elsewhere in the state and nation through their work on WPA/FAP, the Treasury Section, and private commissions. The blossoming of public art in the 1930s culminated with the Golden Gate International Exposition in 1939–1940 and the creation of Diego Rivera's masterpiece there. Except for Refregier's murals, World War II ended the New Deal's art programs. Postwar artists tended to eschew social consciousness and social realism in favor of abstract expressionism. But in the 1970s, San Francisco experienced a revival of interest in public murals that began with the Muralismo of the Latino and Latina artists of the Mission District.

9

New Deal Art and Political Controversy in San Francisco

Franklin D. Roosevelt's New Deal programs for relief, recovery, and reform, including public art projects, often provoked opposition when they were implemented in the 1930s, and some of them have never ceased to be controversial. At their inception, nearly all New Deal programs sparked controversy between Democrats and Republicans, as well as controversy among factions in the two major parties—especially controversy over how and to what degree such programs actually served the public interest. In the decades since, the debates over whether New Deal programs have served the public interest have continued, albeit in a new way that reflects how the two major parties have changed in response to domestic social and cultural developments, as well as the international conditions related to World War II, the Cold War, and post–Cold War globalization.

When the federal government paid artists to paint murals in public buildings, it opened a Pandora's box full of questions about whose priorities in defining the public interest should prevail, questions that came up in many communities with New Deal art, especially art that displayed social consciousness or social realism. San Francisco was no different, but it was distinctive. During the late 1930s and World War II, when demands that Americanism prevail and some nine out of ten San Francisco residents were whites of European descent, controversies about New Deal murals related to the politics of patriotism and loyalty to the United States. Then the city's demography transformed dramatically beginning during World War II and continuing through the 1960s and beyond. From the '60s on, as the buildings that housed murals aged, questions arose about maintenance costs and what to do in the case of demolition as land use patterns changed. At the same time, controversies about public art increasingly related to the politics of recognition of marginalized peoples and respect for their history and culture. San Francisco's distinctive social diversity and hyper-pluralist political culture have compounded the complexity of the post-1960s controversies.

Just as the late 1940s and early 1950s saw a renewal of public criticism of the Coit Tower murals for their supposed Communist bias, so, too, charges that murals in the Rincon Annex post office were Communist propaganda filled headlines in the late 1940s and early 1950s. Refregier completed the murals in 1948, but even as he painted, controversies arose over some of his work. His depiction of an obese priest at Mission Dolores preaching to a crowd of emaciated hardworking Indigenous people drew such complaints that he slimmed the priest down a bit. Refregier's mural originally called *Union Wins 8 Hour Day* drew directly on Ira Cross's account of events in 1868, in a book published by the University of California Press, but because unions and the eight-hour day remained controversial, the title of the mural became *Torchlight Procession*, with marchers' placards positioned so that no message is visible. Refregier planned to include a portrait of Franklin D. Roosevelt in his final mural that presents the victory over fascism, Roosevelt's Four Freedoms, and the founding of the United Nations. However, the federal Public Buildings Administration (which had taken over responsibility from the Treasury Section) directed him to omit Roosevelt, a decision that generated significant protest across the city but to no avail.[1]

The greatest controversy arose over Refregier's mural depicting the 1934 longshore and maritime strikes. In mid-April 1948 the Public Buildings Administration directed him to cover it, pending a review by "experts." The mural depicts an evil-looking figure hiring longshore workers, a union organizer in the center, and the maritime unions' annual "Bloody Thursday" (July 5) memorial service for those killed during the 1934 strikes, an event then held across the street from the Rincon Annex. Based on his attendance at and photographs of the annual commemoration, Refregier included a memorial wreath, union banners, and three men standing at attention, one wearing a Veterans of Foreign Wars (VFW) cap. (A longshoreman killed by police in 1934 was a World War I veteran, and veterans in the longshore union named their VFW post in his honor.) M. C. Herman, the VFW's California adjutant, acknowledged that union members might appropriately honor the man for whom their post was named, but he protested against the VFW insignia in the mural, adding, "We object to the type of all the murals, if you must know." When Refregier was ordered to stop work and cover what he had done, members of the International Longshoremen's and Warehousemen's Union joined local artists in picketing the Rincon Annex in support of Refregier. In the end,

Refregier removed the VFW cap and made a few other modifications, but most of the rest of his original design remained.[2]

In 1954, with Republicans in the White House and in the majority in Congress, Hubert Scudder, a right-of-center Republican Congress member from Sebastopol, north of San Francisco, renewed the controversy when he introduced a joint congressional resolution directing the General Services Administration to remove all the Refregier murals, not just particular ones or particular parts of ones. They were all, he opined, "an insult to the State, an insult to the intelligence of the public and anti-American in motif," and also "communist propaganda . . . intended to promote racial hatred and class warfare." The U.S. House of Representatives Committee on Public Works took up the Scudder Bill on May 1, 1953. Both of San Francisco's U.S. House members defended the murals. John Shelley, a liberal Democrat and former president of the Labor Council, argued that citizens of a democracy were entitled to encounter provocative subject matter: "You cannot change history or a picture of history or a portrayal of it by saying 'But I do not like that.' If we get into that, Mr. Chairman, then we are definitely contributing to thought control and trying to build a nation of conformists." The other Congressman, William Mailliard, a liberal Republican who came from the city's elite, said, "Judging either the painter or the style of art used would be putting Congress in the same position as the totalitarian governments who refused to allow music to be played if the composer's politics do not suit them." The murals also received support from the directors of the city's art museums; the presidents of Stanford University and Mills College; the director of the California School of Fine Arts; the dean of the school of architecture at the University of California, Berkeley; many prominent San Franciscans; and a long list of artists, museum directors, and citizens all across the country. Scudder's bill died in committee.[3] Its defeat marked the last attack on any part of San Francisco's large collection of New Deal art based on claims that it was Communist propaganda.

In a preview of what was to come when other post offices and public buildings that housed New Deal murals were declared obsolete or surplus, the Rincon Annex, including Refregier's murals, was threatened with demolition in the late 1970s. After construction of a new bulk-mail facility, the post office department no longer needed the building. In April 1978, reports that the building was likely to be sold and the site redeveloped set off a two-pronged effort to save the murals. One effort was political. Mayor George Moscone's office contacted the city's delegation in Washington to express concern about the future of the murals; Senator Alan Cranston and Congressman John Burton then convinced the post office department to insist that when the building was sold, it would be with the condition that the murals could not be destroyed or removed. Simultaneously, Emmy Lou Packard and Ruth Asawa, two of the city's most prominent artists, succeeded in having the building listed on the National Register of Historic Places. Later redevelopment of the site took place behind the façade and within the shell of the 1940 building. The lobby was renovated to serve as entry to the new construction, and the murals were cleaned and restored.[4]

In the late 1960s and again in the late 2010s, Victor Arnautoff's murals at George Washington High School came under attack, and the controversies reflected the city's increasingly cultural diversity as well as its hyperpluralist political culture. Though uncontroversial at the time Arnautoff completed his project, two of the large murals attracted the most attention later—those depicting slavery and the genocide and dispossession of Indigenous Americans.[5] The murals first became controversial in 1968, when a faction among the Black students at GWHS, influenced by the Black Power movement, argued that Arnautoff's depiction of enslaved African Americans was denigrating to African American students. The school's Black Student Union demanded that all of Arnautoff's murals be destroyed or changed, but a poll of GWHS students showed that 61 percent of them wanted the murals to be supplemented rather than destroyed. Zuretti Goosby, the first Black member of the board of education, negotiated a compromise that included new murals. Dewey Crumpler, a young Black artist, created a triptych called *Multi-Ethnic Heritage*, sometimes called the *Response* murals, centered on the resistance, struggles, and successes of people of color. Crumpler, who later became a faculty member at the San Francisco Art Institute (formerly the California School of Fine Arts), later reflected on the relation between his presentation of resistance and success and Arnautoff's portrayal of oppression: "Without Arnautoff's murals, my murals are irrelevant. And without my murals, Arnautoff's murals are irrelevant. . . . They are one thing."[6]

In 2016 Arnautoff's GWHS murals again came under criticism when the school district's American Indian Parent Advisory Committee claimed that the depiction of a dead Indigenous American warrior was offensive, even traumatic, to Indigenous American students. Two years later the criticism was repeated when the city's planning department sought to nominate GWHS as a city landmark. Influenced by members of the American Indian Parent Advisory Committee, the board of education refused to accept landmarking of any school, because it did not want to be prohibited from making changes to, or removing, the GWHS mural.[7]

Nine months later, the school district appointed a Reflection and Action Group (R&AG) to formulate a recommendation regarding the GWHS murals. According to Brent Stephens, the school district's chief academic officer, the R&AG was "deliberately small" and "composed deliberately to represent key perspectives and avoid further marginalization." The group was to "consider a variety of perspectives related to the mural images," to "identify options for addressing the social and emotional impact of mural images," and to "make a recommendation—or recommendations—for action . . . about the murals." The R&AG met four times. Throughout, most comments focused primarily on the depiction of the dead Indigenous American and, secondarily, on the enslaved African Americans in the Mount Vernon mural. There were also a few comments about the treatment of Indigenous Americans in the mural depicting Washington's early life and the French and Indian War. Throughout, the thirteen murals were all lumped together as the "*LOW* mural," meaning, *Life of Washington*. There was no consideration of the other ten murals—never, for example, any explanation how the mural showing Washington, Hamilton, and Jefferson discussing the Constitution was offensive or why the ceiling mural of the sun and a rainbow had to be destroyed. I was among several members of the public who explained how Arnautoff had intended the images in question to pose counter-narratives to the celebratory, and racist, received wisdom of his time. We presented alternatives to demolition, including interpretative signage, screening parts or all of the troublesome murals, covering the objectionable murals with curtains, and the creation of new murals. All such options were rejected as unacceptable compromises.[8]

The R&AG announced, "We come to these recommendations due to the continued historical and current trauma of Native Americans and African Americans with these depictions in the mural that glorifies slavery, genocide, colonization, manifest destiny, white supremacy, oppression, etc. . . . It's not a counter-narrative if [the mural] traumatizes students and community members." Even though the statement refers to "the mural" and "this mural," the group recommended that all thirteen *LOW* murals be digitally archived and then destroyed. The vote on these recommendations was eight in favor to one opposed, with two abstentions.[9]

Those critical of the murals explained to reporters why all of them were offensive. Amy Anderson, a member of the Ahkaamaymowin band of Métis, said they represented "American history from the colonizers' perspective." Paloma Flores, a member of the Pit River Nation and coordinator of the San Francisco Unified School District's (SFUSD) Indian Education Program, said, "Intent no longer matters," and that the murals "glorify the white man's role." Mariposa Villaluna, a member of the R&AG committee said, "We need to have them come down. . . . We didn't want anybody to see or re-traumatize or get PTSD again."[10] The argument that Indigenous American students, because of historical trauma, were likely to be traumatized or to experience posttraumatic stress disorder as a result of seeing the image of a dead Indigenous American was repeated throughout the sessions.

The R&AG's recommendation set off a media storm. Articles appeared in the *San Francisco Chronicle, New York Times, Washington Times, Washington Post, National Review, (London) Guardian,* and elsewhere. There were editorials or op-eds opposing destruction of the *LOW* murals in the *San Francisco Chronicle* (several), *Wall Street Journal* (two), *Boston Globe, The Guardian,* and *National Review,* as well as smaller papers.[11]

Few sought out GWHS students for their reactions. Though SFUSD officials made no effort to poll the full student body, a few reporters did so. Carol Pogash, for example, in the *New York Times,* cited an English teacher at GWHS who assigned forty-nine freshmen to write essays about the frescoes, only four of whom favored removal.[12]

Various organizations announced their opposition to destruction of the *LOW* murals, led by the George Washington High School Alumni Association. Others included San Francisco Heritage (the city's leading organization for architectural and cultural preservation), the San Francisco–based Russian Community Council, the National Coalition Against Censorship/Arts Advocacy Program, the College Art Association of America, and the Living New Deal. Among those endorsing the R&AG recommendations were the Richmond District Democratic Club and the American Indian Movement West. At the school board meetings, many who spoke against the murals were associated with Coleman Advocates, a community organization that defines its purpose as "fighting to advance rights, safety, and full inclusion of low-income people of color."[13]

Many, if not most, of those who opposed destruction of the murals acknowledged the concerns of those on the other side but sought alternatives to destruction, ranging from the addition of interpretative signage, to screening parts of murals or placing curtains over the murals considered offensive.

Support for the *LOW* murals came from a wide range of individuals. Lope Yap Jr., of Filipino descent and vice president of the GWHS Alumni Association, was prominent. Robert Tamaka Bailey, a Choctaw language instructor who participated in the Indigenous American occupation of Alcatraz in 1969, said, "The ones who should be offended by these murals should be the descendants of these settlers, who did these horrific atrocities. . . . I would be offended if you took them down, because then I would see you as those who say, 'it didn't happen and there are no Indians left to offend.'" Both Carol Roland Nawi, a former State Historic Preservation officer, and I explained that any action taken by the board had to comply with state law, especially the California Environmental Quality Act (CEQA).[14]

Mayor London Breed, most members of the board of supervisors, Nancy Pelosi (the city's member of Congress), the two U.S. senators (both San

Franciscans), the chamber of commerce, university presidents, corporate leaders—unlike their counterparts in 1953—all remained silent in public, even though several privately sided with defenders of the murals.

On June 18, 2019, the San Francisco school board received a staff report on the options available to deal with the murals: conservation, placing a curtain over the murals, placing solid panels over the murals, and painting out the murals. All had sizable price tags, with the panels costing an estimated $645,000–$825,000 and painting over them at more than $600,000. During public comment, Amy Anderson said, in part, "The mural is already depicting a whitewashed history, where everything within it was based on the story and the telling and the writing of people who are . . . [ellipsis in original] white," and she urged the board members to "be woke! . . . end white supremacy!"[15] More than one speaker attributed any defense of the murals to "the white supremacy culture." One claimed that those who were not white and were defending the murals had been "colonized."[16]

After the hour of public comment, board members spoke, fully embracing the arguments of those seeking to destroy the murals. Board president Stevon Cook, who is Black, had announced his support for destroying the murals two months earlier, long before the board meeting at which board members were to receive staff recommendations and hear public comments. He came to the June 18 board meeting with a long resolution justifying destruction of the murals as did other board members.[17]

On June 25, the day the school board voted, the *San Francisco Chronicle* carried statements opposing destruction of the murals from Bay Area art leaders: Stephen Beal, president of the California College of Art; Neal Benezra, director of the San Francisco Museum of Modern Art; Thomas Campbell, director of the Fine Arts Museums of San Francisco; and Gordon Knox, president of the San Francisco Art Institute. Knox said, "Our anger should be directed not at [Arnautoff] a courageous artist, or at this irreplaceable work of art, but at the systems of oppression and subjugation on which this country was founded and which we must fight each day to dismantle."[18]

At the board meeting that day, the board took up the staff's recommendation to cover "the mural"—meaning all the murals—with solid panels. The resolution was amended by a unanimous vote of the board (one member was absent) to specify that painting over all of the murals was the preference, but that the board would be satisfied with solid panels if that choice were more expeditious.[19]

The GWHS Alumni Association made clear that it would take legal action to protect the murals. After the board's vote in favor of destroying all the murals, support for the murals gradually increased. More articles and editorials in national publications and in online and broadcast media appeared in both the United States and internationally. On July 14, 2019, former mayor and former speaker of the California Assembly, Willie Brown, who is Black, defended the murals: "I'm the father of a Washington High graduate. My daughter was never traumatized by Arnautoff's painting—as a matter of fact, it generated conversations at home that otherwise would not have occurred. It was a learning experience for her, and for me." Others defending the murals included Dewey Crumpler; Jon Golinger; Matt Gonzalez, a Green Party member, former supervisor, and vice presidential candidate with Ralph Nader in 2008; Art Agnos, a former mayor; Henry Der, former director of Chinese for Affirmative Action; and Rocco Landesman, chairman of the National Endowment for the Arts during the Obama administration. They united under the banner of a new group led by Golinger called Coalition to Protect Public Art, which quickly announced it would begin gathering petition signatures to place a measure on the March 2020 ballot that would prevent the school board from destroying the Arnautoff murals, or any other New Deal mural in San Francisco, without first getting approval from the Arts Commission, the board of supervisors, or the voters.[20]

By late July, some among the city's political leadership began to intervene behind the scenes, first to block a resolution supporting the school board that had been proposed for the Democratic County Central Committee and then to push the school board leadership to compromise and avoid a high-profile ballot fight on this issue.[21] On August 6, officers of the local and regional NAACP chapter joined with other leaders of the Black community and Dewey Crumpler to hold a press conference in support of keeping the murals. That same day, Golinger released the results of a poll indicating that 76 percent of city voters opposed the school board's decision, and only 12 percent favored destroying the murals, making it appear highly likely that the proposed ballot measure would pass if it were on the ballot. Soon after, school board president Cook announced that he would propose a resolution at the next board meeting that would replace the previous resolution and seek a solution that would not destroy the murals.[22]

At the August 13 meeting, Cook proposed to rescind the previous resolution and to endorse covering the murals with solid panels. With the exception of Cook, board members did not speak to matters of state law and instead addressed their comments to those they apparently considered to be their political base. They accepted Cook's resolution by a vote of 4–3; those opposed favored the earlier approach.[23]

The controversy continued. On August 14, the day after the board voted, U.S. senator Dianne Feinstein wrote to each school board member saying she could not support removing the murals from view and expressing her hope that the process in state CEQA law would "bring a greater level of rationality to this discussion." On August 19 Alice Walker, the renowned Black novelist, issued a public defense of the murals. On August 21 the city's Historic Preservation Commission unanimously agreed to send a letter to the school board in defense of the murals.[24]

The GWHS Alumni Association sued the San Francisco school district on the grounds that the board's resolutions were in violation of CEQA, which helped to delay the planned destruction of the murals, as did the intense political and media backlash followed by the outbreak of the COVID-19 pandemic in March 2020. On July 27, 2021, California Superior Court judge Anne-Christine Massullo ruled that the board had violated CEQA and ordered them to "set aside all actions and approvals relating to destroying or removing the murals form public view." Among many other grounds, the judge cited my letter to the school board explaining that there were thirteen separate murals and that the board's proposed action was in violation of CEQA.[25] Though the board was facing a significant financial deficit, board members initially decided to appeal the decision.

Then, in a special election in February 2022, voters recalled the only three board members eligible for recall, all of whom had voted to destroy the murals, by majorities ranging from 69 to 76 percent. The murals played some part in the recall, but other significant issues included many parents' dissatisfaction with the board's handling of student learning early on during the pandemic, a decision to change the names of forty-four schools (based on questionable research in Wikipedia), and a decision to convert admission to Lowell High School, the city's academic high school, from a merit system (based on middle-school GPA) to a lottery system, which brought lawsuits that the school district lost. The last especially angered many members of the city's Asian community. After the recall and appointment of three new board members, the reconstituted board withdrew its appeal of Judge Massullo's decision, followed her order to revoke all of its resolutions back to the naming of the R&AG committee, ended the renaming controversy, and returned Lowell to its previous admission status.[26]

In August 2021, as the legal and political battles over the George Washington High School murals were playing out, another set of San Francisco New Deal murals came under threat when the University of California, San Francisco, planned to demolish the building in which they were located and was unwilling to pay to have them removed. The murals, twelve separate panels by Bernard Zakheim, were funded by the WPA/FAP and depicted the history of medicine in California. A public outcry led the San Francisco Board of Supervisors to declare the murals a city and county landmark. Though the UCSF administration noted that UC's constitutional autonomy meant they were not bound by such an ordinance, they nonetheless found the funds necessary to remove the murals from the building and place them in storage.[27]

Controversies over San Francisco's New Deal art since the 1930s have reflected local manifestations of national and international debates over how to define the public interest and who should participate in the debate about making the definition. The resolution approved by the Council of the American Historical Association (AHA) in 2017, at the time of controversy over Confederate monuments, and since endorsed by twenty-four other professional associations, is relevant for such debates over New Deal art. That resolution includes this statement:

> We also encourage communities to remember that all memorials remain artifacts of their time and place. They should be preserved, just like any other historical document, whether in a museum or some other appropriate venue. Prior to removal they should be photographed and measured in their original contexts. These documents should accompany the memorials as part of the historical record. . . . Decisions to remove memorials to Confederate generals and officials who have no other major historical accomplishment does not necessarily create a slippery slope towards removing the nation's founders, former presidents, or other historical figures whose flaws have received substantial publicity in recent years. George Washington owned enslaved people, but the Washington Monument exists because of his contributions to the building of a nation. There is no logical equivalence between the builders and protectors of a nation—however imperfect—and the men who sought to sunder that nation in the name of slavery. There will be, and should be, debate about other people and events honored in our civic spaces. And precedents do matter. But so does historical specificity, and in this case the invocation of flawed analogies should not derail legitimate policy conversation.[28]

When considering New Deal art that is deemed controversial, the most relevant part of the AHA statement is "all memorials remain artifacts of their time and place. They should be preserved, just like any other historical document, whether in a museum or some other appropriate venue." So, too, New Deal art remains an artifact of its time and place, and should be preserved, just like other historical documents.

When a building that includes mural art becomes obsolete or hazardous in some way, preserving the art should be a high priority. The best way to deal with a structurally sound but obsolete building may be to repurpose the building and preserve the art. This was done in San Francisco in the cases of the Rincon Annex and the Alemany Health Center.[29] Post office murals were often oil on canvas that were glued to post office walls. Such murals have been successfully removed and relocated when the original site was to be razed or significantly modified.[30] To save the murals at the

Rincon Annex, the development project was designed to save the part of the building with the murals. The Zakheim murals at UCSF were successfully removed from a building that has now been demolished. That project also demonstrates that at least some New Deal murals, even fresco murals, may be portable. And New Deal art that is portable is protected by federal law.

Perhaps the most important lesson to take away from the San Francisco experience is that New Deal art should be preserved regardless of the objections of today's critics. Public officials should not destroy yesterday's public art, because that would deprive people tomorrow from drawing their own conclusions about the art. New Deal art, considered in the context of its time and with appreciation for the intent of the artists, will continue to be reinterpreted in the future, but that will not happen if the art is destroyed.

If there is a general consensus that a work of New Deal art is in some way objectionable because of its depiction of people or events, there are alternatives to destruction. First and foremost, there needs to be interpretive signage, identifying the artist and explaining, as far as known, the artist's purpose. Such signage might include a forthright statement of what is considered objectionable in the mural. In some cases, it may be appropriate to cover the mural or part of the mural with a curtain or other screen that can be removed to study the art and replaced to cover the objectionable features. Some museums have found creative ways to deal with such situations, notably the New-York Historical Society's treatment of a diorama in such a way that instructs viewers regarding its historical inaccuracies.[31]

Protecting New Deal public art by means of existing or future laws may not be sufficient to preserve such cultural heritage treasures. Some New Deal art projects raised objections when they were created, and some have been decried since, and some will no doubt draw objections in the future. If representative democracy is to serve a broadly defined and long-term-focused public interest in decisions about public art, then, as the American Historical Association recommended, "Communities faced with decisions about monuments [should] draw upon the expertise of historians both for understanding the facts and chronology underlying such monuments and for deriving interpretive conclusions based on evidence."[32]

APPENDIX

The Coit Tower Artists

Ruth Zakheim Gottstein, the daughter of Bernard Zakheim the muralist, was eleven years old when her father was painting his mural at Coit Tower and included a portrait of her. She recalled in 2012:

> They were artists . . . first and foremost. Not politicians, not intellectuals, not economists. They came from vastly different backgrounds. . . . Via their murals, this eclectic group of artists was able to capture the rich tapestry of an emerging California in the 1930s. This was their San Francisco and their California—their hopes for a positive future for many generations to come.[1]

Though some of the artists were well known before the start of the undertaking, the Coit Tower project helped to launch many of the others on productive careers. Many of them went on to create more public art under New Deal art program auspices, and several developed distinguished careers as artists. The following paragraphs briefly summarize their contributions, especially their work on public murals.

Maxine Albro (1903–1966)

Albro was among the more experienced fresco painters at Coit Tower. Born in Iowa, she grew up in Los Angeles. After graduating from high school, she moved to San Francisco and began working as a commercial artist to raise funds for her study at the Art Students League in New York, in Paris, and at the California School ofFine Arts (CSFA). She and Parker Hall traveled widely in Mexico and painted many scenes of Mexican life. Although she did not study formally with Diego Rivera, she watched him as he painted and talked with him. She also watched José Clemente Orozco, another of the leading Mexican muralists, and studied fresco painting with Pablo O'Higgins, one of Rivera's assistants and a significant muralist in his own right. She was influenced by Rivera's style, and upon returning from Mexico, she painted several privately commissioned fresco murals. She assisted Rivera in his San Francisco murals. After her Coit Tower mural, she received commissions for other New Deal art projects, including a mosaic mural (no longer extant) at San Francisco State College and a mural for Vallejo High School. Albro married fellow Coit Tower artist Parker Hall in 1938. They moved to Carmel, California, and became leaders and highly influential members of the Carmel artists' colony.[2]

Victor Mikhail Arnautoff (1896–1979)

Arnautoff was one of the most experienced fresco painters at Coit Tower. He grew up in Mariupol, now in Ukraine but then part of the Russian Empire. He studied at the CSFA in the late 1920s and then went to Mexico, where he assisted Diego Rivera for two years, including the murals at Cuernavaca and at the National Palace. Arnautoff returned to San Francisco in 1931. As technical coordinator for the Coit Tower project, he advised his fellow artists at the same time he painted the mural *City Life*. He produced the most New Deal art of any of the Coit Tower artists: a large mural at the Protestant chapel at the Presidio of San Francisco (funded by SERA and contributor to the National Historic Landmark District), thirteen panels on the life and era of George Washington at George Washington High School, San Francisco (funded by the WPA/FAP and listed in Historic American Buildings Survey #CA-2939; local landmark nomination pending), post office murals at College Station, Texas (no longer extant); Linden, Texas; Pacific Grove, California; Richmond, California (now in that city's history museum); and South San Francisco, California. He also produced public murals at the Old Cathedral of the Holy Virgin (City of San Francisco Landmark No. 28), the former Palo Alto Medical Clinic (National Register #10000357; also listed in the Palo Alto Historic Buildings Inventory), and three fresco lunettes in the library of the San Francisco Art Institute (National Register #15000950; City of San Francisco Landmark No. 85). He taught at Stanford University for twenty-four years after a short time teaching at the CSFA. Toward the end of his life, he returned to Mariupol and produced three large mosaic murals there, now likely destroyed along with most of that city. After completing those murals, he moved to Leningrad (St. Petersburg), where he died.[3]

Jane Clara Berlandina (1898–1970)

Born in France, Berlandina studied in Paris at the École nationale supérieure des Arts Décoratifs with Henri Matisse and Raoul Dufy and exhibited at the Paris Salon. She came to New York in 1928 and soon had an exhibition at a prestigious gallery. She married Henry Temple Howard, and they came to California in 1931. By 1933 she was well known for her modernist watercolors and had exhibited at the Museum of Modern Art in New York. At Coit Tower her work is quite abstract compared to the prevalent American Scene style and was painted using egg-based tempera rather than the fresco technique and the palette used by the others. After her Coit Tower work, she continued to paint in oils and watercolors, exhibiting at prestigious galleries in San Francisco and New York as well as at San Francisco art museums. She also created a mural for the Golden Gate International Exposition.[4]

Raymond Clarence Bertrand (1909–1986)

Bertrand, a native San Franciscan, studied at the CSFA. In 1936 he became the lead printer for the Graphics Arts Division of the California WPA/FAP, where he developed a new transfer paper for lithography. He later taught lithography at the CSFA and made a reputation as an easel artist, especially of landscapes, and a lithographer. One of his works is held by the National Gallery of Art.[5]

Ray Sceptre Boynton (1883–1951)

Among the Coit Tower artists, Boynton may have had the most prior experience with fresco. He grew up on an Iowa farm, studied at the Chicago Academy of Fine Arts, and then spent seven years at manual labor in eastern Washington before coming to San Francisco in 1915, where he made a name for himself as an artist. He began to experiment with fresco in 1917, created perhaps the earliest successful outdoor fresco in the West, and joined the faculty of the CSFA in the early 1920s. There he taught fresco, among other courses, the first such course in the area if not the region. In 1926 he traveled to Mexico to observe Rivera at work. In 1928, at Mills College in Oakland, he created large-scale fresco murals. Boynton's expertise and seniority made him the "dean of the fresco painters" at Coit Tower, where younger artists sought his advice. His subsequent New Deal–funded projects included twelve lunettes at the post office in Modesto, California. He was privately commissioned to do two fresco lunettes in the library of the California School of Fine Arts (National Register #15000950; City of San Francisco Landmark No. 85). Later, Boynton became a faculty member at the University of California, Berkeley; he retired to New Mexico.[6]

Ralph (Raphael Alexandre) Chessé (1900–1991)

Chessé was born in New Orleans to Creole (mixed-race) parents. He grew up in New Orleans and Chicago, attended the Chicago Art Institute in 1918, but was largely self-taught as an artist. A sculptor, painter, and puppeteer, he moved to California in 1923. In the 1920s he divided his time among acting, marionette shows, and exhibiting his paintings, drawings, and block prints. His Coit Tower mural, *Children at Play*, presents its characters in an almost puppet-like manner. He later reflected that he had been influenced by American colonial portraits of children. Following the Coit Tower project, Chessé became the official director of puppetry for the San Francisco, Oakland, and Los Angeles districts of the WPA. Chessé, along with his son Bruce, worked extensively for decades as a professional puppeteer, creating and performing the marionettes for the pioneering Bay Area children's television show *Brother Buzz*. His Coit Tower mural was his first and only work in that medium.[7]

Rinaldo Cuneo (1877–1939)

Cuneo was one of the four Coit Tower muralists who chose not to work in fresco. He was born in San Francisco's North Beach neighborhood, center of the city's Italian community. After three years in the U.S. Navy, he studied at the Mark Hopkins Institute of Art (later the CSFA). He then traveled to London and Paris to study art. Upon returning to San Francisco, he specialized in painting landscapes, especially mountains. He had a number of exhibitions in the mid- and late 1920s, usually of landscapes, including one in Rome, and he occasionally taught painting at the CSFA. He exhibited a still life at the Museum of Modern Art in New York in 1933; his works are held by the San Francisco Museum of Modern Art, the Los Angeles County Museum of Art, the Huntington, and the Museo Italo-Americo of San Francisco.[8]

Benjamin Frazier Cunningham (1904–1975)

Born in Colorado, Cunningham studied briefly at the University of Nevada and then at the CSFA. Under various New Deal arts programs, he produced murals for the San Francisco City Assessor's Office, the post office at Ukiah, California, and the Golden Gate International Exposition. He also served as the supervisor for mural painting for the Northern California WPA/FAP. He then moved to the New York City area, where he taught in several art schools. His work was acquired by the Museum of Modern Art, the Guggenheim, and the Whitney.[9]

Harold Mallette Dean (1907–1975)

Born in Washington, Dean came to California and studied at the CSFA beginning in 1927. He later painted a mural in the Sebastopol post office, worked as a book illustrator, and taught printmaking at the CSFA. His works are held by the San Francisco Museum of Modern Art, de Young Museum, New York Public Library, Library of Congress, Smithsonian American Art Museum, and the University of San Francisco Library.[10]

Parker Lee Hall (1898–1982)

Born in Colorado, Hall graduated from the University of California, Berkeley, and then attended the CSFA. He and Maxine Albro traveled to Mexico, where they watched Rivera at work on the murals at Cuernavaca. Hall later recalled, "The thing to do there was just to sit all day and watch him paint," and then return to the United States and "experiment." After Coit Tower, he worked on WPA/FAP projects as a sculptor and became an accomplished etcher and lithographer. He and Albro married in 1938 and moved to Carmel, California.[11]

Edith Anne Hamlin (1902–1992)

Born in Oakland, Edith Hamlin attended the CSFA from 1922 to 1924 and later Columbia University Teacher's College in New York City. She exhibited landscapes and scenes of the Southwest in the early 1930s and executed a few private commissions for murals. After the Coit Tower project, she created two large murals at Mission High School, San Francisco (City of San Francisco Landmark No. 256); three murals at the Tracy, California, post office; and a mural, jointly with her husband, Maynard Dixon, at the Martinez, California, post office. She and Dixon moved to Tucson, Arizona, where she painted four public murals, along with one in Phoenix, between 1947 and 1952. After Dixon's death, Hamlin returned to San Francisco.[12]

George Albert Harris (1912–1991)

The youngest of the Coit Tower muralists, Harris was a student at the CSFA at the time he painted his mural in Coit Tower. In his mural of a law library, he used fanciful or humorous titles for law books, and attributed many of them to his fellow artists. He later did other murals for private commissions and established a reputation with his easel paintings. In 1950 he created a twenty-seven-foot-long mural for the San Francisco

Chamber of Commerce. He earned a PhD at Stanford University and became professor of art there. His works are represented in the San Francisco Museum of Modern Art, the Library of Congress, and the National Gallery of Art in Washington, D.C. In later life he moved to England and then to southern France.[13]

William Jurgen Hesthal (1908–1985)

Born in San Francisco, Hesthal began attending classes at the CSFA at age nine and first exhibited at age ten. Following the Coit Tower project, Hesthal was one of the six Coit Tower muralists commissioned by Albert Bender in 1936 to paint lunettes in the library at the CSFA (National Register #15000950; City of San Francisco Landmark No. 85). Hesthal completed a mural for Tamalpais High School in Mill Valley, California, and a series of lithographs through the WPA/FAP program. He later studied in China and Mexico before moving to Santa Barbara, where he became a curator at Santa Barbara Museum and taught at Moorpark and Ventura colleges before retiring.[14]

John Langley Howard (1902–1999)

Born in New Jersey, Howard moved to California with his parents as an infant. At the University of California, Berkeley, he majored in engineering and English and then enrolled at the California College of Arts and Crafts. Later he continued his studies at the Art Students League in New York City. As the son of an architect, John Galen Howard, and brother to an architect, Henry Temple Howard, and a sculptor, Robert Boardman Howard, he was part of a large and talented family well known for their contribution to the arts. At the time of the Coit Tower project, he was convinced that he could contribute to the advancement of society through his art. He thought Zakheim was "a punster and a jokester" and that the depiction of him reaching for *Das Kapital* was "a joke." This was his only fresco mural. He later specialized in easel painting, including illustrations of fishing equipment for magazines and specialized machines for *Scientific American*.[15]

Lucien Adolphe Labaudt (1880–1943)

A native of Paris, France, Labaudt began as a designer, especially costumes and stage scenery, but was inspired by a work by Cézanne to begin painting. He came to the United States in 1906 and to San Francisco in 1910, hoping to create murals, but found that costume design paid the bills. He taught costume and fashion design at the CSFA and then opened his own school of design. At the same time, his paintings—landscapes, still lifes, nudes, and abstracts—were included in exhibitions in San Francisco, Los Angeles, New York, and Paris and some received prizes. After Coit Tower, he continued to create murals and easel paintings. His murals depicting outdoor life in San Francisco cover all the walls of the first floor of the Beach Chalet, San Francisco (City of San Francisco Landmark No. 179; National Register #81000172). Labaudt also did one mural at George Washington High School, San Francisco (HABS #CA-2939) and two murals for what was then the Los Angeles Post Office and Courthouse and is now the Spring Street Courthouse (National Historic Landmark as of 2012). Though his public murals are examples of realism, his easel paintings of the same period provide examples of surrealism. He died in World War II while on assignment as an artist war correspondent.[16]

Gordon Langdon (1910–1963)

Born in San Francisco, Langdon left his studies at Stanford to study at the CSFA. His family's ranch at Olema, California, provided the subject for his Coit Tower mural, in which he painted a self-portrait as well as portraits of Labaudt (with a cow) and Stackpole (peeking in the window). Langdon later painted a small fresco mural funded by the WPA/FAP at George Washington High School (HABS #CA-2939) and was one of six of the Coit Tower artists commissioned to paint fresco lunettes inside the library at the CSFA (National Register #15000950; City of San Francisco Landmark No. 85). After serving in World War II, he abandoned his art career and entered the hardware business.[17]

José Moya del Pino (1891–1969)

A native of Spain, Moya del Pino graduated from the Academy of Fine Arts in Madrid and had important commissions in Spain, including a portrait of the king, before coming to the United States with a traveling exhibition. He remained in San Francisco, where he worked as a portrait painter, did easel paintings for exhibitions, and was commissioned to do three large murals for the Merchants' Exchange Club. Soon after the Coit Tower project, he was commissioned to do a series of murals in the Aztec Brewery in San Diego, parts of which are now in a San Diego public library, three murals in the Acme Brewery in San Francisco, which are still extant and have recently been restored, and three large murals for the Biltmore Hotel in Santa Barbara. He also received Treasury Section commissions for two murals in the Stockton Federal Building, and for murals in post offices, at Lancaster, California; Alpine, Texas; and Redwood City, California.[18]

Otis Oldfield (1890–1969)

Oldfield was born in Sacramento. Desiring to become an artist, he studied at a private art school in San Francisco and then went to Paris in 1911, studied at the Académie Julian, exhibited at Salon d'Automne and the Société des Artistes Indépendants, and remained in Paris, with his work interrupted by service in the French army during World War I, for which he received the French War Cross. He returned to the United States in 1924, began teaching at the CSFA in 1925, but continued to exhibit, including watercolors of San Francisco scenes in New York. A near-nude he painted was awarded first prize at the 1933 California State Fair. After Coit Tower, Oldfield continued to teach and also worked in the WPA/FAP lithograph projects in San Francisco. He served as a draftsman on military projects during World War II, then resumed his artistic career and began teaching at the California College of Arts and Crafts in Oakland, California. He is remembered for his figure paintings and his many depictions of scenes of San Francisco in his oils, watercolors, lithographs, and drawings. The Achenbach Foundation of the Palace of the Legion of Honor in San Francisco has a large collection of his works on paper, and his works are also represented in the National Gallery of Art, San Francisco Museum of Modern Art, Oakland Museum, de Young Museum, Brooklyn Museum, Smithsonian American Art Museum, Los Angeles County Museum of Art, and Metropolitan Museum of Art.[19]

Frederick Erskine Olmsted Jr. (1911–1990)

Olmsted was born in San Francisco and was the great nephew of Frederick Law Olmsted, the landscape architect who designed New York's Central Park. He was educated at Stanford University and later studied with Ralph Stackpole. A painter and sculptor, the twenty-three-year-old Olmsted initially came to the Coit Tower project as an assistant artist to Frede Vidar, George Harris, and John Langley Howard. Howard later assigned him the small panel above the main entrance, where Olmsted created his own mural, *Power*, depicting a left fist bursting through flames. He received one of the commissions for a fresco lunette in the CSFA library (National Register #15000950; City of San Francisco Landmark No. 85). Olmsted later completed a mural and two sculptures, which were subsequently moved to San Francisco City College, both done initially as part of the *Art in Action* exhibition at the Golden Gate International Exposition. Olmsted eventually abandoned his art career and became a successful biophysicist, specializing in designing medical and oceanographic equipment.[20]

Suzanne Scheuer (1898–1984)

Scheuer was born in San Jose, California, graduated from the California College of Arts and Crafts, and later studied mural painting with Boynton at the CSFA. She did a few small murals before her Coit Tower project. Her mural *Newsgathering* on the tower's west wall was restored by the artist herself in 1963, twenty-nine years after she first painted it. She took the initiative to change the name of the fictional newspaper she painted in the mural to *Chronicle*. She did three post office murals commissioned by the Treasury Section, in Eastland, Texas; Caldwell, Texas; and Berkeley, California. She later taught art at the College of the Pacific in Stockton, California, before retiring to Santa Cruz, California, where she designed six houses.[21]

Ralph Ward Stackpole (1885–1973)

Stackpole grew up in Oregon. He began to study at the Mark Hopkins Art Institute (predecessor of the CSFA) at the age of sixteen, then went to Paris to study at the École des Beaux-Arts. While in Paris, he began a lifelong friendship with Diego Rivera. He returned to the United States and studied with Robert Henri in New York before coming back to San Francisco, where he began his career as a sculptor, muralist, etcher, and educator. He became one of the city's leading artists during the 1920s and 1930s, based on his sculptures at the Panama-Pacific International Exposition in 1915, the Paramount Theater in Oakland (1931, National Register #73000395; HABS CAL,1-OAK,9-; Oakland City Landmark #9), and the remodeled Pacific Coast Stock Exchange (1932), and his teaching at the California School of Fine Arts. After visiting Rivera in Mexico and observing his work in 1924, Stackpole was primarily responsible for bringing Diego Rivera to San Francisco in 1930. In addition to Stackpole's Coit Tower mural, he also did a mural at George Washington High School, San Francisco (HABS #CA-2939), and two lunettes in the library of the CSFA (National Register #15000950; City of San Francisco Landmark No. 85) before returning to sculpture. In 1938, at the request of President Franklin D. Roosevelt, he did a recreation of his sculpture *Reverence*, from 1915. His other works include an eighty-foot-high sculpture, *Pacifica*, for the Golden Gate International Exposition (1938–1941) and a large bas-relief sculpture of John Wesley Powell for the U.S. Department of the Interior Building in Washington, D.C. (1940). He served on the U.S. Commission of Fine Arts in 1941–1945, the first person from the West Coast to do so. In 1949 he moved to France and remained there for the rest of his life.[22]

Takeo Edward Terada (1908–1993)

Born in Japan, Terada immigrated to California with his family in 1922. He studied briefly at the University of California, Berkeley, and then at the California School of Fine Arts. Terada returned to Japan in 1935, initially intending to stay briefly, but found his art was popular and decided to stay. He settled in Tokyo, where he became a leading force in the Japanese art world. In 1984 one of his paintings won the Emperor's Award.[23]

Frede Jensen Vidar (1911–1967)

Vidar was born in Denmark and came to the Bay Area with his parents as a teenager. He studied at the CSFA and in Paris. He returned to Paris for further study after the Coit Tower project. A combat artist during World War II, he received a prestigious Guggenheim grant in 1946. He exhibited widely and became a member of the art faculty at the University of Michigan in 1950. His work is represented in New York City's Museum of Modern Art.[24]

Clifford Seymour Wight (ca. 1900–1961)

Wight was born in England and immigrated to Canada, where he became a Mountie before joining the military in World War I. He studied with Stackpole in San Francisco in the mid-1920s and then went to Mexico, where he met Diego Rivera. He worked as Rivera's secretary, translator, and assistant in San Francisco, New York, and Detroit. Wight returned to England and later had a career teaching sculpture and as a secretary in the British House of Commons.[25]

Bernard Baruch Zakheim (1896–1985)

Zakheim, along with Albro, Arnautoff, and Boynton, were the most experienced in fresco before the Coit Tower project. He arrived in San Francisco in 1920 seeking political asylum from his native Poland, where he had been imprisoned at the end of World War I. He found work as a furniture maker while he continued to look for opportunities to pursue art. In 1929 Diego Rivera, to whom Zakheim had sent some sketches, invited him to Mexico City for six months to collaborate and to study Aztec and Mayan art in the National Museum of Mexico. In 1932 Zakheim spent a year in Europe studying art; he learned to paint fresco murals during that time. Upon his return to San Francisco, he won a competition to create a fresco in the courtyard of the city's new Jewish Community Center. After the Coit Tower project, he produced two murals at the Alemany Health Center, San Francisco, and two projects—one of two mural panels and the other of ten mural panels—at what became the University of California, San Francisco. He also produced post office murals at Rusk and Mineola, Texas. In later life he turned to sculpture and produced six wooden sculptures commemorating the Holocaust.[26]

Notes

Chapter 1. The Origin of the Coit Tower Murals

1. Among the standard treatments of the era are William E. Leuchtenburg, *Franklin D. Roosevelt and the New Deal* (New York: Harper, 1963), and David M. Kennedy, *Freedom from Fear: The American People in Depression and War, 1929–1945* (New York: Oxford University Press, 1999).

2. Paul Webbink, "Unemployment in the United States, 1930–1940," *Papers and Proceedings of the American Economic Association* 30 (1941): 250–251; Emily H. Huntington, *Unemployment Relief and the Unemployed in the San Francisco Bay Region: 1929–1934* (Berkeley: University of California Press, 1939), esp. pp. 7, 9, 34; William H. Mullins, *The Depression and the Urban West Coast, 1929–1933: Los Angeles, San Francisco, Seattle, and Portland* (Bloomington: Indiana University Press, 1991), 36–38, 52, 73–75, 92, 102–104, 118; Christopher VerPlanck and Donna Graves, "San Francisco New Deal Historic Context Statement: Rebuilding the City, 1933 to 1943" (approved by the Historic Preservation Commission on March 1, 2023). Some of the bond issues were approved before 1929, but the actual work came after; the Bay Bridge also benefited from funds from the federal Reconstruction Finance Corporation.

3. Katherine Petrin, Robert W. Cherny, and Jon Golinger, National Register of Historic Places Nomination Form for Coit Tower, Nov. 2017, section 7, p. 5. For a summary of information about Lillie Hitchcock Coit and the construction of the tower, see Masha Zakheim, *Coit Tower, San Francisco: Its History and Art*, 2nd ed. (Volcano, CA: Volcano Press, 2009), pp. 4–11.

4. Webbink, "Unemployment in the United States, 1930–1940"; for CP demonstrations, see, e.g., *San Francisco Chronicle*, Jan. 7, 8, 20, 1931, and Louise Todd Lambert, interviewed by Lucy Kendall, May 27, 1975, tape 2, Labor Archives and Research Center, San Francisco State University. Party membership data can be tracked from 1931 to early 1934 in f7, b1, Samuel Adams Darcy Papers, Wagner Labor Archives, New York University; *Chronicle*, Nov. 4, 1931, p. 1; Nov. 9, 1933, p. 11. See also Robert W. Cherny, *San Francisco Reds: Communists in the Bay Area, 1919–1958* (Urbana: University of Illinois Press, 2024), ch. 3.

5. Robert W. Cherny, *Victor Arnautoff and the Politics of Art* (Urbana: University of Illinois Press, 2017), pp. 45–46, 75; Idwal Jones, *Ark of Empire: San*

Francisco's Montgomery Block (Garden City, NY: Doubleday, 1951), esp. pp. 233–38; Harvey Smith, "The Art Culture of the New Deal in the San Francisco Bay Area," https://www.foundsf.org/index.php?title=New_Deal_Artists_and_Programs_During_the_Depression. The location of various artists' studios can be traced through the Crocker-Langley City Directory. See also Thomas Albright, *Art in the San Francisco Bay Area, 1945–1980: An Illustrated History* (Berkeley: University of California Press, 1985), p. 4; Linda Gordon, *Dorothea Lange: A Life beyond Limits* (New York: W. W. Norton, 2009), chs. 3–5.

6. Cherny, *Victor Arnautoff*, ch 4. The social status of the SFAA board members can be traced through the *San Francisco Blue Book and Club Directory* (San Francisco: Alexander Dulfer and Jed J. Hoag, Publishers, 1925).

7. For Boynton's murals, see Howard Putzel, "Ray Boynton's Mural Decorations at Mills College," *American Magazine of Art* 20 (1929): 335–338; "Ray Boynton," *California Art Research*, ed. Gene Hailey (San Francisco: Works Progress Administration, 1936–1937, https://digitalassets.lib.berkeley.edu/cara/ucb/text/, v. 9, pp. 1–29, esp. 18–19 (repaginated online as 1226–1258). For Piazzoni's murals, see "Gottardo Piazzoni," in Hailey, *California Art Research*, v. 7, pp. 31–87, esp. 75–77 (repaginated online as 0971–1033). The library murals are now installed at the De Young Museum, San Francisco.

8. *California Art Research*, First Series, v. 14, W.P.A. Project 2874, O.P. 650303632 (mimeographed, San Francisco, 1937). There is a thick file of letters from Rivera to Stackpole, all in French, in the Ralph Stackpole Papers, box 1, folder "Rivera, Diego," Bancroft Library, University of California, Berkeley.

9. Albright, *Art in the San Francisco Bay Area*, p. 4.

10. *San Francisco Chronicle*, Nov. 9, 1932, p. 1; Leuchtenburg, *FDR and the New Deal*, pp. 121–124.

11. There is a rich literature on the Mexican muralists and Mexican Modernism more generally. See, e.g., Desmond Rochfort, *Mexican Muralists: Orozco, Rivera, Siqueiros* (London: Laurence King, 1993); Leonard Folgarait, *Mural Painting and Social Revolution in Mexico, 1920–1940: Art of the New Order* (Cambridge: Cambridge University Press, 1998); Alejandro Anreus et al., eds., *Mexican Muralism: A Critical History* (Berkeley: University of California Press, 2012); Laura Almeida, "What Is Mexican Modernism," Denver Art Museum, https://www.denverartmuseum.org/en/blog/what-mexican-modernism/; James Oles, *Diego Rivera's America* (San Francisco: San Francisco Museum of Modern Art in association with University of California Press, 2022).

12. On the influence of the Mexican muralists on American artists, see, e.g., Francis V. O'Connor, "The Influence of Diego Rivera on the Art of the United States During the 1930s and After," in *Diego Rivera: A Retrospective*, ed. Cynthia Newman Helms (New York: W. W. Norton, 1986); Peter Selz, "The Impact from Abroad: Foreign Guests and Visitors," in *On the Edge of America: California Modernist Art, 1900–1950*, ed. Paul J. Karlstrom (Berkeley: University of California Press, 1996). A recent account is Barbara Haskell, ed., *Vida Americana: Mexican Muralists Remake American Art, 1925–1945* (a joint publication of Whitney Museum of American Art, New York, and Yale University Press, New Haven, 2020), the catalog for an exhibition at the Whitney Museum; Maria Castro, "Diego Rivera's New American Art: San Francisco, 1930–31," in Oles, ed., *Diego Rivera's America*, pp. 110–161. For Orozco's study at the CSFA, see Enrollment Records Collection, 1917, San Francisco Art Institute Legacy Foundation+Archive, San Francisco; and John Crosse, "Orozco in San Francisco, 1917–1919," *Southern*

California Architectural History (March 21, 2017), https://socalarchhistory.blogspot.com/2017/03/orozco-in-san-francisco-1917.html/.

13. Letter, George Biddle to Franklin D. Roosevelt, May 9, 1933, quoted in O'Connor, "Influence of Diego Rivera on the Art of the United States," p. 170.

14. For the creation of the PWAP, see, e.g., Lenore Clark, *Forbes Watson: Independent Revolutionary* (Kent, OH: Kent State University Press, 2001), pp. 104–109; Richard D. McKinzie, *The New Deal for Artists* (Princeton, NJ: Princeton University Press, 1973), ch. 3–11. The photo appears in Clark, *Forbes Watson*, p. 106, and in McKinzie, *New Deal for Artists*, p. 11. Ben Davis, in "The Myths about FDR's New Deal Arts Programs Are Misleading: Here Are the Real Lessons for Struggling Artists Today," *artnet*, Feb. 25, 2021 (https://news.artnet.com/art-world-archives/new-deal-art-projects-lessons-1946590), argues that pressures from left intellecturals and artists were as significant as Biddle's letter.

15. Form letter, in file "Form Letters from Edward Bruce to Dr. Walter Heil," PWAP files, De Young Museum, San Francisco, CA.

16. Form letter, Bruce to all regional directors, May 2, 1934, PWAP files, De Young Museum.

17. Marlene Park and Gerald E. Markowitz, *Democratic Vistas: Post Offices and Public Art in the New Deal* (Philadelphia: Temple University Press, 1984), p. 6.

18. Belisario R. Contreras, *Tradition and Innovation in New Deal Art* (Lewisburg, PA: Bucknell University Press, 1983), pp. 22–23; Karal Ann Marling, *Wall-to-Wall America: A Cultural History of Post-Office Murals in the Great Depression* (Minneapolis: University of Minnesota Press, 1982), p. 45.

19. Clark, *Forbes Watson*, p. 111.

20. Park and Markowitz, *Democratic Vistas*, p. 5.

21. E.g., *New Deal Art in Georgia: A Guide to Post Office Murals and Sculpture* (Athens: Georgia Museum of Art, University of Georgia, 1990); Philip Parisi, *Texas Post Office Murals: Art for the People* (College Station: Texas A&M Press, 2016); Bernice L. Thomas, *The Stamp of FDR: New Deal Post Offices in the Mid-Hudson Valley* (Fleischmanns, NY: Purple Mountain Press, 2002); Nicholas A. Calcagno, *New Deal Murals in Oklahoma: A Bicentennial Project* (Miami, OK: Pioneer Printing, 1976); Eileen Toutant, *New Deal Murals in Kentucky Post Offices* (Louisville, KY: University of Louisville, 2000); *A Common Canvas: Pennsylvania's New Deal Post Office Murals* (Harrisburg: Pennsylvania Historical and Museum Commission, 2008); Mary Motian-Meadows, *Western Visions: Colorado's New Deal Post Office Murals* (Denver: Colorado Historical Society, 1991); L. Robert Puschendorf, *Nebraska's Post Office Murals: Born of the Depression, Fostered by the New Deal* (Lincoln: Nebraska State Historical Society, 2012).

22. The sixty-eight murals at the Department of Justice Building in Washington were created by fourteen artists over six years; the forty-six murals in the Department of the Interior Building were done by twenty-one artists over five years, and twenty-two murals in the former Post Office Department Building were done by thirteen artists over four years.

23. I arrive at the figure of twenty-eight by considering Wight's figures around the east windows to be one mural, and similarly for Wight's figures around the west windows and Dean's figures around the south windows; Berlandina's mural on four walls to be one mural; Hamlin's mural on three walls to be one mural; Oldfield's lunettes over the doors in the lobby to be one mural; and that Cuneo did two murals. By counting each panel or wall separately and including the three that had been destroyed, Heil identified forty-two murals in his final report. See

"Public Works of Art Project: Region No. 15, mimeographed report of artists, their work, Costs, etc., December 1933 to 1934," Walter Heil Papers, Archives of American Art, Smithsonian Institution.

Chapter 2. Creating the Coit Tower Murals

1. Tape-recorded interview by Lewis Ferbrache with Bernard Baruch Zakheim, Sebastopol, California, 1964, Archives of American Art; hereafter, AAA.

2. Zakheim oral history, AAA; on Zakheim's unwillingness to acknowledge his CP membership, see Joseph Danysh interviewed by Lewis Ferbrache, Dec. 3, 1964, AAA.

3. Edward Bruce to Walter Heil, telegram, Dec. 10, 1933, Region 15 papers, National Archives; *San Francisco Chronicle*, Dec. 14, 1933, p. 6; Zakheim oral history, AAA.

4. Walter Heil to Edward Rowan, January 12, 1934, Region 15 papers, National Archives; Raymond L. Wilson, "The Northern Scene," in *American Scene Painting: California, 1930s and 1940s*, ed. Ruth Westphal and Janet Blake Dominik (Irvine, CA: Westphal Publishing, 1991; available online at https://tfaoi.org/aa/3aa/3aa52.htm); Masha Zakheim, *Coit Tower, San Francisco: Its History and Art*, 2nd ed. (Volcano, CA: Volcano Press, 2009), pp. 14–15; Jeffrey T. Tillman, *Arthur Brown Jr.: Progressive Classicist* (New York: W. W. Norton, 2006), 187–191. There are a number of accounts of the December 8 meeting; see, e.g., Belisario R. Contreras, *Tradition and Innovation in New Deal Art* (Lewisburg, PA: Bucknell University Press, 1983), pp. 40–41; or, on the relation to the CWA, see Bonnie Fox Schwartz, *The Civil Works Administration, 1933–1934: The Business of Emergency Employment in the New Deal* (Princeton, NJ: Princeton University Press, 1984), pp. 137–138.

5. Anthony Lee, in his book *Painting on the Left: Diego Rivera, Radical Politics, and San Francisco's Public Murals* (Berkeley: University of California Press, 1999), pp. 130–134, draws upon Zakheim's 1964 interview to conclude that Zakheim was in charge of organizing the artists. That claim is refuted both in the press and in several oral histories by the artists; see *San Francisco Chronicle*, Dec. 15, 1933, 25, and oral history interviews with Suzanne Scheuer, July 29, 1964; Maxine Albro and Parker Hall, July 27, 1964; William Hesthal, Dec. 22, 1964; and Ralph Chessé, Oct. 22, 1964, all AAA, Smithsonian Institution.

6. All the master artists, assistant artists, and assistants are listed in Heil's final report, Public Works of Art Project, Region 15, a mimeographed report of artists, their work, costs, etc., December 1933 to 1934; Walter Heil Papers, AAA, hereafter PWAP Region 15 final report. Heil's notebook and final report indicate that one of the master artists, William Gaw, withdrew but served as a volunteer assistant, and that one assistant artist, Frederick Olmsted, was briefly raised to a master artist, leaving the total at twenty-five. Olmsted thus appears in the final report as both a master artist and an assistant. The three artists who worked with oil and canvas had no assistants. See also Nadia Lavrova, "Forty-Six Artists—One Palette," *Christian Science Monitor*, Weekly Magazine Section, Aug. 1, 1934, pp. 8–9; oral history interview with Otis Oldfield, May 21, 1965; oral history interview with John Langley Howard and Mary Howard, Sept. 5, 1991, both in AAA, Smithsonian Institution; see also Robert W. Cherny, "Controversy at Coit Tower, 1934: Communist Conspiracy or Tempest in a Teapot," *The Argonaut* 28, no. 1 (Summer 2017): 73; Cherny, *Victor Arnautoff and the Politics of Art* (University of Illinois Press, 2017), pp. 82–83.

7. Francis V. O'Connor, "The Influence of Diego Rivera on the Art of the United States During the 1930s and After," in *Diego Rivera: A Retrospective*, ed. Cynthia Newman Helms (New York: W. W. Norton, 1986), pp. 170–171.

8. The most extensive treatment of the three murals Rivera created in the Bay Area in 1930–1931 is that by Maria Castro, "Diego Rivera's New American Art: San Francisco, 1930–31," in Oles, *Diego Rivera's America,* pp. 110–161.

9. Lavrova, "Forty-Six Artists—One Palette"; oral history interview with John Langley Howard and Mary Howard, Sept. 5, 1991, both in AAA, Smithsonian Institution; see also Cherny, "Controversy at Coit Tower," p. 73; Cherny, *Victor Arnautoff,* pp. 82–83.

10. U.S. Department of Commerce, Bureau of the Census, *Fifteenth Census of the United States,* Table 15, vol. 3, *1930 Census of Population,* https://www.census.gov/library/publications/1932/dec/1930a-vol-03-population.html/; Table 4, vol. 4, *1930 Census of Population,* https://www2.census.gov/library/publications/decennial/1930/population-volume-4/41129482v4ch03.pdf/. For the members of the Artists Council, see *San Francisco Art Association Bulletin* (June 1934), p. 5, available through the Internet Archive and at the SFAI Legacy Foundation+Archive, San Francisco.

11. Oldfield oral history, AAA; José Moya del Pino interviewed by Mary Fuller McChesney, Sept. 10, 1964, AAA; Stacey Moss, *The Howards: First Family of Bay Area Modernism* (Oakland, CA: Oakland Museum, 1988), pp. 68–69.

12. PWAP Region 15 final report; minutes of the Art Commission of the City and County of San Francisco, 1934 http://archive.org/stream/minutesofartcomm1934sanf#page/n0/mode/1up/, pp. 159, 161, 179; Cherny, "Controversy at Coit Tower," p. 77.

13. Albro and Hall oral history, AAA.

14. Francis V. O'Connor, a leading art historian of New Deal art, later commented on the relation of the largest murals to the "exterior world" and related that to the influence of Rivera; see O'Connor, "Influence of Diego Rivera," p. 122.

15. Evelyn Seeley, "A Frescoed Tower Clangs Shut amid Gasps," *Literary Digest,* Aug. 25, 1934, pp. 24, 31.

16. Petrin et al., National Register Nomination Additional Information (https://npgallery.nps.gov/NRHP/GetAsset/NRHP/07001468_text); Zakheim, *Coit Tower* (2009), p. 18; Shirley Staschen Triest, *A Life on the First Waves of Radical Bohemianism in San Francisco,* oral history, Regional Oral History Office, Bancroft Library, University of California, Berkeley, 1997, p. 65; Suzanne Scheuer oral history, July 29, 1964, AAA, Smithsonian Institution.

17. Mack to Bruce, Jan. 9, 1934, Region 15 papers.

18. Art Commission Minutes, pp. 159, 161, 179; Letter, Heil to Forbes Watson, Jan. 23, 1934, Region 15 papers; PWAP Region 15 final report. The surviving half-inch to one-foot drawings and a number of other preliminary sketches, drawings, and watercolors are in the Achenbach Foundation of the California Palace of the Legion of Honor; regarding the significance of the half-inch to one-foot drawings, see Zakheim interview, 1964, AAA. As evidence that Oldfield, Moya del Pino, and Cuneo had substantially completed their murals by mid-February, see the article and photograph "Marine Murals for Coit Tower," *San Francisco Examiner,* Feb. 11, 1934, p. 8W, which misidentifies the mural as by Cuneo instead of Moya del Pino; and also the March 17 photo of Oldfield in this chapter.

19. As will be discussed in chapter 4, the areas over all three windows no longer have the original frescoes.

20. As will be discussed in chapter 4, the areas over all three windows no longer have the original frescoes.

21. As will be discussed in chapter 4, the areas over all three windows no longer have the original frescoes.

22. I found no explanation by Olmsted of the left fist arising from flames. It may be of relevance that a left-fist salute was then in use by Trotskyists, to distinguish themselves from the right-fist salute then in use by Communists. In 1930 and 1933, Rivera depicted Trotsky giving a left-fist salute; for description and photos, see John Lear, "Diego Rivera Paints the Proletariat," in Oles, *Diego Rivera's America*, pp. 185, 188–189.

23. Zakheim, *Coit Tower* (2009), pp. 41–111, presents color photographs of each mural and brief biographies of each muralist.

24. Letter, Mack to Bruce, Jan. 9, 1934, Region 15 papers; "Coit Artists Still Creating after 50 Years," *Oakland Tribune*, Oct. 5, 1983, D1, D3; Albro and Hall oral history; oral history interview with George Gaethke, Sept. 26, 1964; oral history interview with Hebe Daum Stackpole and Jack Moxom, Jan. 9, 1965; oral history interview with Otis Oldfield, May 21, 1965, all in AAA, Smithsonian Institution; Annie Nakao, "Hoopla for Coit Mural Painters," *San Francisco Examiner*, Oct. 6, 1983, A1-A3.

25. Zakheim, *Coit Tower* (2009), pp. 41–111, identifies many of the figures modeled on identifiable individuals.

26. Zakheim, *Coit Tower* (2009), p. 38.

27. Arnautoff's papers at the Archives of American Art include at least one sketch of a city scene in preparation for his mural; Scheuer, oral history, AAA.

28. Zakheim put current news into local papers but did not copy the papers themselves; his *Western Worker* headlines never appeared in that publication. Arnautoff copied an actual paper, and the paper itself is in his papers at the Archives of American Art.

29. The ground-floor plan of murals that includes the notation "Various Races of Population" is part of the collection of sketches at the Achenbach Foundation; see fig. 3.1. California Tables 14, 15, vol. 3, 1930 Census of Population, https://www.census.gov/library/publications/1932/dec/1930a-vol-03-population.html/.

30. There are a number of accounts of the destruction of Rivera's mural at Rockefeller Center; for Rivera's own account, see his *My Art, My Life: An Autobiography* (1960; New York: Dover Press, 1991), pp. 124–129. A recent account is John Lear, "Diego Rivera Paints the Proletariat," in Oles, *Diego Rivera's America*, pp. 168–169. For coverage by the San Francisco press, see "Rockefeller City Rivera Mural of Lenin Destroyed," *San Francisco Examiner*, Feb. 13, 1934, p. 29; *San Francisco Chronicle*, Feb. 13, 1934, p. 6. See also "Daughters Back an Artful End to the Rivera-Rockefeller Rivalry Story," NPR Morning Edition, Feb. 24, 2015, https://www.npr.org/2015/02/24/387310019/daughters-back-an-artful-end-to-the-rivera-rockefeller-rivalry-story/; and "Destroyed by Rockefellers, Mural Trespassed on Political Vision," NPR Weekend Edition, Sunday, Mar. 9, 2014, https://www.npr.org/2014/03/09/287745199/destroyed-by-rockefellers-mural-trespassed-on-political-vision/.

31. "Destruction of Rivera Mural in N.Y. Termed 'Murder,'" *San Francisco News*, Feb. 14, 1934, p. 5. For Rivera's previous identification with calla lilies, see Luis-Martin Lozano and Juan Rafael Coronel Rivera, *Diego Rivera: The Complete Murals* (Hong Kong: Taschen, 2008), p. 147; James Oles, "From Murals to

Paintings: Scenes of Everyday Life," in Oles, *Diego Rivera's America*, pp. 60, 63, which presents examples from 1923–1924 and 1932.

32. Helen White to Edward Bruce, May 10, 1934, Region 15 papers, National Archives; PWAP Region 15 final report, pp. 17–19, indicates the number of weeks each artist worked and the source of their payment. Those paid from SERA funds, i.e., those still working after April 28, were Albro, Arnautoff, Boynton, Cunningham, Howard, Labaudt, Langdon, and Stackpole and their assistants. The Walter Heil papers, available on microfilm from the Archives of American Art, include some handwritten notes indicating that most of the artists were commissioned on or near December 13 and that many of them received their first paychecks the next week, on or near December 20. The most weeks for which any of the artists was paid from PWAP funds was nineteen: two weeks in December and seventeen weeks through April 28. For the report of some artists still at work in mid-June, see *San Francisco News*, June 23, 1934, p. 10.

33. Letter, Mack to Roosevelt, May 3, 1934, Region 15 papers, National Archives.

Chapter 3. The Murals

1. The Howard family included John Galen Howard, a leading architect in the Bay Area, and his four sons: Henry Temple Howard, an architect and member of the firm of Arthur Brown Jr, who designed Coit Tower; Robert Boardman Howard, a sculptor, who created the bas-relief sculptures over the entrance to Coit Tower; John Langley Howard, who did the *California Industrial Scenes* mural; and Charles Houghton Howard, another artist. The editors of *California Art Research* devoted an entire volume, 17, to the Howard family, including Adeline Kent, wife of Robert Boardman Howard, and a significant artist in her own right; see Gene Hailey, ed., *California Art Research*, 20 vols., W.P.A. Project 2874, O.P. 650303632. San Francisco, 1937; updated and digitized by the Bancroft Library, University of California, Berkeley (https://digitalassets.lib.berkeley.edu/cara/ucb/text/Cara_Volume_17.pdf/).

Chapter 4. Political Controversy, 1934

1. Junius Cravens, *San Francisco News*, July 7, 1934.

2. The standard treatment of the 1934 strikes is David F. Selvin's *A Terrible Anger: The 1934 Waterfront and General Strikes in San Francisco* (Detroit: Wayne State University Press, 1996); see also Robert W. Cherny, *Harry Bridges: Labor Radical, Labor Legend* (Urbana: University of Illinois Press, 2023), chs. 4, 5.

3. Many of the original sketches are in the Achenbach Foundation collection, California Palace of the Legion of Honor, San Francisco Fine Arts Museums; Ralph Chessé, "The WPA & The Great Coit Tower Controversy: The Artists Look Back," *City of San Francisco*, Feb. 4, 1976, p. 22; Bernard Baruch Zakheim interviewed by Lewis Ferbrache, 1964, Archives of American Art (AAA); oral history interview with John Langley Howard and Mary Howard, Sept. 5, 1991, AAA, Smithsonian Institution.

4. Zakheim interview; Heil's pay records show that Zakheim was paid for fifteen and a half weeks, concluding with the week of March 31–April 7.

5. Howard oral history, AAA.

6. Heil's pay records show that Wight was paid for six murals—that is, the

four figures and the two panels above the windows—and that Dean was paid for three, PWAP Region 15 final report. Regarding lack of prior approval of the sketches for the locations over the windows, see letter, Harold Mack to Ned [Bruce], July 16, 1934, Harold Mack file, Edward Bruce Papers, AAA, Microfilm Reel D87:805–860; hereafter, Bruce Papers. Wight's drawings for his agricultural symbols over the east windows are in the Achenbach Foundation. No drawings or photographs have been located of Dean's painting over the south windows.

7. For Wight's explanation, see Clifford Wight, "Statement in Defense of the Coit Tower Mural," box 1, Clifford Wight Collection Relating to Diego Rivera, Special Collections Research Center, Syracuse University. See also *New York Times*, July 29, 1934, p. E7.

8. Victor Arnautoff with Leonid Sanin, *Zizn' zanobo* (Life Anew) (Donetsk: Izdatel'stvo Donbas, 1972), 2nd ed., translated by Lloyd Kramer, Labor Archives and Research Center, San Francisco State University, pp. 32–33; hereafter, Arnautoff, *Life Anew*.

9. Cherny, *Victor Arnautoff*, p. 89; Tillman, *Arthur Brown Jr.*, 192. It is not clear when Wight completed his work above the west windows. He was paid only from PWAP funds, meaning he was not paid for work past the end of April. However, no one seems to have taken notice of his hammer and sickle until Brown on June 23. Brown may have been inspired to make his "casual" visit on the twenty-third after reading an article by John Barry in the *San Francisco News* of the same date (p. 10). The article described the Coit Tower murals in some detail, and generally very positively, with no hint of controversy or mention of Wight's mural. The *News* article also described seeing Stackpole, Boynton, and Labaudt still at work when the reporter visited "the other afternoon," although all of them had received their final pay some weeks before (see chapter 2).

10. Telegram, Heil to Bruce, June 28, 1934; telegram, Forbes Watson to Heil, June 29, 1934, Region 15 papers.

11. "Statement of the Executive Committee of the Artists & Writers Union," undated, Region 15 papers. The source of the orders is not clear, but the only possibilities were Heil, as PWAP regional director, or someone from the Art Commission, although there is no indication of that in the commission's minutes.

12. Evelyn Seeley, "A Frescoed Tower Clangs Shut," *Literary Digest*, Aug. 25, 1934, suggests that the tower was locked on approximately June 25. Nothing about the locking of the tower appears in the minutes of the Board of Park Commissioners (http://archive.org/stream/parkrecreat1930sanf#page/n1/mode/1up/), pp. 42–43.

13. *San Francisco Call-Bulletin*, July 2, 1934; "Statement of the Executive Committee of the Artists & Writers Union," undated, Region 15 papers; *San Francisco Chronicle*, July 4, p. 15. The "Closed" sign was probably brought by the protesters.

14. *San Francisco Chronicle*, July 4, p. 15; form letter, in file "Form Letters from Edward Bruce to Dr. Walter Heil," PWAP files, De Young Museum, San Francisco, CA.

15. *San Francisco Chronicle*, July 3, 1934, 13.

16. Selvin, *Terrible Anger*, pp. 193–194.

17. *San Francisco Examiner*, July 5, 1934, p. 7.

18. Joseph Danysh interviewed by Lewis Ferbrache, Dec. 3, 1964, AAA. See also Joseph Danysh, "The WPA & the Great Coit Tower Controversy," *City of San Francisco*, Feb. 4, 1976, pp. 20, 21. For Zakheim's one-man show, see *San*

Francisco Chronicle, July 1, 1934, p. D3; *San Francisco Examiner*, July 17, 1934, second section, page 1.

19. Junius Cravens, "Artists Fight to Prevent Changes," *San Francisco News*, July 7, 1934, p. 8. The erroneous reading of the legend "United Workers of the World" was to be repeated by many subsequent historians, even though the photograph in Masha Zakheim's book (1983) makes clear the actual wording.

20. Cravens, "Artists Fight to Prevent Changes."

21. *New York Times*, July 29, 1934, p. E7.

22. Cravens, "Artists Fight to Prevent Changes."

23. Letter, Bruce to Mack, July 9, 1934, Bruce Papers. I am grateful to Jon Golinger for drawing my attention to these letters.

24. Selvin, *Terrible Anger*, pp. 193–194; telegram, McIntyre to the president, July 17, 1934, file: 1934 Pacific Coast Longshoremen's Strike, b11, OF407b, Franklin D. Roosevelt Papers, Franklin D. Roosevelt Library; minutes of the Board of Park Commissioners (http://archive.org/stream/parkrecreat1930sanf#page/n1/mode/1up/).

25. Letter, Mack to Bruce, July 16, 1934, Bruce Papers; all punctuation errors are in the original.

26. Letter, Bruce to Mack, July 27, 1934; letter, Bruce to Rowan, July 27, 1934, Region 15 papers.

27. "Statement of the Executive Committee of the Artists & Writers Union," undated, Region 15 papers; Zakheim, *Coit Tower* (2009), 29–32; Seeley, "Frescoed Tower Clangs Shut," 24. According to the *San Francisco Chronicle*, July 4, p. 15, Lewis Hobart, president of the Art Commission, issued a reply to the Artists and Writers Union on July 3; that article carried much of the text of the union's statement.

28. Statement, Parker Hall et al. to the Regional Committee, the Public Works of Art Project, July 30, 1934, attached to Parker Hall et al. to Edward Bruce, Aug. 17, 1934, copy provided by Andrew Hemingway, who, in his *Artists on the Left: American Artists and the Communist Movement, 1926–1956* (New Haven: Yale University Press, 2002), 300n93, provides the citation AAA DC7.

29. Selvin, *Terrible Anger*, pp. 228–29; *San Francisco Examiner*, July 24, 1934, 1, 2.

30. Art Commission minutes, 1931–1935, http://archive.org/stream/minutesofartcomm1934sanf#page/n0/mode/1up/, p. 213.

31. Wight's drawing of his symbols for the area of the east windows is in the Achenbach Foundation collections at the California Palace of the Legion of Honor, accession number FA9500.

32. When the murals were restored in 2012–2014, an effort was made to scrape off later layers of paint to see if the original murals still existed; they were not found. Members of the restoration team told me this. However, the change to Howard's mural seems to have been accomplished by painting over the *Western Worker* banner; see Howard's oral history. If the *Western Worker* banner in Zakheim's mural was changed, as seems likely, it was probably accomplished in the same way.

33. Junius Cravens, "Coit Tower Row," *San Francisco News*, Aug. 11, 1934, 3. For examples of the press coverage, see *New York Times*, July 29, 1934; *Los Angeles Daily News*, July 2, 1934; *Oakland Tribune*, July 3, 1934; *San Bernardino Sun*, July 4, 1934; *California Arts and Architecture* 46 (Aug. 1934): 4.

34. Arnautoff, *Life Anew*, 34.

35. Victor Arnautoff, "A Vital Question," *San Francisco Art Association Bulletin* 1 (Sept. 1934): 1.

36. Minutes of the Board of Park Commissioners, 46, 64 (http://archive.org/stream/parkrecreat1930sanf#page/n1/mode/1up/). Leaks have continued to pose dangers to the murals ever since 1934. The most recent restoration, completed in spring 2014, included extensive waterproofing intended to prevent future damage, but it, too, has been less than fully successful.

37. John Langley Howard oral history; *San Francisco Chronicle*, Oct. 13, 1934.

38. Karal Ann Marling, *Wall-to-Wall America: A Cultural History of Post-Office Murals in the Great Depression* (Minneapolis: University of Minnesota Press, 1982), pp. 46–48. Marling's book is filled with examples of how the staff in Washington closely managed the content of Treasury Section murals. Edward Lucie-Smith reached similar conclusions in *American Realism* (1994; paperback ed., New York: Thames and Hudson, 2002), pp. 112–113: "The furor over Coit Tower bred a determination in Washington that in the future no government-sponsored mural project must be allowed to slip from the grasp of the central bureaucracy."

39. John Langley Howard oral history, AAA.

Chapter 5. Contemporary Reactions

1. *San Francisco Chronicle*, Oct. 13, 1934, p. 11.

2. Lavrova, "Forty-Six Artists—One Palette."

3. Lavrova, "Forty-Six Artists—One Palette"; Public Works of Art Project, *Report of the Assistant Secretary of the Treasury to Federal Emergency Relief Administrator: December 8, 1933–June 30, 1934* (Washington, D.C.: Government Printing Office, 1934), p. 8. However, Heil's final report listed thirty-eight frescoes; Public Works of Art Project, Region No. 15, a mimeographed report of artists, their work, costs, etc. Date: December 1933, to 1934, Public Works of Art Project–California, Archives of American Art, Smithsonian Institution. That report listed thirty-one frescoes at Coit Tower, including two for Boynton, three for Dean, three for Labaudt, and six for Wight. Lavrova also claims a total of thirty-one frescoes at Coit Tower. PWAP artists produced several other fresco murals in San Francisco, but there were no more than three in the same location, and no other location had more than two artists.

4. Lavrova, "Forty-Six Artists—One Palette."

5. Lavrova, "Forty-Six Artists—One Palette."

6. Heil quoted in Lavrova, "Forty-Six Artists—One Palette."

7. Seeley, "Frescoed Tower Clangs Shut."

8. Seeley, "Frescoed Tower Clangs Shut."

9. Seeley, "Frescoed Tower Clangs Shut." The Mooney case involved Tom Mooney and Warren Billings, convicted of a bombing in 1916 and still in prison as of 1934 even though a key witness was subsequently shown to have committed perjury; see Richard Frost, *The Mooney Case* (Stanford: Stanford University Press, 1968). The reference to strikes was, of course, to the longshore, maritime, and general strikes of 1934 and, perhaps, to the agricultural strikes of the year before. The reference to lynchings was likely to the lynching of two murder suspects in San Jose in 1933.

10. *San Francisco News*, Oct. 20, 1934. Arthur Miller, in the *Los Angeles Times*, also seems to have had access to the tower before it was closed. In an article on

June 24, he described the site and the murals, noting that "the general technique stems from Rivera," and gave special attention to the murals by Arnautoff and Labaudt.

11. *New York Times*, April 24, April 25, April 29, Sept. 24, 1934; *National Exhibition of Art* [exhibition guide], Corcoran Gallery, pp. 23, 24, file CWA & PWA, Edwart B. Rowan Papers, AAA.

12. Forbes Watson, "Art and the Government in 1934," *Parnassus* 6 (1935): 12–16.

13. Oral history interview with Dorothy Cravath, May 13–27, 1964, AAA, Smithsonian Institution.

Chapter 6. Later Controversies

1. *San Francisco Chronicle*, Aug. 23, p. 23; Aug. 31, p. 10; Sept. 4, 1935, p. 14.

2. For a recent account of the HUAC hearings that resulted in the termination of the Writers' Project, see Scott Borchert, *Republic of Detours: How the New Deal Paid Broke Writers to Rediscover America* (New York: Farrar, Scott, and Giroux, 2021), ch. 6. For the continuing attacks on maritime union leaders, especially Bridges, see my *Harry Bridges: Labor Radical, Labor Legend* (Urbana: University of Illinois Press, 2023), chs. 9, 10; for various attacks on the local Communist Party, see my *San Francisco Reds: Communists in the Bay Area, 1919–1958* (Urbana: University of Illinois Press, 2024), chs. 7, 8.

3. Art Commission minutes, June 14, 1941, https://archive.org/details/minutesofartcomm1941sanf/page/n111/mode/2up/.

4. Information on Lermen from Ancestry.com; *San Francisco Chronicle*, July 22, pp. 1, 10; July 23, 1941, p. 11.

5. *San Francisco Chronicle*, July 25, 1941, p. 14; Oct. 4, 1941, p. 9.

6. *San Francisco Chronicle*, July 23, 1941, p. 11; Park Commission minutes for August 28, 1941, https://archive.org/details/minutesboardofpa1941sanf/. The issue of the actual ownership of New Deal art—whether it belongs to a local governmental agency or to the federal government—returned to San Francisco recently, with controversies over WPA art projects at George Washington High School and at the University of California, San Francisco. See Federal Property and Administrative Services Act of 1949 and General Services Administration Bulletins regarding ownership of New Deal Art (summarized in a memorandum from the U.S. General Services Administration, https://www.gsa.gov/cdnstatic/legal_fact_sheet_final_I.pdf/.

7. Park Commission minutes for Aug. 28, 1941.

8. Art Commission minutes for 1941 and 1942 are available at https://archive.org/details/minutesofartcomm1941sanf/page/n111/mode/2up/ and https://archive.org/details/minutesofartcomm1942sanf/mode/1up/.

9. See, e.g., Thomas Doherty, *Show Trial: Hollywood, HUAC, and the Birth of the Blacklist* (New York: Columbia University Press, 2018); David M. Oshinsky, *A Conspiracy So Immense: The World of Joe McCarthy* (New York: Oxford University Press, 2005.

10. *San Francisco Examiner*, Sept. 23, Oct. 1, 1953, *San Francisco Examiner* clippings file, envelope marked San Francisco/Telegraph Hill/Coit Tower, History Center, San Francisco Public Library.

11. *Efflorescence* occurs when water comes through the plaster from behind the mural, depositing minerals on the surface of the mural, where they present as white or gray powder.

12. *San Francisco Chronicle*, April 22, 1946, p. 13; Katherine Petrin et al., "National Register of Historic Places Registration Form for Coit Memorial Tower," 2017 ((https://npgallery.nps.gov/NRHP/GetAsset/NRHP/07001468_text/); hereafter, "Petrin report." I was a coauthor of the Petrin report.

13. Petrin report, 2017; *San Francisco Examiner*, Jan. 6, March 12, 1961, *San Francisco Examiner* clippings file, Envelope: San Francisco/Telegraph Hill/Coit Tower, History Center, San Francisco Public Library; oral history interview with Suzanne Scheuer, July 29, 1964, AAA, Smithsonian Institution.

14. Petrin report, 2017.

15. Chiori Santiago, "Mural, Mural on the Wall: The Restoration of Coit Tower," *SF: The Magazine of Design and Style* 2, no. 6 (June 1990): 88–91.

16. *San Francisco Chronicle*, Oct. 17, 2013, A1; *New York Times*, Feb. 3, 2012, A21A; *Los Angeles Times*, Jan. 3, 2012, AA1.

17. *SF Business Times*, Nov. 11–12, 2011, 5.

18. Press release, Dec. 8, 2011, courtesy of Jon Golinger; *San Francisco Chronicle*, Dec. 8, 2011, C1; Jon Golinger, *Saving San Francisco's Heart: How to Win Elections, Reclaim Our City, and Keep SF a Special Place* (San Francisco: Bay Guardian Books, 2017), 68–69.

19. Golinger, *Saving*, 69–70; *New York Times*, Feb. 3, 2012, A21A; San Francisco Voter Information Pamphlet, April 11, 2012, https://webbie1.sfpl.org/multimedia/pdf/elections/June_5_2012.pdf/, 77, 80–82. The artists whose relatives came out in support of Prop. B were Arnautoff, Oldfield, Hesthal, and Zakheim; see https://www.nbcbayarea.com/news/local/group-fights-for-coit-towers-decaying-murals/1946511/.

20. San Francisco Voter Information Pamphlet, April 11, 2012, https://webbie1.sfpl.org/multimedia/pdf/elections/June_5_2012.pdf/, 78–79, 82; email from Jon Golinger to Robert Cherny, Aug. 20, 2022.

21. City and County of San Francisco, Department of Elections, Results Summary, June 5, 2012, Consolidated Presidential Primary Election (https://sfelections.org/results/20120605/). Other propositions also had a higher level of participation than in the primaries, and Prop. B drew the fewest voters among the two state-level and two local propositions. The highest level of participation was on a state proposition to increase cigarette taxes. For the symbolic check, see Sam Whiting's obituary of Ruth Zakheim Gottstein at https://www.sfchronicle.com/sf/article/ruth-gottstein-17457887.php/.

22. Email from Anne Rosenthal to Robert Cherny, Aug. 6, 2019; *San Francisco Chronicle*, Feb. 12, np; March 21, A1; May 15, 2014, A1. I was present during the reopening and talked with the muralists' descendants. That work also included roof repairs that, it was hoped, would prevent future efflorescence; like all previous roof repairs, it has failed to do so.

23. Coit Tower is National Register #07001468. The 2017 amendment to the nomination was intended not only to revise the information on the 2008 form but also to provide the basis for a National Historic Landmark designation, a process still in progress.

Chapter 7. Subsequent Perspectives on the Coit Tower Murals

1. Jonathan Harris, *Federal Art and National Culture: The Politics of Identity in New Deal America* (New York: Cambridge University Press, 1993), p. 5.

2. Martin R. Kalfatovic, *The New Deal Fine Arts Projects: A Bibliography, 1933–1992* (Metuchen, NJ: Scarecrow Press, 1994).

3. Biographical information on O'Connor from the Archives of American Art (AAA), https://www.aaa.si.edu/collections/francis-v-oconnor-papers-9095/, accessed Sept. 6, 2022. *Federal Support for the Visual Arts: The New Deal and Now* (Greenwich, CT: New York Graphic Society, 1969); *The New Deal Art Projects: An Anthology of Memoirs* (Washington, D.C.: Smithsonian Institution, 1972); *Art for the Millions: Essays from the 1930s by Artists and Administrators of the WPA Federal Art Project* (Greenwich, CT: New York Graphic Society, 1973).

4. Richard McKinzie, *The New Deal for Artists* (Princeton, NJ: Princeton University Press, 1973), pp. 24–27. McKinzie also erroneously identified Coit Tower as a "memorial to volunteer firemen."

5. Steven M. Gelber et al., *New Deal Art: California* (Santa Clara, CA: de Saisset Art Gallery and Museum, Santa Clara University, 1976), esp. p. 7.

6. The film that is available online in the its uncut and unedited version is at https://californiarevealed.org/islandora/object/cavpp%3A12266/. Summer Olsen, of the de Saisset, confirmed that there is no edited version in an email to me on Sept. 7, 2022.

7. Editor's Notes, *California Living*, magazine of the *San Francisco Sunday Examiner and Chronicle*, Dec. 14, 1975, p. 4; Masha Zakheim Jewett, "The Murals in Coit Tower," *California Living*, Dec. 14, 1975., pp. 30–34.

8. Gelber et al., *New Deal Art: California*, esp. pp. 69–79, 81–107.

9. Steven M. Gelber, "The Irony of San Francisco's 'Commie Art': An Artistic and Political Appraisal," *City of San Francisco*, Feb. 4, 1976, pp. 24, 28, 37. Gelber explained the title to me in an email on Sept. 10, 2022.

10. Steven M. Gelber, "Working to Prosperity: California's New Deal Murals," *California History* 58 (1979): 98–127, esp. pp. 104, 106, 108.

11. Masha Zakheim Jewett, *Coit Tower, San Francisco: Its History and Art*, 1st ed. (San Francisco: Volcano Press, 1983); Masha Zakheim, *Coit Tower, San Francisco: Its History and Art*, 2nd ed. (Volcano, CA: Volcano Press, 2009).

12. "Coit Artists Still Creating after 50 years," *Oakland Tribune*, Oct. 5, 1983, D1, D3; Annie Nakao, "Hoopla for Coit Mural Painters," San Francisco *Examiner*, Oct. 6, 1983, zA1-zA3.

13. Belisario R. Contreras, *Tradition and Innovation in New Deal Art* (Lewisburg: Bucknell University Press, 1983). Though Contreras's book appeared the year after Marling's, Contreras did not cite her work; it is highly unlikely that he knew of Marling's book at the time he was completing the revision of his 1967 dissertation. Similarly, he could not have known of Masha Zakheim Jewett's book.

14. Contreras, *Tradition and Innovation*, pp. 44–49.

15. Contreras, *Tradition and Innovation*, pp. 45–46.

16. Contreras, *Tradition and Innovation*, p. 46.

17. Contreras, *Tradition and Innovation*, pp. 79, 104, 140.

18. Contreras, *Tradition and Innovation*, p. 171.

19. Karal Ann Marling, *Wall-to-Wall America: A Cultural History of Post-Office Murals in the Great Depression* (Minneapolis: University of Minnesota Press, 1982), pp. 46–48. Marling's book is filled with examples of how the staff in Washington closely managed the content of Treasury Section murals.

20. Marlene Park and Gerald E. Markowitz, *Democratic Vistas: Post Offices and Public Art in the New Deal* (Philadelphia: Temple University Press, 1984), p. 5.

21. O'Connor, "Influence of Diego Rivera," p. 156, 159–174.

22. O'Connor, "Commentary," in Zakheim, *Coit Tower* (2009), p. 121.

23. O'Connor, ""Influence of Diego Rivera," pp. 171–173; O'Connor, "Commentary," pp. 121–122.

24. O'Connor, "Influence of Diego Rivera," p. 172; O'Connor, "Commentary," p. 122.

25. O'Connor, "Influence of Diego Rivera," p. 174.

26. O'Connor, "Commentary," p. 123.

27. Mercilee Jenkins and Richard Talavera were able to locate a copy of the play for me. I have given it to the San Francisco History Center at the San Francisco Public Library. For press coverage and criticism, see *San Francisco Chronicle*, March 15, 1987, Datebook section, pp. 34, 35; April 2, 1987, p. 68. Though the script identifies the main character as "Lydia," which was the name of Arnautoff's wife, the review calls her "Elena," so perhaps there was a change in that character's name. It seems likely that McNutt may have interviewed Arnautoff's son, Vasily, who lived near that community center. Contact with Vasily is also suggested by her reference to Arnautoff as distributing leaflets during the general strike; Vasily would have had copies of two block prints his father had created at that time, depicting the violence of July 3 and 5, the presence of the National Guard, and a third created either then or later depicting the funeral procession on Market Street; see Cherny, *Victor Arnautoff*, pp. 97–98.

28. Peter Selz, "The Impact from Abroad: Foreign Guests and Visitors," in *On the Edge of America: California Modernist Art, 1900–1950*, ed. Paul J. Karlstrom (Berkeley: University of California Press, 1996), p. 105.

29. Anthony W. Lee, *Painting on the Left: Diego Rivera, Radical Politics, and San Francisco's Public Murals* (Berkeley: University of California Press, 1999).

30. Lee, *Painting on the Left*, pp. 95–96. When Danysh asked Zakheim if he was a Communist in July 1934, Zakheim said no; Danysh oral history, AAA.

31. I have reviewed all of Lee's citations regarding Arnautoff except one without finding any evidence for such a claim. The one not available to me is an interview with Arnautoff's son, Vasily, whom I was not able to interview. My sources include letters to Arnautoff from his wife during 1925–1929; interviews with his son, Michael, who was in San Francisco from 1925 to 1929; Arnautoff's memoirs; Arnautoff's FBI file; the autobiographies that Arnautoff submitted with his applications to emigrate to the Soviet Union that are now in the State Archive of the Russian Federation (GARF); and the files of CP District 13 (California) in the Russian State Archive for Social and Political History (RGASPI); all of these are detailed in my *Victor Arnautoff and the Politics of Art* (Urbana: University of Illinois Press, 2017). If Arnautoff had been involved in party activities in the 1920s and early 1930s, he would surely have mentioned it in the autobiographies filed as part of his applications to emigrate to the Soviet Union. Instead, the GARF documents state that he joined the CP in 1937; his FBI file claims that he joined in 1938, based on documents viewed by an informant. Arnautoff's memoirs, published in the Soviet Union in 1965 and in a revised edition in 1972, indicate that he was radicalized by the 1934 strikes and by the Spanish Civil War. In my biography of Arnautoff, I also suggest possible other factors in his decision to join the CP.

32. Lee, *Painting on the Left*, p. 122.

33. Cherny, *Victor Arnautoff*, ch. 6, esp. 75–78.

34. Cherny, *Victor Arnautoff*, ch. 6, esp. 75–78. On the disarray of the local CP, see my *San Francisco Reds: Communists in the Bay Area, 1919–1958* (Urbana: University of Illinois Press, 2024), chs. 2, 3.

35. Lee, *Painting on the Left*, p. 146. One can see the difference between the traffic police officers' uniforms and those of other city police in the photographs in the photos section of San Francisco Police Department records, History Center, San Francisco Public Library, notably photo AAG-0177.

36. Lee, *Painting on the Left*, pp. 130–131.

37. I searched the oral histories of Ben Cunningham, Ralph Chessé, Dorothy Cravath, Hebe Daum, George Gaethke, William Hesthal, John Langley Howard, Otis Oldfield, Suzanne Scheuer, Shirley Staschen Triest, and Herman Volz, all at AAA; none mentioned Zakheim in the role that Lee describes. Chessé, Gaethke, and Scheuer all mention Stackpole; Chessé and Gaethke also mention Mack. Scheuer, who worked side by side with Zakheim at Coit Tower, states flatly, "Stackpole . . . was in charge, pretty much in charge of picking the artists." Zakheim was not as close to the CSFA as nearly all the other artists; he once enrolled at the CSFA but left after a short time.

38. Lee, *Painting on the Left*, p. 138; there is no citation. A search on "National Guard" in all issues of the *San Francisco Chronicle* between July 5 and July 31 produces not a single account of fighting between strikers and the National Guard. On July 13, in fact, the *Chronicle* described the Embarcadero as "steeped in the calm that has prevailed since the National Guard troops were moved to the water front"; July 13, 1934, p. 2. The four days with major conflicts between strikers and the police are described in my *Harry Bridges: Labor Radical, Labor Legend* (Urbana: University of Illinois Press, 2023), pp. 66–68, 81–88.

39. *San Francisco Examiner*, Feb. 11, 1934, p. 8W; PWAP Region 15 final report. The *Examiner* photo is of Moya del Pino's mural but identifies it as Cuneo's.

40. Lee, *Painting on the Left*, pp. 145–146. A careful examination of Hesthal's mural indicates that the workers are *not* removing spikes from the tracks but instead removing weeds; my interpretation is that the workers are preparing the rails for the resumption of economic activity under the stimulus of the New Deal. Hesthal's sketch is available in the Achenbach Foundation materials, San Francisco Palace of the Legion of Honor; his completion date is based on the number of weeks for which he was paid, as indicated in the PWAP final report.

41. Lee, *Painting on the Left*, p. 151.

42. See, esp., the letter from Ruth Zakheim to Edward Bruce, April 7, 1934, announcing that her father had completed his mural and needed more work; the letter is reproduced in Bruce J. Bustard, *A New Deal for the Arts* (Seattle: University of Washington Press, 1997), p. 2.

43. Lee, *Painting on the Left*, pp. 147, 148. A comparison of the headlines in that newspaper with those in the *Western Worker* from December through mid-May finds no similarities, and certainly none that refer positively to Roosevelt or Secretary of Labor Frances Perkins, as the headlines in Howard's mural do. The *Western Worker* is available at https://www.marxists.org/history/usa/pubs/westernworker/index.htm/.

44. Shirley Staschen Triest, "A Life on the First Waves of Radical Bohemianism in San Francisco," Oral History Transcript, 1997, Regional Oral History Office, Bancroft Library, pp. 71–72.

45. Matthew Baigell and Julia Williams, *Artists against War and Fascism: Papers of the First American Artists' Congress* (New Brunswick: Rutgers University Press, 1986), pp. 6–11, 47–52.

46. Howard's work appears on the covers of Cybelle Fox's *Three Worlds of Relief: Race, Immigration, and the American Welfare State from the Progressive*

Era to the New Deal (Princeton University Press, 2012) and Elizabeth E. Sine's *Rebel Imaginaries: Labor, Culture, and Politics in Depression-Era California* (Duke University Press, 2021). Stackpole's work is on the cover of Robert W. Cherny, Gretchen Lemke-Santangelo, and Richard Griswold del Castillo's *Competing Visions: A History of California*, 2nd ed. (Cengate, 2013). For the Roosevelt University program, see https://www.roosevelt.edu/centers/new-deal-studies/history-fair/new-deal-art/.

47. "Courtroom Murals: Images of New Deal Era Art from Coit Tower," March 3, 2020, U.S. District Court for the Northern District of California Historical Society, https://ndhistoricalsociety.org/presentation/courtroom-murals-images-of-new-deal-era-art-from-coit-tower/.

48. "Hard Times: Andrew Hemingway on Cultural Democracy and the New Deal Art Programs," *Art Forum*, April 30, 2020, https://www.artforum.com/slant/andrew-hemingway-on-cultural-democracy-and-the-new-deal-art-programs-82962/.

Chapter 8. Legacies

1. Oral history interview with Maxine Albro and Parker Hall, July 27, 1964, Archives of American Art (AAA), Smithsonian Institution.

2. The eleven were Maxine Albro, Victor Arnautoff, Ben Cunningham, Hebe Daum (an assistant artist at Coit Tower), Parker Hall, Edith Hamlin, Lucien Labaudt, Gordon Langton, Fred Olmsted, Ralph Stackpole, and Bernard Zakheim. Through the WPA/FAP, Albro created a mosaic mural; Arnautoff created fourteen fresco murals in two projects; Cunningham created one photo mural; Daum created several murals, but the exact number is uncertain since only fragments survive; Hall created a wooden sculpture; Hamlin created three murals in one project; Labaudt created twelve fresco murals and two mosaic murals in three projects; Langton did one mural; Olmsted did one mural and two sculptures in one project; Stackpole did two murals and a large sculpture in three projects; and Zakheim did fourteen murals in three projects. The various artists and their work can be traced through the New Deal Art Registry, online at https://newdealartregistry.org, which is sometimes incomplete; and in Christopher VerPlanck and Donna Graves, "San Francisco New Deal Historic Context Statement" (approved by the San Francisco Historic Preservation Commission, March 1, 2023), which includes as complete a list of projects in San Francisco as is ever likely to be compiled. See also biographical information in the appendix. Arnautoff's work at the Presidio of San Francisco is included in the documentation for the Presidio's listing as a National Historic Landmark District (see Alley, Barker, Chappell, et al., pp. 7-130, 8-53); Arnautoff's, Labaudt's, Langdon's, and Stackpole's murals at George Washington High School are part of that building's listing in the Historic American Buildings Survey; Daum's surviving mural at the former San Francisco State College is listed in those buildings' local landmarking documentation (San Francisco Article 10 landmark); Hamlin's murals at Mission High School are part of that building's listing as an Article 10 landmark; and Zakheim's murals at the Alemany Health Center and those formerly at Toland Hall, University of California San Francisco, are Article 10 landmarks.

3. See note 2 for their work in WPA/FAP; for their Treasury Section work, see the various artists' listings in the New Deal Art Registry.

4. Arnautoff had five projects each with one mural; Moya del Pino had three

projects each with one mural; Hamlin, Scheuer, and Zakheim each had two projects each for one mural; Boynton had one project with fourteen murals; Labaudt had one project with two murals; Cunningham, Harris, and Stackpole each had one project for one mural; for details see the New Deal Art Registry.

5. VerPlanck and Graves, "San Francisco New Deal Historic Context Statement," pp. 46–48, 166.

6. VerPlanck and Graves, "San Francisco New Deal Historic Context Statement," pp. 46–48, 166. For the Bruton sisters, see Wendy Van Wyck Good, *Sisters in Art: The Biography of Margaret, Esther, and Helen Bruton* (n.p.: West Margin Press, 2021), pp. 85–91, esp. 90. For Puccinelli, see "Dorothy Wagner Puccinelli," in Hailey, *California Art Research* v. 20, pp. 67–73B, renumbered for the digital version as pp. 3005–3015, esp. 70–71 (3008–3009).

7. Exceptions include the art at the Beach Chalet, what is now the Maritime Museum, and at the Rincon Annex post office and also the mostly temporary art at the Golden Gate International Exposition (see below for a summary of later New Deal art).

8. Christopher VerPlanck, "Landmark Designation Report: Theodore Roosevelt Middle School" (San Francisco Article 10 landmark nomination, approved by SF HPC, Oct. 17, 2017, approved by the San Francisco Board of Supervisors on March 15, 2019), pp. 6, 49, 57, 58.

9. Arnautoff listed all of his assistants in the lower left corner of the mural; oral history interview with Richard Ayer, Sept. 26, 1964, AAA; *San Francisco Examiner*, Dec. 30, 1934, p. E8; June 23, 1935, p. E7; Charles I. Schottland and Frank Y. McLaughlin, *Review of Activities: State Relief Administration of California: 1933–1935* (Sacramento: California State Printing Office, 1936), p. 22; and Cherny, *Victor Arnautoff*, pp. 102–103. Though the loggia was originally open, it is now enclosed by a glass wall.

10. San Francisco Planning Department, *Landmark Case Report: Alemany Emergency Hospital and Health Center, 35–45 Onondaga Avenue* (San Francisco: 2016), https://sfplanning.s3.amazonaws.com/commissions/hpcpackets/2015-003877DES.pdf/.

11. VerPlanck and Graves, *SF New Deal HCS*, pp. 102–103; The Living New Deal, https://livingnewdeal.org/projects/mission-high-school-civilization-arts-crafts-taught-neophyte-indians-mural-san-francisco-ca/; Sally Swope, *Edith Hamlin: WPA Muralist*, Found SF.org., (https://www.foundsf.org/index.php?title=Edith_Hamlin:_WPA_Muralist/. Hamlin's murals have recently been criticized as depicting cultural genocide.

12. Annette Melville et al., *George Washington High School*, Historic American Buildings Survey (hereafter, HABS) No. CA-2939 (2020), pp. 6–7, http://memory.loc.gov/master/pnp/habshaer/ca/ca4400/ca4411/data/ca4411data.pdf/; Christopher VerPlanck, "Landmark Nomination Report: George Washington High School," Oct. 18, 2017 (approved by the San Francisco Historic Preservation Commission, Dec. 6, 2017), p. 39, https://commissions.sfplanning.org/hpcpackets/George%20Washington%20HS.pdf/. Other sources inaccurately credit those sculptures to Arnautoff. It's not clear that Howard's sculptures were funded by WPA/FAP; see VerPlanck and Graves, *SF New Deal HCS*, p. 157.

13. Cherny, *Victor Arnautoff*, pp. 108–110; Melville, HABS, pp. 13–15, 17, and appendix 4; VerPlanck, "Landmark Nomination Report: George Washington High School," pp. 39–41.

14. Cherny, *Victor Arnautoff*, pp. 108–110; Melville, HABS, pp. 13–15, 17, and

appendix 4; VerPlanck, "Landmark Nomination Report: George Washington High School," pp. 39–41.

15. Melville, HABS, pp. 17–19, and appendix 3; VerPlanck, "Landmark Nomination Report: George Washington High School," pp. 45–46.

16. Melville, HABS, pp. 5, 24 and appendix 5, and appendix 3; VerPlanck, "Landmark Nomination Report: George Washington High School," pp. 42–45.

17. Molly Blauvelt, "Beach Chalet," National Register Nomination Form, 1980, entered July 22, 1981, https://npgallery.nps.gov/NRHP/GetAsset/396ce0d5-c9b3-4168-805c-2692db2e8809/.

18. VerPlanck and Graves, *SF New Deal HCS*, pp. 162–164; James P. Delgado, "Aquatic Park Historic District," National Register of Historic Places Inventory Nomination Form, Feb. 1, 1984, pp. 7–3 to 7–6, http://npshistory.com/publications/goga/nr-aquatic-park-hd.pdf/; Jeff Rosato Jr., "Aquatic Park Bathhouse Marks 80th with Restored Murals," NBC Bay Area, May 16, 2019, https://www.nbcbayarea.com/news/local/aquatic-park-bathhouse-marks-80th-with-restored-murals/190346/.

19. James P. Delgado, "Aquatic Park Historic District"; VerPlanck and Graves, *SF New Deal HCS*, pp. 162–164.

20. James P. Delgado, "Aquatic Park Historic District"; VerPlanck and Graves, *SF New Deal HCS*, pp. 162–163.

21. James P. Delgado, "Aquatic Park Historic District"; VerPlanck and Graves, *SF New Deal HCS*, pp. 162, 164.

22. Robert S. Sherins, ed. and comp., "History of Medicine in California Articulated in Frescoes: The Story behind the Murals of Toland Hall, UCSF," http://robertssherinsmd.com/files/books/7-Toland%20Manuscript.4.pdf/; San Francisco Planning Department, Article 10 Landmark Designation Fact Sheet History of Medicine in California (approved by the Historic Preservation Commission on August 19, 2020), p. 23.

23. Sherins, "History of Medicine in California Articulated in Frescoes"; San Francisco Planning Department, Article 10 Landmark Designation Fact Sheet History of Medicine in California (approved by the Historic Preservation Commission on August 19, 2020), pp. 24, 26–37; https://sfplanninggis.org/docs/landmarks_and_districts/LM289.pdf. See also Carl Nolte, "UCSF to Let Public See Trove of Medical History Murals," *San Francisco Chronicle*, March, 1, 2015, C1.

24. In Maxine Albro and Parker Hall oral history, July 27, 1964, AAA, Hall explained that he did most of the work but that it was completed by Michael von Meyer, who usually received the credit in later descriptions.

25. Carol Roland, National Register of Historic Places Registration Form for San Francisco State Teacher's College, certified Jan. 7, 2008, pp. 7–10 and 7–11, https://npgallery.nps.gov/nrhp/GetAsset?assetID=b459deb2-7f3d-4211-a842-762f77aeed43/; oral history interview with Maxine Albro and Parker Hall, July 27, 1964, AAA, Smithsonian Institution; oral history interview with Hebe Daum Stackpole and Jack Moxom, Jan. 9, 1965, AAA, Smithsonian Institution; "Haight Street Art Center to Dedicate Completely Restored Significant Reuben Kadish Mural," https://haightstreetart.org/blogs/news/reuben-kadish-mural/.

26. For overviews of the creation of Treasure Island and the exposition, see Andrew M. Shaken, *Into the Void Pacific: Building the 1939 San Francisco World's Fair* (Berkeley: University of California Press, 2014); Lisa Rubens, "The 1939 San Francisco World's Fair: The New Deal, the New Frontier and the Pacific Basin" (PhD diss., University of California, Berkeley, 2004); VerPlanck and Graves, *SF*

New Deal HCS, section 6; Richard Reinhardt, *Treasure Island: San Francisco's Exposition Years* (Mill Valley, CA: Squarebooks, 1978).

27. For a list of artists who worked on the Golden Gate International Exposition, see Eugen Neuhaus, *The Art of Treasure Island* (Berkeley: University of California Press, 1939), pp. 139–151. That book also includes many photographs of the artwork of the exposition; unfortunately, the list is at least somewhat incomplete, failing to list Jo Mora, who does appear elsewhere in the book, and there is no index.

28. Neuhaus, *Art of Treasure Island*, pp. 139–151; VerPlanck and Graves, *SF New Deal HCS*, p. 182.

29. Neuhaus, *Art of Treasure Island*, pp. 139–151; VerPlanck and Graves, *SF New Deal HCS*, pp. 182, 184; Gordon H. Chang, Mark Dean Johnson, and Paul J. Karlstrom, eds., *Asian American Art: A History, 1850–1970* (Stanford, CA: Stanford University Press, 2008), p. 443.

30. VerPlanck and Graves, *SF New Deal HCS*, pp. 186–187.

31. *Diego Rivera Mural Project*, City College of San Francisco, https://riveramural.org/fullmural/.

32. *Diego Rivera Mural Project*.

33. *Diego Rivera Mural Project*, especially "Diego's Assistants"; VerPlanck and Graves, *SF New Deal HCS*, pp. 188–189; Letter, Emmy Lou Packard to Ken Maley, July 10, 1990, Coit Tower Preservation Fund, City of San Francisco Department of Recreation and Parks, as cited in Petrin, National Register Nomination Form, p. 33.

34. VerPlanck and Graves, *SF New Deal HCS*, pp. 189–190.

35. VerPlanck and Graves, *SF New Deal HCS*, p. 189.

36. VerPlanck and Graves, *SF New Deal HCS*, p. 171.

37. The most complete account of the Rincon Annex murals is Gray Brechin, "Politics and Modernism: The Trial of the Rincon Annex Murals," in *On the Edge of America: California Modernist Art, 1900–1950* (Berkeley: University of California Press, 1996), ed. Paul J. Karlstrom, pp. 68–93, esp. 74–93. See also Emmy Lou Packard, Case Report on Rincon Annex, San Francisco Landmarks Preservation Advisory Board, Nov. 1, 1978, Emmy Lou Packard Papers, AAA, Smithsonian; National Register of Historic Places Inventory—Nomination Form: Rincon Annex, 1979, https://npgallery.nps.gov/GetAsset/71f080f2-84c3-4329-badf-0f36e39fbdbe/; VerPlanck and Graves, *SF New Deal HCS*, p. 172.

38. Packard's case report and the National Register Nomination Form list the various murals by title and provide some description; photos of most of the murals in the Library of Congress are available online.

39. The *Torchlight Procession* and *Beating the Chinese* murals, and perhaps others, strongly suggest that Refregier was drawing on Ira Cross, *A History of the Labor Movement in California* (Berkeley: University of California Press, 1935).

40. There are multiple treatments of the topic of both these murals. For Mooney and Billings, see Richard J. Frost, *The Mooney Case: The San Francisco Preparedness Day Bombing of 1916 and Its Aftermath* (Stanford: Stanford University Press, 1967), and Curt Gentry, *Frame-Up: The Incredible Case of Tom Mooney and Warren Billings* (New York: Norton, 1967). For the 1934 strikes, see David Selvin, *A Terrible Anger: The 1934 Waterfront and General Strikes in San Francisco* (Detroit: Wayne State University Press, 1996) and Robert W. Cherny, *Harry Bridges: Labor Radical, Labor Legend* (Urbana: University of Illinois Press, 2023), chs. 3–5.

41. Cherny, *Victor Arnautoff,* p. 111–112; "The Art of José Moya del Pino," Ross Historical Society/Moya del Pino Library, https://www.moya-rhs.org/the-art-of-moya.html/; Chang et al., *Asian American Art,* p. 432. Earlier, Moya del Pino had done a series of murals in the Aztec Brewery in San Diego, parts of which are now in a San Diego public library.

42. Wendy Van Wyck Good, *Sisters in Art: The Biography of Margaret, Esther, and Helen Bruton* (n.p.: West Margin Press, 2021), esp. pp. 69–103; Therese Poletti, *Art Deco San Francisco: The Architecture of Timothy Pflueger* (New York: Princeton Architectural Press, 2008), p. 176.

43. Mark Dean Johnson, "Uncovering Asian American Art in San Francisco, 1850–1940," in Chang et al., *Asian American Art,* pp. 21–22; "Biographies," in Chang et al., *Asian American Art,* pp. 397–398, 407–408.

44. Nancy Dustin Wall Moure, *California Art: 450 Years of Painting and Other Media* (Los Angeles: Dustin Publications, 1998), p. 267; Richard Candida Smith, *Utopia and Dissent: Art, Poetry, and Politics in California* (Berkeley: University of California Press, 1995), pp. 90–126; David Beasley, *Douglas MacAgy and the Foundations of Modern Art Curatorship* (Simcoe, Ontario, Canada: Davis Publishing, 1998), pp. 29–44; Susan Landauer, "Painting under the Shadow: California Modernism and the Second World War," in *On the Edge of America: California Modernist Art, 1900–1950,* ed. Paul J. Karlstrom (Berkeley: University of California Press, 1996), pp. 40–62, esp. pp. 42, 61. For the recovery of some of the murals at the former CSFA, later the San Francisco Art Institute, see "1930s-Era Murals Found under Painted Hallways at SF Art Institute," NBC Bay Area (https://www.nbcbayarea.com/news/local/1930s-era-murals-found-under-painted-hallways-at-sf-art-institute/2195201/).

45. Frances Stonor Saunders, *The Cultural Cold War: The CIA and the World of Arts and Letters* (New York: New Press, 1999), esp. pp. 1, 97–99, 148–151, 259–261, 228–276.

46. Carlos Cordova, "Latino Visual Arts" (unpublished draft in possession of the author, 2020); see also Cary Cordova, *The Heart of the Mission: Latino Art and Politics in San Francisco* (Philadelphia: University of Pennsylvania Press, 2017), esp. ch. 5.

47. John Natsoulas, "Foreword," *Emmy Lou Packard* (Davis: John Natsoulas Press, 2022), esp. p. 15; Cordova, "Latino Visual Arts"; Anne Cervantes provided the information about the 1984 program at Galería de las Raza. Soon after, Packard led a restoration of the Coit Tower murals (ch. 6) and helped to lead efforts to save the Rincon Annex murals (ch. 9).

48. Lavrova, "Forty-Six Artists—One Palette."

Chapter 9. New Deal Art and Political Controversy in San Francisco

1. Gray Brechin, "Politics and Modernism: The Trial of the Rincon Annex Murals," in *On the Edge of Ameria: California Modernist Art, 1900–1950,* ed. Paul J. Karlstrom (Berkeley: University of California Press, 1996), pp. 69–93, esp. 75; Cherny, *Victor Arnautoff,* pp. 157–159; (San Francisco) *People's World,* Nov. 15, 1947, p. 1.

2. Brechin, "Politics and Modernism," pp. 77–78; Cherny, *Victor Arnautoff,* pp. 158–159; *San Francisco News,* May 14, 1948, p. 6; *People's World,* April 12, 1948, p. 5.

3. *Rincon Annex Murals: San Francisco: No. 83-5: Hearing before the Subcommittee*

on Public Buildings and Grounds of the Committee on Public Works, House of Representatives, May 1, 1953 (Washington, D.C.: United States Government Printing Office, 1953), esp. pp. 47, 54; Brechin, "Politics and Modernism," pp. 79–85; Cherny, *Victor Arnautoff*, pp. 173–175.

4. Michael Semler told me of his, the mayor's office's, and Cranston's roles in an email; *San Francisco Chronicle*, April 19, 1978, p. 49; Nov. 25, *This World* section, pp. 41–42; Dec. 4, 1979, p. 12; Dec. 10, 1979, p. 4; *San Francisco Chronicle, California Living Magazine* section, May 2, 1982, p. 33; *San Francisco Chronicle*, June 26, 1984, p. 47; March 25, 1998, p. A22; folder 21, Restoration of Murals by Anton Refregier, Rincon Annex post office, San Francisco, California, box 7, Emmy Lou Packard Papers, Archives of American Art (AAA), esp. "The Rincon Annex Post Office, San Francisco, California, preliminary report for the Landmarks Advisory Board," Nov. 1, 1978.

5. Cherny, *Victor Arnautoff*, pp. 108–110. In his use of grisaille to depict the "westward march of the white race," Arnautoff was explicitly drawing upon lessons learned from Diego Rivera at Cuernavaca. There, Rivera depicted some of the most atrocious practices of the Spanish conquistadors in grisaille panels below his major panels, which were in color. Arnautoff did something similar with separate grisaille panels in two of his earliest murals, those at the Palo Alto clinic and in a fellow artist's studio. At GWHS, however, he moved the grisaille into the middle of a color mural; for the Cuernavaca murals, see, e.g., Desmond Rochfort, *The Murals of Diego Rivera* (London: Journeyman Press, 1987), pp. 63–64; and Cherny, *Victor Arnautoff*, pp. 65–66, for Arnautoff's participation at Cuernavaca, and pp. 78–79 for Arnautoff's earlier San Francisco murals using grisaille to denote objectionable features related to the central presentation in color.

6. Crumpler, quoted in "For SF Muralist Dewey Crumpler, the Controversial Past Is Present," by Alex Lash, at *The Frisc*, April 19, 2019, https://thefrisc.com; Sam Lefebvre, "'This Is Reparations,'" KQED radio, June 25, 2019, https://www.kqed.org/arts/13860237/this-is-reparations-s-f-school-board-votes-to-paint-over-controversial-high-school-mural/.

7. Christopher VerPlanck, "Landmark Nomination Report George Washington High School," https://commissions.sfplanning.org/hpcpackets/George%20Washington%20HS.pdf/. I was present at the school board meeting when the nomination was rejected. The school board meeting was reported in the *Richmond Review/Sunset Beacon* on March 7, 2019. A recording of the board meeting (there are apparently no transcripts of minutes) was once online at http://www.sfusd.edu/en/about-sfusd/board-of-education/meeting-documents.html/ but is no longer. The other two schools that were part of the original recommendation for landmarking have since been declared landmarks by action of the board of supervisors.

8. The quotations are from the fourth session PowerPoint slides prepared by Brent Stephens. I was present for the second, third, and fourth sessions as well as all the school board meetings.

9. As quoted by Alex Lash, "At SF's Washington High, an 80-Year-Old Mural Depicting People of Color Is Again Under Fire," *The Frisc*, April 5, 2019, https://thefrisc.com/; also quoted in Sarah B, "Historic WPA Murals at George Washington High School Are Facing Destruction Due to Controversial Depictions of Native Americans and African-Americans," *Richmond District Blog*, April 9, 2019, https://richmondsfblog.com/.

10. *New York Times*, April 13, 2019, p. C2, and online in a slightly different form at https://www.nytimes.com/2019/04/11/arts/design/george-washington-murals-ugly-history-debated.html?searchResultPosition=1/; *Richmond Review*, May 4, 2019, https://sfrichmondreview.com/2019/05/04/mural-opponents-meet-defenders-at-tour-of-george-washington-h-s-artwork/.

11. For examples of news accounts, see, e.g., CNN, June 9, 2019; *The Guardian*, May 20, 2019; *Washington Post*, May 8, 2019; *San Francisco Examiner*, May 7, 2019; *Washington Times*, May 2, 2019; (San Francisco) KQED Radio *Forum*, April 23, 2019; *New York Times*, April 11, 2019; *San Francisco Chronicle*, April 8, 2019; NBC Bay Area, April 8, 2019; KTVU-Fox, April 8, 2019; *Richmond Review/Sunset Beacon*, April 5, March 29, March 7, 2019; (San Francisco) *The Frisc*, April 5, 2019. For a sampling of editorials and op-eds, see Michael Henry Adams, *The Guardian*, May 26, 2019; *Conservative Zone*, May 21, 2019; Roberta Sutton, *Wall Street Journal*, May 16, 2019; Tom Ciccotta, *Breitbart.com*, May 13, 2019; Katherine Timpf, *National Review*, May 7, 2019; Barry Tompkins, *Marin Independent Journal*, May 4, 2019; Renee Loth, *Boston Globe*, April 29, 2019; Fergus Bordewich, *Wall Street Journal*, April 26, 2019; Therese Poletti, *Timothy Pflueger Blog*, April 23, 2019; Will Doolittle, Glens Fall, NY, *Post Star*, April 12, 2019; *San Francisco Chronicle* editorial board, *San Francisco Chronicle*, April 9, 2019; Charles Desmarais, *San Francisco Chronicle*, April 8, 2019. All are available online, but I have omitted the URLs for space and clarity.

12. *New York Times*, April 11, 2019. In the midst of the media coverage, I spoke to the History Club at Lowell High School, San Francisco's high school where admission is based on a high GPA in middle school; there, the students were most upset that no one had asked GWHS students for their opinions.

13. "Purpose," Coleman Advocates, https://colemanadvocates.org/about/.

14. Copies of letters, Bailey to Dr. Vincent Matthews, March 29, 2019; Roland Nawi to Matthews, June 2, 2019; Cherny to Matthews, March 26, 2019; copies of all these letters and more are held by the GWHS Alumni Association; Lope Yap Jr., vice president of GWHSAA, quoted in *The Frisc*, April 5, 2019.

15. Labor Video Project, "Arnautoff Mural Debate at SFUSD Board Meeting over Proposed Destruction of Murals," YouTube (June 20, 2019), https://www.youtube.com/watch?v=rG6x4JS76j0/. A fifty-three-minute documentary film about the controversy, *Town Destroyer*, produced and directed by Alan Snitow and Deborah Kaufmann, was released in 2022.

16. For one definition of white supremacy culture and its characteristics, see Tema Okun, "White Supremacy Culture," Dismantling Racism, https://www.dismantlingracism.org/. Or see "White Supremacy Culture," https://surjpoliticaledsite.weebly.com/white-supremacy-culture.html/. This description is taken from the second source: "White supremacy culture is reproduced by all the institutions of our society. In particular the media, the education system, western science . . . , and the Christian church have played central roles in reproducing the idea of white supremacy (i.e. that white is 'normal,' 'better,' 'smarter,' 'holy' in contrast to Black and other People and Communities of Color. . . . The list of white supremacy characteristics includes: perfectionism, a sense of urgency, defensiveness, valuing quantity over quality, worship of the written word, belief in only one right way, paternalism, either/or thinking, power hoarding, fear of open conflict, individualism, belief that I'm the only one (who can do this 'right'), the belief that progress is bigger and more, a belief in objectivity, and claiming a right to comfort."

17. This account is based in major part on my own observation of the meeting. See also *San Francisco Chronicle*, June 19, 2019, p. C4; Jeanne Elle, "George Washington Mural Causes Controversy in SF High School," NBC Bay Area, June 23, 2019, https://www.nbcbayarea.com/news/local/George-Washington-Mural-Causes-Controversy-in-SF-High-School-511501432.html/. The official recordings of the meetings are at http://www.sfusd.edu/en/about-sfusd/board-of-education/meeting-documents.html/. Cook announced his position on KQED on April 23. For his long resolution justifying destruction of the murals, see the official recording of the June 18, 2019, meeting.

18. The article appeared in the online edition of the *San Francisco Chronicle*, the afternoon of June 25, 2019; see Charles Desmarais, "Bay Area Art Leaders on Censorship of George Washington High Mural," June 25, 2019, *SF Chronicle*, Datebook, https://datebook.sfchronicle.com/art-exhibits/bay-area-art-leaders-on-censorship-of-george-washington-high-mural#/.

19. I also attended the June 25 meeting. The recording is at the same URL noted in note 7. See also *San Francisco Chronicle*, June 26, pp. C1, C3; June 27, 2019, pp. C1, C2; Lefebvre, "'This Is Reparations'" (see note 6); *Richmond Review*, July 2019, p. 12. Cook and Sanchez, response to an editorial in the *New York Times*, July 6, 2019, posted to the Facebook page of Allison Collins on July 7, 2019. The actual letter to the editor of the *New York Times* was considerably abbreviated; see July 14, 2019, https://www.nytimes.com/2019/07/14/opinion/letters/san-francisco-mural.html/; see also Stevon Cook, "Keep Those Slaves on that Wall!" *Medium.com*, July 11, 2019, at https://medium.com/@stevon.cook/keep-those-slaves-on-that-wall-5369a63a2a7/.

20. *San Francisco Chronicle*, July 14, 2019, p. C1; July 16, 2019, p. C1.

21. As an active participant in efforts to protect the murals, I received confidential information about the involvement of various public figures who were unwilling to make public announcements but who were involved in efforts to save the murals.

22. *San Francisco Chronicle*, Aug. 7, 2019, pp. C1, C2, C3; Aug. 10, 2019, pp. C1, C4.

23. *San Francisco Chronicle*, Aug. 14, 2019, pp. C1, C4; *New York Times*, Aug. 14, 2019, at https://www.nytimes.com/2019/08/14/arts/san-francisco-murals-george-washington.html?smid=nytcore-ios-share/.

24. I was provided a copy of the Feinstein letter; https://news.artnet.com/art-world/alice-walker-mural-interview-san-francisco-1630942/.

25. *George Washington High School Alumni Association v. San Francisco Unified School District*, Case No. CPF-19-516880/.

26. *San Francisco Chronicle*, Feb. 6 and 15, 2022, https://www.sfchronicle.com/projects/2022/sf-school-board-recall-timeline/; Feb. 23, 2022, https://www.sfchronicle.com/projects/2022/election-results-sfusd-recall/.

27. As a resident of the neighborhood, I was involved in all phases of this controversy, from joining with another neighborhood resident and Adam Gottstein, grandson of Zakheim, to publicize the issue and mobilize supporters, through the decision of the Historic Preservation Commission and board of supervisors to landmark the murals. We continue to monitor the situation as UCSF considers what to do with the murals.

28. AHA Statement on Confederate Monuments (Aug. 2017), https://www.historians.org/news-and-advocacy/aha-advocacy/aha-statement-on-confederate-monuments/.

29. Lisa Dunseth, "The Alemany Emergency Hospital and Health Center: The Hidden History behind the New Deal Era Buildings," 2016 (no longer available online); Nashelly Chavez, "Community Hopes to Revive Former Hospital for Public Use," *San Francisco Examiner*, March 20, 2016, https://www.sfexaminer.com/news/community-hopes-to-revive-former-hospital-for-public-use/; San Francisco Planning Department, *Landmark Case Report*, pp. 35–45 Onondaga Avenue, https://sfplanninggis.org/docs/landmarks_and_districts/LM272.pdf/.

30. Arnautoff's mural at the Richmond, California, post office was removed during remodeling, placed in storage for many years, and later restored and installed at the Richmond Museum of History; see https://richmondmuseum.org/news/press-release-victor-arnautoff-mural/. Scheuer's mural in the post office in Caldwell, Texas, has been moved to the Burleson County courthouse; see https://livingnewdeal.org/projects/burleson-county-courthouse-mural-caldwell-tx/.

31. "What's Wrong with This Diorama? You Can Read All about It," *New York Times*, March 20, 2019, https://www.nytimes.com/2019/03/20/arts/design/natural-history-museum-diorama.html/.

32. The AHA resolution originated in the controversies over the removal of Confederate statuary. It is online at https://www.historians.org/news-and-advocacy/aha-advocacy/aha-statement-on-confederate-monuments/.

Appendix: The Coit Tower Artists

1. Ruth Gottstein, "Who Were the Artists Who Painted the Murals at Coit Tower?" in *The Semaphore*, a publication of the Telegraph Hill Dwellers, Issue 198, Spring 2012, p. 4.

2. Oral history interview with Maxine Albro and Parker Hall, July 27, 1964, Archives of American Art (AAA), Smithsonian Institution; "The Women Who Painted Coit Tower" (Dec. 6, 2017), Living New Deal, https://livingnewdeal.org/women-painted-coit-tower/; *California Art Research*, ed. Gene Hailey (San Francisco: WPA Project 2874, 1937), v. 20, part two, pp. 1–15.

3. Robert W. Cherny, *Victor Arnautoff and the Politics of Art* (Urbana: University of Illinois Press, 2017).

4. "Jane Berlandina," in *California Art Research*, v. 17, pp. 110–183; Masha Zakheim, *Coit Tower, San Francisco: Its History and Art* (Volcano, CA; Volcano Press, 2009), 2nd ed., p. 108. See also "Women Who Painted Coit Tower."

5. Zakheim, *Coit Tower*, 2nd ed., p. 81; National Gallery of Art, https://www.nga.gov/collection/artist-info.33187.html/; Jon Golinger, computer research on the twenty-five lead Coit Tower artists for exhibitions in 2015 and 2016, copy in author's possession; hereafter, Golinger, exhibition notes.

6. "Ray Boynton," in *California Art Research*, v. 9, pp. 1–29; Zakheim, *Coit Tower*, 2nd ed., pp. 42, 45; Golinger, exhibition notes.

7. Oral history interview with Ralph Chessé, Oct. 22, 1964, AAA, Smithsonian Institution; "Chessé, Ralph," Amistad Research Center, https://amistad-finding-aids.tulane.edu/agents/people/1376/; Zakheim, *Coit Tower*, 2nd ed., p. 103; Lettie Connell Schubert and Randal J. Metz, "*An Incomplete History of the San Francisco Bay Area Puppeteers Guild*" (1996, rev. 2010), http://www.sfbapg.org/about/history/; Golinger, exhibition notes.

8. "Rinaldo Cuneo," in *California Art Research*, v. 11, pp. 61–100; Zakheim, *Coit Tower*, 2nd ed., p. 89; Golinger, exhibition notes; Cuneo obituary, *San Francisco*

Examiner, Dec. 28, 1939, p. 13; and the websites of the museums that hold Cuneo's work.

9. Obituary of Benjamin Cunningham in *New York Times*, April 6, 1975; Zakheim, *Coit Tower*, 2nd ed., p. 107.

10. Zakheim, *Coit Tower*, 2nd ed., p. 62; "H. Mallette Dean Biography," Annex Galleries, https://www.annexgalleries.com/artists/biography/3267/Dean/H.%20 Mallette?mc_cid=55c7df414d&mc_eid=UNIQID/; Golinger, exhibition notes.

11. Oral history interview with Maxine Albro and Parker Hall, July 27, 1964, AAA, Smithsonian Institution; Zakheim, *Coit Tower*, 2nd ed., p. 98; Golinger, exhibition notes.

12. Phil Kovinick and Marian Yoshiki-Kovinick, eds., *An Encyclopedia of Women Artists of the American West* (Austin: University of Texas Press, 1998), 123–124; Zakheim, *Coit Tower*, 2nd ed., p. 105; "Edith Anne Hamlin," in *California Art Research*, v. 16, pp. 94–114. See also "Women Who Painted Coit Tower."

13. Zakheim, *Coit Tower*, 2nd ed., p. 69; "George Albert Harris," Artist Auction Records, askART, https://www.askart.com/auction_records/George_Albert_Harris/10023296/George_Albert_Harris.aspx; Golinger, exhibition notes.

14. Oral history interview with William Hesthal, Dec. 22, 1964, AAA, Smithsonian Institution; Zakheim, *Coit Tower*, 2nd ed., p. 51; *California Art Research*, vol. 20, part one, pp. 8–13; "William Hesthal," Artist Auction Records, askART, https://www.askart.com/auction_records/William_Jurgen_Hesthal/4494/William_Jurgen_Hesthal.aspx; Golinger, exhibition notes.

15. Stacy Moss, *The Howards: First Family of Bay Area Modernism* (Oakland, CA: Oakland Museum, 1988), 59; oral history interview with John Langley Howard and Mary Howard, Sept. 5, 1991, AAA, Smithsonian Institution; Zakheim, *Coit Tower*, 2nd ed., p. 49; *California Art Research*, v. 17, pp. 53–92; Golinger, exhibition notes.

16. Oral history interview with Marcelle Labaudt, Sept. 16, 1964, AAA, Smithsonian Institution; "Lucien Labaudt," in *California Art Research*, v. 19, pp. 1–28; Zakheim, *Coit Tower*, 2nd ed., p. 96.

17. Zakheim, *Coit Tower*, 2nd ed., p. 85; "Gordon Langdon," Artist Auction Records, askART, https://www.askart.com/artist/Gordon_Langdon/10031293/Gordon_Langdon.aspx/; Golinger, exhibition notes.

18. Zakheim, *Coit Tower*, 2nd ed., p. 88; "José Moya del Pino," in *California Art Research*, v. 13, pp. 100–139; "Who Was José Moya del Pino?" Ross Historical Society/José Moya del Pino Library, https://www.moya-rhs.org/moya-del-pino .html/; Fran Cappelletti, "The Moya Brewery Murals: From Acme to Aztec," *Brewery History* 164 (2016): 33–36; Miguel Forada Serrano and Paola Coa-Nunsiznte, *José Moya del Pino: Two Lives of an Artist* (n.p.: Paola Coda Nunziante (2021).

19. Zakheim, *Coit Tower*, 2nd ed., p. 86; oral history interview with Otis Oldfield, May 21, 1965, AAA, Smithsonian Institution; "Otis Oldfield," in *California Art Research*, v. 19, pp. 29–74; Otis Oldfield biography, https://www.otisoldfield .net/biography/.

20. Zakheim, *Coit Tower*, 2nd ed., p. 86; "Fredrerick Olmsted," Artist Auction Records, askART, https://www.askart.com/artist/Frederick_Olmsted/10040195/Frederick_Olmsted.aspx/.

21. Oral history interview with Suzanne Scheuer, July 29, 1964, AAA, Smithsonian Institution; "Women Who Painted Coit Tower"; "Suzanne Scheuer," Fine Arts Museums of San Francisco, https://art.famsf.org/suzanne-scheuer/; Zakheim, *Coit Tower*, 2nd ed., p. 57; Golinger, exhibition notes.

22. "Ralph Stackpole," in *California Art Research*, v. 14, pp. 1–62; Zakheim, *Coit Tower*, 2nd ed., p. 55; "Ralph Stackpole," U.S. Commission of Fine Arts, https://www.cfa.gov/about-cfa/who-we-are/ralph-stackpole/.

23. Zakheim, *Coit Tower*, 2nd ed., p. 101; Golinger, exhibition notes.

24. Zakheim, *Coit Tower*, 2nd ed., p. 73; Golinger, exhibition notes.

25. "Biographical History," Clifford Wight Collection, Syracuse University, https://library.syr.edu/digital/guides/w/wight_rivera.htm#d2e94/; Julian Baker, "Clifford Wight—An Extraordinary Life," https://swindonlibraries.wordpress.com/2015/03/20/clifford-wight-an-extraordinary-life-a-talk-by-julian-baker/; Zakheim, *Coit Tower*, 2nd ed., p. 74; Golinger, exhibition notes.

26. "Bernard Zakheim," in *California Art Research*, v. 20, part 2, pp. 32–113; Elizabeth M. Boone, "'Something of His Own Soil': Jewish History, Mural Painting, and Bernard Zakheim in San Francisco," *American Jewish History* 90, no. 2 (2002): 123–140; Zakheim, *Coit Tower*, 2nd ed., p. 61.

Selected Bibliography

Archival Sources

Achenbach Foundation for Graphic Arts Study Center, Palace of the Legion of Honor, Fine Arts Museums of San Francisco, CA:
WPA Prints and Drawings [including Coit Tower artists' drawings]

Archives of American Art (AAA), Smithsonian Institution, Washington, D.C.:
Victor Arnautoff Papers
Edward Bruce Papers
Walter Heil Papers
Emmy Lou Packard Papers
Oral Histories and Interviews:
Maxine Albro and Parker Hall, July 27, 1964
Ralph Chessé, Oct. 22, 1964
Dorothy Cravath, May 13–27, 1964
Joseph Danysh, Dec. 3, 1964
Hebe Daum Stackpole and Jack Moxom, Jan. 9, 1965
George Gaethke, Sept. 26, 1964
William Hesthal, Dec. 22, 1964
John Langley Howard and Mary Howard, Sept. 5, 1991
José Moya del Pino, Sept. 10, 1964
Otis Oldfield, May 21, 1965
Suzanne Scheuer, July 29, 1964
Herman Volz, June 27, 1964
Bernard Baruch Zakheim, 1964

De Young Museum, San Francisco, CA:
Public Works of Art Project (PWAP) files

National Archives, Washington, D.C.:
Public Works of Art Project, Region 15 papers

Regional Oral History Office, Bancroft Library, University of California, Berkeley:
Shirley Staschen Triest, *A Life on the First Waves of Radical Bohemianism in San Francisco*, 1997

San Francisco Art Institute Legacy Foundation+Archive, San Francisco:
Enrollment Records

San Francisco History Center, San Francisco Public Library:
San Francisco Art Commission minutes, online at Internet Archive:

https://archive.org/details/minutesofartcomm1934sanf/mode/1up?view=theater/
https://archive.org/details/minutesofartcomm1941sanf/mode/1up?view=theater/
https://archive.org/details/minutesofartcomm1942sanf/mode/1up/

San Francisco city directories, online at Internet Archive:

https://sfpl.org/locations/main-library/magazines-newspapers-center/bay-area-city-directories-and-phone-books/san-0/

San Francisco Examiner clippings file, envelope marked San Franciso/Telegraph Hill/Coit Tower/
San Francisco Park Commission minutes, online at Internet Archives:

https://archive.org/details/parkrecreat1930sanf/mode/1up?view=theater
https://archive.org/details/minutesboardofpa1941sanf/page/n5/mode/2up/

Syracuse University, Syracuse, New York, Special Collections Research Center:
Clifford Wight, "Statement in Defense of the Coit Tower Mural," Clifford Wight Collection Relating to Diego Rivera

Newspapers

Los Angeles Times
New York Times
Oakland Tribune
San Francisco Chronicle
San Francisco Examiner
San Francisco News
(San Francisco) *People's World*
(San Francisco) *Richmond Review/Sunset Beacon*
Washington Post

Online Databases

Art Works, The Living New Deal. University of California, Berkeley. https://livingnewdeal.org/new-deal-categories/art-works/.
New Deal Art Registry. https://www.newdealartregistry.org/renderartists/.

Published Primary Sources

Arnautoff, Victor. "A Vital Question." *San Francisco Art Association Bulletin* 1 (Sept. 1934).
Arnautoff, Victor, with Leonid Sanin. *Zizn' zanobo* [Life Anew] (Donetsk:

Izdatel'stvo Donbas, 1972), 2nd ed. Translated by Lloyd Kramer, Labor Archives and Research Center, San Francisco State University.
Baigell, Matthew, and Julia Williams. *Artists against War and Fascism: Papers of the First American Artists' Congress*. New Brunswick: Rutgers University Press, 1986.
Chessé, Ralph. "The WPA & The Great Coit Tower Controversy: The Artists Look Back." *City of San Francisco*, Feb. 4, 1976, p. 22.
Danysh, Joseph. "The WPA & the Great Coit Tower Controversy." *City of San Francisco*, Feb. 4, 1976, pp. 20, 21.
Lavrova, Nadia. "Forty-Six Artists—One Palette." *Christian Science Monitor*, Weekly Magazine Section, Aug. 1, 1934, 8–9.
Rivera, Diego. *My Art, My Life: An Autobiography*. 1960; reprint, NY: Dover Press, 1991.
Seeley, Evelyn. "A Frescoed Tower Clangs Shut amid Gasps." *Literary Digest*, Aug. 25, 1934, pp. 24.
U.S. Congress. House of Representatives. *Rincon Annex Murals: San Francisco: No. 83-5: Hearing before the Subcommittee on Public Buildings and Grounds of the Committee on Public Works, May 1, 1953*. Washington, D.C.: United States Government Printing Office, 1953.
U.S. Department of Commerce. Bureau of the Census. Fifteenth Census of the United States: 1930. v. 3, Population, Reports by States, Part II, "California." https://www2.census.gov/library/publications/decennial/1930/population-volume-3/10612963v3p1ch03.pdf/
Watson, Forbes. "Art and the Government in 1934." *Parnassus* 6 (1935): 12–16.

Secondary Works

Albright, Thomas. *Art in the San Francisco Bay Area, 1945–1980: An Illustrated History*. Berkeley: University of California Press, 1985.
Alley, Paul, Leo R. Barker, Gordon Chappell, et al. "Presidio of San Francisco." USDI/NPS NRHP Registration Form. Submitted Oct. 16, 1992. https://npgallery.nps.gov/NRHP/GetAsset/NHLS/66000232_text/.
Almeida, Laura. "What Is Mexican Modernism." Denver Art Museum. https://www.denverartmuseum.org/en/blog/what-mexican-modernism/.
Anreus, Alejandro, et al., eds. *Mexican Muralism: A Critical History*. Berkeley: University of California Press, 2012.
Blauvelt, Molly. "Beach Chalet." National Register Nomination Form, 1980, entered July 22, 1981. https://npgallery.nps.gov/NRHP/GetAsset/396ce0d5-c9b3-4168-805c-2692db2e8809/.
Boone, Elizabeth M. "'Something of His Own Soil': Jewish History, Mural Painting, and Bernard Zakheim in San Francisco." *American Jewish History* 90, no. 2 (2002): 123–140.
Brechin, Gray. "Politics and Modernism: The Trial of the Rincon Annex Murals." In *On the Edge of America: California Modernist Art, 1900–1950*, edited by Paul J. Karlstrom. Berkeley: University of California Press, 1996.
Bustard, Bruce I. *A New Deal for the Arts*. Seattle: University of Washington Press, 1997.
Castro, Maria. "Diego Rivera's New American Art: San Francisco, 1930–31." In Oles, *Diego Rivera's America*.
Chang, Gordon H., Mark Dean Johnson, and Paul J. Karlstrom, eds. *Asian*

American Art: A History, 1850–1970. Stanford, CA: Stanford University Press, 2008.

Cherny, Robert W. "The Controversy at Coit Tower, 1934: Communist Conspiracy or Tempest in a Teapot." *The Argonaut* 28, no. 1 (Summer 2017): 68–91.

Cherny, Robert W. *Harry Bridges: Labor Radical, Labor Legend*. Urbana: University of Illinois Press, 2023.

Cherny, Robert W. *San Francisco Reds: Communists in the Bay Area, 1919–1958*. Urbana: University of Illinois Press, 2024.

Cherny, Robert W. "San Francisco's New-Deal Murals in Long-Term Perspective: Controversy, Neglect, and Restoration." *California History* 97 (Feb. 2020): 3–32.

Cherny, Robert W. *Victor Arnautoff and the Politics of Art*. Urbana: University of Illinois Press, 2017.

Clark, Lenore. *Forbes Watson: Independent Revolutionary*. Kent, OH: Kent State University Press, 2001.

Contreras, Belisario R. *Tradition and Innovation in New Deal Art*. Lewisburg: Bucknell University Press, 1983.

Cordova, Cary. *The Heart of the Mission: Latino Art and Politics in San Francisco*. Philadelphia: University of Pennsylvania Press, 2017,

"Courtroom Murals: Images of New Deal Era Art from Coit Tower." U.S. District Court for the Northern District of California Historical Society, March 3, 2020. https://ndhistoricalsociety.org/presentation/courtroom-murals-images-of-new-deal-era-art-from-coit-tower/.

Delgado, James P. "Aquatic Park Historic District." National Register of Historic Places Inventory Nomination Form, Feb. 1, 1984. http://npshistory.com/publications/goga/nr-aquatic-park-hd.pdf/.

Dustin Wall Moure, Nancy. *California Art: 450 Years of Painting and Other Media*. Los Angeles: Dustin Publications, 1998.

Folgarait, Leonard. *Mural Painting and Social Revolution in Mexico, 1920–1940: Art of the New Order*. Cambridge: Cambridge University Press, 1998.

Gelber, Steven M. "The Irony of San Francisco's 'Commie Art': An Artistic and Political Appraisal." *City of San Francisco*, Feb. 4, 1976, pp. 24, 28, 37.

Gelber, Steven M. "Working to Prosperity: California's New Deal Murals." *California History* 58 (1979): 98–127.

Gelber, Steven M., et al., *New Deal Art: California*. Santa Clara, CA: de Saisset Art Gallery and Museum, University of Santa Clara, 1976.

Golinger, Jon. *Saving San Francisco's Heart: How to Win Elections, Reclaim Our City, and Keep SF a Special Place*. San Francisco: Bay Guardian Books, 2017.

Gordon, Linda. *Dorothea Lange: A Life beyond Limits*. New York: W. W. Norton, 2009.

Gottstein, Ruth. "Who Were the Artists Who Painted the Murals at Coit Tower?" *The Semaphore*, Issue 198, Spring 2012.

Hailey, Gene, ed. *California Art Research*, 20 vols., W.P.A. Project 2874, O.P. 650303632. San Francisco, 1937; updated and digitized by the Bancroft Library, University of California, Berkeley. https://digicoll.lib.berkeley.edu/record/52113/.

Harris, Jonathan. *Federal Art and National Culture: The Politics of Identity in New Deal America*. New York: Cambridge University Press, 1993.

Haskell, Barbara. "America: Mexican Muralism and Art in the United States, 1935–1945." In *Vida Americana: Mexican Muralists Remake American Art*,

1925–1945, edited by Barbara Haskell. New Haven: Yale University Press, 2020.
Haskell, Barbara, ed. *Vida Americana: Mexican Muralists Remake American Art, 1925–1945*. New Haven: Yale University Press, 2020.
Hemingway, Andrew. *Artists on the Left: American Artists and the Communist Movement, 1926–1956*. New Haven: Yale University Press, 2002.
Hemingway, Andrew. "Hard Times: Andrew Hemingway on Cultural Democracy and the New Deal Art Programs." *ArtForum*, April 30, 2020. https://www.artforum.com/slant/andrew-hemingway-on-cultural-democracy-and-the-new-deal-art-programs-82962/.
Hinkle, Warren, ed. "When Art Was Fun and Fabulous: The Treasures of the WPA: The Forgotten Great Public Art of the Bay Area." *City of San Francisco*, Feb. 4, 1976.
Hughes, Edan Milton. *Artists in California*, 2nd ed. San Francisco: Hughes Publishing, 1989.
Huntington, Emily H. *Unemployment Relief and the Unemployed in the San Francisco Bay Region: 1929–1934*. Berkeley: University of California Press, 1939.
Jones, Idwal. *Ark of Empire: San Francisco's Montgomery Block*. Garden City, NY: Doubleday, 1951.
Kalfatovic, Martin R. *The New Deal Fine Arts Projects: A Bibliography, 1933–1992*. Metuchen, NJ: Scarecrow Press, 1994.
Karlstrom, Paul J., ed. *On the Edge of America: California Modernist Art, 1900–1950*. Berkeley: University of California Press, 1996.
Kennedy, David M. *Freedom from Fear: The American People in Depression and War, 1929–1945*. New York: Oxford University Press, 1999.
Lear, John. "Diego Rivera Paints the Proletariat." In Oles, *Diego Rivera's America*.
Lee, Anthony. *Painting on the Left Painting on the Left: Diego Rivera, Radical Politics, and San Francisco's Public Murals*. Berkeley: University of California Press, 1999.
Leuchtenburg, William E. *Franklin D. Roosevelt and the New Deal*. New York: Harper, 1963.
Lozano, Luis-Martin, and Juan Rafael Coronel Rivera. *Diego Rivera: The Complete Murals*. Hong Kong: Taschen, 2008.
Lucie-Smith. Edward. *American Realism*. 1994; paperback ed., New York: Thames and Hudson, 2002.
Marling, Karal Ann. *Wall-to-Wall America: A Cultural History of Post-Office Murals in the Great Depression*. Minneapolis: University of Minnesota Press, 1982.
McKinzie, Richard D. *The New Deal for Artists*. Princeton: Princeton University Press, 1973.
Melville, Annette, et al., *George Washington High School*. Historic American Buildings Survey No. CA-2939 (2020). http://memory.loc.gov/master/pnp/habshaer/ca/ca4400/ca4411/data/ca4411data.pdf/.
Moss, Stacey. *The Howards: First Family of Bay Area Modernism*. Oakland, CA: Oakland Museum, 1988.
Mullins, William H. *The Depression and the Urban West Coast, 1929–1933: Los Angeles, San Francisco, Seattle, and Portland*. Bloomington: Indiana University Press, 1991.
Musher, Sharon Ann. *Democratic Art: The New Deal's Influence on American Culture*. Chicago: University of Chicago Press, 2015.

Natsoulas, John, et al. *Emmy Lou Packard*. Davis: John Natsoulas Press, 2022.

Neuhaus, Eugen. *The Art of Treasure Island*. Berkeley: University of California Press, 1939.

O'Connor, Francis V. "Commentary." In Masha Zakheim, *Coit Tower, San Francisco: Its History and Art*. Volcano, CA: Volcano Press, 2009.

O'Connor, Francis V. "The Influence of Diego Rivera on the Art of the United States During the 1930s and After." In *Diego Rivera: A Retrospective*, edited by Cynthia Newman Helms. New York: W. W. Norton, 1986.

Oles, James, ed. *Diego Rivera's America*. San Francisco: San Francisco Museum of Modern Art in association with University of California Press, 2022.

Oles, James. "From Murals to Paintings: Scenes of Everyday Life." In Oles, *Diego Rivera's America*.

Park, Marlene, and Gerald E. Markowitz. *Democratic Vistas: Post Offices and Public Art in the New Deal*. Philadelphia: Temple University Press, 1984.

Petrin, Katherine, Robert W. Cherny, and Jon Golinger, National Register of Historic Places Nomination Form for Coit Tower, Nov. 2017. https://npgallery.nps.gov/NRHP/GetAsset/NRHP/07001468_text/.

Poletti, Therese. *Art Deco San Francisco: The Architecture of Timothy Pflueger*. New York: Princeton Architectural Press, 2008.

Putzel, Howard. "Ray Boynton's Mural Decorations at Mills College." *American Magazine of Art* 20 (1929): 335–338.

Reinhardt, Richard. *Treasure Island: San Francisco's Exposition Years*. Mill Valley, CA: Squarebooks, 1978.

Rochfort, Desmond. *Mexican Muralists: Orozco, Rivera, Siqueiros*. London: Laurence King, 1993.

Roland, Carol. National Register of Historic Places Registration Form for San Francisco State Teacher's College, certified Jan. 7, 2008. https://npgallery.nps.gov/nrhp/GetAsset?assetID=b459deb2-7f3d-4211-a842-762f77aeed43/.

Rubens, Lisa. "The 1939 San Francisco World's Fair: The New Deal, the New Frontier and the Pacific Basin" (PhD diss., University of California, Berkeley, 2004).

San Francisco Planning Department. *Landmark Case Report: Alemany Emergency Hospital and Health Center, 35–45 Onondaga Avenue*, San Francisco. 2016. https://sfplanning.s3.amazonaws.com/commissions/hpcpackets/2015-003877DES.pdf/).

San Francisco Planning Department. Article 10 Landmark Designation Fact Sheet History of Medicine in California (approved by the Historic Preservation Commission on August 19, 2020). https://sfplanninggis.org/docs/landmarks_and_districts/LM289.pdf/.

Santiago, Chiori. "Mural, Mural on the Wall: The Restoration of Coit Tower." *SF: The Magazine of Deign and Style* 2, no. 6 (June 1990): 88–91.

Schwartz, Bonnie Fox. *The Civil Works Administration, 1933–1934: The Business of Emergency Employment in the New Deal*. Princeton, NJ: Princeton University Press, 1984.

Selvin, David F. *A Terrible Anger: The 1934 Waterfront and General Strikes in San Francisco*. Detroit: Wayne State University Press, 1996.

Selz, Peter. "The Impact from Abroad: Foreign Guests and Visitors." In *On the Edge of America: California Modernist Art, 1900–1950*, edited by Paul J. Karlstrom. Berkeley: University of California Press, 1996.

Shaken, Andrew M. *Into the Void Pacific: Building the 1939 San Francisco World's Fair*. Berkeley: University of California Press, 2014.

Sherins, Robert S., ed. and comp. "History of Medicine in California Articulated in Frescoes: The Story behind the Murals of Toland Hall, UCSF." http://robertssherinsmd.com/files/books/7-Toland%20Manuscript.4.pdf/.

Smith, Harvey. "The Monkey Block: The Art Culture of the New Deal in the San Francisco Bay Area." http://foundsf.org/index.php?title=The_Monkey_Block/.

Tillman, Jeffrey T. *Arthur Brown Jr.: Progressive Classicist*. New York: W. W. Norton, 2006.

U.S. Department of the Interior. National Register of Historic Places Inventory Nomination Form: Rincon Annex, 1979. https://npgallery.nps.gov/GetAsset/71f080f2-84c3-4329-badf-0f36e39fbdbe/.

Van Wyck Good, Wendy. *Sisters in Art: The Biography of Margaret, Esther, and Helen Bruton*. n.p.: West Margin Press, 2021.

VerPlanck, Christopher. "Landmark Designation Report: Theodore Roosevelt Middle School" (approved by the San Francisco Historic Preservation Commission on Oct. 17, 2017, and by the San Francisco Board of Supervisors on March 15, 2019). https://sfplanning.s3.amazonaws.com/commissions/hpcpackets/New%20Deal%20Schools_101817.pdf/.

VerPlanck, Christopher. "Landmark Nomination Report: George Washington High School," Oct. 18, 2017 (approved by the San Francisco Historic Preservation Commission, Dec. 6, 2017), p. 39. https://commissions.sfplanning.org/hpcpackets/George%20Washington%20HS.pdf/.

VerPlanck, Christopher, and Donna Graves. "San Francisco New Deal Historic Context Statement: Rebuilding the City, 1933 to 1943" (approved by San Francisco City and County Historic Preservation Commission on March 1, 2023), access through San Francisco City Planning website: https://sfplanning.org/project/citywide-historic-context-statement#completed/.

Wagner, Ann Prentice. *1934: A New Deal for Artists*. London: D. Giles Limited for Smithsonian American Art Museum, 2009.

Webbink, Paul. "Unemployment in the United States, 1930–1940." *Papers and Proceedings of the American Economic Association* 30 (1941): 250–251.

Webster, Sally, and Sylvia Rhor. "Modern Mural Painting in the United States: Shaping Spaces/Shaping Publics." In *A Companion to Public Art*, edited by Cher Krause Knight and Harriet F. Senie. n.p.: John Wiley & Sons, 2016.

Wilson, Raymond L. "The Northern Scene." In *American Scene Painting: California, 1930s and 1940s*, edited by Ruth Westphal and Janet Blake Dominik. Irvine, CA: Westphal Publishing, 1991.

Zakheim Jewett, Masha. *Coit Tower, San Francisco: Its History and Art*. 1st ed. San Francisco: Volcano Press, 1983.

Zakheim Jewett, Masha. "The Murals in Coit Tower." *California Living*, Dec. 14, 1975, pp. 30–34.

Zakheim, Masha. *Coit Tower, San Francisco: Its History and Art*. 2nd ed. Volcano, CA: Volcano Press, 2009.

Index

ROBERT W. CHERNY is a professor emeritus of history at San Francisco State University. His many books include *Victor Arnautoff and the Politics of Art* and *Harry Bridges: Labor Radical, Labor Legend.*

The University of Illinois Press
is a founding member of the
Association of University Presses.

Designed by Jim Proefrock
Composed in 11/14 Mercury Text
with Trade Gothic and Montreal display
at the University of Illinois Press
Manufactured by Versa Press, Inc.

University of Illinois Press
1325 South Oak Street
Champaign, IL 61820-6903
www.press.uillinois.edu